Polishing the Dragons

Making Epcot's "Wonders of China"

by Jeff Blyth

COPYRIGHT 2020, JEFF BLYTH
COVER DESIGN: JEFF BLYTH AND SHANNON LASKEY
PHOTO SPREADS: JEFF BLYTH
INTERIOR LAYOUT: SHANNON LASKEY
PROOFREADER: HUGH ALLISON

All Rights Reserved. No part of this book may be reproduced in any form or by any electronic or mechanical means including information storage and retrieval systems, without permission in writing from the author. The only exception is by a reviewer, who may quote short excerpts in a review.

This book is neither authorized nor sponsored nor endorsed by the Disney Company or any of its subsidiaries. It is an unofficial and unauthorized book and not a Disney product. The mention of names and places associated with the Disney Company and its businesses are not intended in any way to infringe on any existing copyrights or registered trademarks of the Disney Company but are used in context for educational purposes. The opinions and statements expressed in the quotations and text are solely the opinions of the author or those people who are quoted and do not necessarily reflect the opinions and policy of the Disney Company and its businesses nor Bamboo Forest Publishing.

Although the Publisher and the Author of this book have made every effort to ensure the information was correct at the time of going to press, the Publisher and the Author do not assume and herby disclaim any liability to any party for any loss or damage caused by errors, omissions, misleading information, or any potential travel disruption due to labor or financial difficulty, whether such errors or omissions result from negligence, accident, or any other cause.

Printed in the United States of America
ISBN: 978-0-9910079-9-8
Bamboo Forest Publishing

TABLE OF CONTENTS

1	DEDICATION
3	FOREWORD
4	CHAPTER ONE 开始 (Action!)
12	CHAPTER TWO The Chinese Way
19	CHAPTER THREE Little Miss Pu
28	CHAPTER FOUR No One Ever Says "Yes"
33	CHAPTER FIVE Off the Deep End
41	CHAPTER SIX Step by Step, Brick by Brick
47	CHAPTER SEVEN Chopsticks and Charred Birds
56	CHAPTER EIGHT A Train Ride from Hell
63	CHAPTER NINE The Long March
73	CHAPTER TEN A Wastebasket Story
82	CHAPTER ELEVEN Porcelain Footprints
91	CHAPTER TWELVE A Renovation in Bamboo
99	CHAPTER THIRTEEN Iron Rice Bowl
107	CHAPTER FOURTEEN Scattered Dragon's Teeth
115	CHAPTER FIFTEEN Mayor of Helicopter Town

Table of Contents

- **123** CHAPTER SIXTEEN
  Above the Clouds and Off a Cliff

- **132** CHAPTER SEVENTEEN
  Ernie Haller's Hat

- **137** CHAPTER EIGHTEEN
  Distant Lands

- **147** CHAPTER NINETEEN
  Polishing the Dragons

- **156** CHAPTER TWENTY
  Phony Receipts

- **161** CHAPTER TWENTY-ONE
  Bear Paw and Moose Nose

- **169** CHAPTER TWENTY-TWO
  To Yi, or Not To Yi

- **178** CHAPTER TWENTY-THREE
  The Dragon's Head

- **185** CHAPTER TWENTY-FOUR
  The Dragon's Tail

- **194** CHAPTER TWENTY-FIVE
  Beyond the Bund

- **200** CHAPTER TWENTY-SIX
  Suzhou Unrefined

- **206** CHAPTER TWENTY-SEVEN
  A Great Poet Rewritten

- **214** CHAPTER TWENTY-EIGHT
  Number One Son

- **222** CHAPTER TWENTY-NINE
  Patchwork

- **230** CHAPTER THIRTY
  One Thing Wrong

- **235** CHAPTER THIRTY-ONE
  Reflections

- **246** ABOUT THE AUTHOR

Dedication

    This book represents a personal journey and is told not just from recollections but my obsessive daily journal entries. I want to dedicate this to the memory of Bob Gibeaut, a former Vice President of Production at Walt Disney Studios in Burbank.

    During the making of "Wonders of China," after we'd overcome several unique problems and confronted significant cross-cultural issues, Bob gave me his blessing to write a book about my experiences.

    I said at the time, "Bob, why would I want to write a book? I'm a filmmaker."

Foreword

Consider this book a kind of time machine, an up close and very personal view of a People's Republic of China (PRC) that no longer exists. The historic places I visited are still there but now you may find them overlaid with steel and glass, paved with parking lots, and choked with tourists in their own cars. The fascinating Chinese people I encountered have had their traditional practices and customs altered, reshaped, and constrained by a modern world and an evolving government. Despite the vast changes the past four decades have brought, my experiences included the discovery of enduring elements of a classic and timeless China that will outlive us all.

My adventures in filmmaking for "Wonders of China" happened between 1980 and 1982, not long after President Nixon's trip to "open up" the country, a time still shadowed by the Cultural Revolution. This was an era when being welcomed within China's borders was a unique and highly sought privilege. During banquets in one remote province or another, I'd often be asked by some proud party official to make a little speech, "Tell us what you think of China." I had done a lot of research and kept my eyes open, but I was no authority. I'd quote Mao Zedong's well-known (and apocryphal) words from the nation's founding in 1949: "The Chinese people have stood up." I'd follow that by saying, "From what I've seen traveling the countryside, the Chinese people are not standing, or even walking. They have learned to run." That never failed to please because it was true. Vestiges of China's immediate and ancient past remained visible, but so were glimpses of its future. My little crew and I saw for ourselves the first stumbling steps from doctrinaire Communism to a more market-driven economy.

One of the great honors of my life has been the responsibility granted to me by Walt Disney Productions to introduce the China I personally witnessed to Western audiences. The resulting 360-degree film, "Wonders of China," was viewed by over 100 million visitors since it opened at EPCOT's China Pavilion. Many of the film's iconic scenes remained an integral part of "Reflections of China," the film that replaced it in 2003 and played there for many more years.

Waiting for "action"

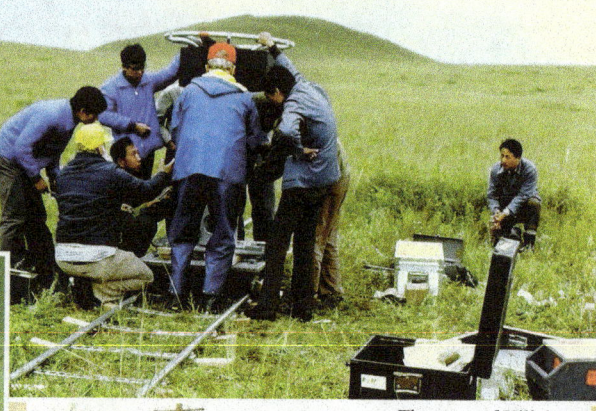
Our American-Chinese crew

The author directing Shih Kuan

Local transport

A Mongolian family

The town of Xilinhot

The "Sheep Dip" Hotel

Shih Kuan as Li Po

Mongolian horsemen

开始 (Action!)

It was the first day of my dream job directing for Disney and I was certain I'd be undone by either millions of black flies or a dozen surly Mongolian horsemen.

Two months of scouting across China had come down to this. Our five-man American crew was matched by local Chinese technicians as we worked together to set up the complex Circle-Vision cameras. The location was a little hollow among the green rolling hills of Inner Mongolia, about an hour's drive north of the town of Xilinhot and the other side of the universe from Burbank, California. Every step we took through the ankle-length grass stirred up swarms of angry flies who thrived on the leftover cow, sheep, and horse dung. Joe Nash, our camera technician, was growing concerned as they landed on our nine front surface mirrors. They'd look like huge moving black blobs, ruining any shot. He'd already gone through several cans of Dust-Off trying to chase them away with bursts of compressed air.

Having set my crew in motion to get ready to film our first shot for "Wonders of China," I was MIA.

In truth I was out of sight a few hundred yards away over a gentle rise, trying to sort out a horseman issue. These wiry nomadic riders had been hired as extras and they'd ridden for four hours through the night to arrive on time. We'd been able to track their approach from miles away across the wide-open grassy plains and slopes. But since their arrival they'd been crouched down, muttering to themselves, rolling crude cigarettes with a practiced hand.

These were tough old birds with leathery, coffee-colored skin, squinting at me through the haze of their shared smokes, figuring out why this "foreign devil" was trying to tell them what to do. My directions had to go from English to Chinese to Mongolian and then back again, so I expected communication to be somewhat hit and miss, like a perverted game of telephone. I'd been trying to express myself through drawings in the dirt with lots of arm waving, but my intentions had to pass through layers of filtered translation and cultural interpretation. Why weren't they *getting* what I was asking: ride at speed over the hill and circle our cameras while they chased down a few stray horses, an activity they did every day of their lives. After an hour of failed negotiations, all I was getting was more squinting, squatting, and smoking. I'd spent two years in the Peace Corps in West Africa and prided myself on cross-cultural communication skills, so this failure weighed heavily on me.

My Chinese negotiators were upset by the growing stalemate, particularly Tan Shi Gui, our production manager. He may have risked losing face, but he wasn't the one who would have to answer to studio executives. For whatever reasons, Disney had put their trust in me to deliver a film in time for EPCOT's grand opening. He Bao Zhang and Ding Hai Hua were my two translators, my only lifeline to understanding what was really going on. A couple of months earlier Bao (as he preferred to be called) and Ding had been students studying English in the Foreign Language Institute. They were hardly wise to the world, never having traveled outside of Beijing before this film. They had to be thinking: "What did we get ourselves into?" I know I was.

China of 1981 was a little like rural America of 1951. When my American crew arrived in Beijing, it felt like we'd stepped back in time, and Xilinhot was even further removed, a dusty little outpost with dirt streets filled with horse carts and the rare bicycle. This is a place where Chinese movies were sometimes projected with battery-operated devices on a bed sheet. We'd flown into this remote area a couple of days earlier in a chartered Russian-made aircraft that looked like it was left over from Lend-Lease. The vintage plane was most remarkable for a full-sized refrigerator attached inside the fuselage with a simple come-along strap. If we'd had to make a hard landing, that appliance would have torn loose and wiped us out like bowling pins.

We'd recently checked into the best hotel Xilinhot had to offer, a dusty concrete edifice of functional Stalinist design that seemed unfinished: no tile or carpets, bare light bulbs, no hot water and the smell, oh that smell! We'd instantly dubbed the place the Sheep Dip Hotel because the stench of wet mutton permeated every corner of the building. A lot more black flies, too. At least the staff supplied thick comforters to make up for the lack of heat. Hotel food was another challenge. It wasn't just Chinese, it was Mongolian. Fermented mare's milk tea was served with every meal and left a greasy coating on the tongue. A taste for this beverage had to be acquired over generations, certainly not on a brief visit.

At a local banquet served in our honor, my young translators had a difficult time naming food they didn't recognize. Sometimes the best they could come up with was "three kinds of beef." In those days the Chinese didn't make much of a distinction between cow brain, cow tongue, or filet mignon. The dessert was announced by Ding as "some kind of cheese" but it turned out to be caramelized camel hump. Believe me, it tasted much better when we thought it was cheese.

I'm sure those horsemen slouching on the hillside would've considered our banquet to be a feast, washed down with more mare's milk tea, please. Now they huddled together in their colorful silk outfits, smoking or tending to their grazing Mongolian ponies. I made particular note of the wooden saddles. They weren't carved and artistic but rather crude, like something you might make in ninth-grade woodshop out of plywood and two-by-fours. Somehow these men could travel for hours every day on these awkward saddles, although I wasn't surprised they spent most of their time standing in the stirrups. Bao took me aside to whisper what he suspected was happening. He thought Tan was embarrassed to say that the Mongolian horseman would only take directions from an American if I first *showed* them what I wanted.

"Bao, I've been showing them. I drew diagrams and… Wait, you mean they want me to ride one of their ponies?" I hadn't been on a horse since high school and that would've been a broken-down rental nag on a tourist trail.

A thought flashed into my mind that these riders were setting me up, daring me to get on a horse whose name would translate from Mongolian as "Dynamite" not "Buttercup." At this point I figured I had nothing to lose. Besides, their ponies were so short I couldn't fall very far. I climbed onto the designated pony under the watchful gaze of these skeptical horsemen, looking for signs of silent laughter. I radioed my crew over a walkie-talkie to tell them to get ready to take some still photographs because I was only going to do this once.

The horse was surprisingly docile, and I urged it faster and faster as it carried me up the hill. As I cleared the rise, I could see my crew busily preparing the Circle-Vision cameras and swatting away black flies. Not one of them paid any attention. Was an LA director riding a Mongolian pony nothing out of the ordinary? I swung around the camera rig with as much skill as I could and then guided the horse back over the hill. I found the horsemen standing around smiling. A few even gave me a pat on the back. That broke the cultural logjam and from there we were able to begin filming.

I was certain I had a few splinters from that saddle but that was a small price to pay to get my first shot. I joined Joe Nash in hiding under the

360-degree camera rig and we were each armed with two cans of Dust-Off. The only real problem on the first take was not the flies. A few of the riders became confused and their horses ran into each other making the big turn. Once that was sorted out, we filmed three more times. To have an actual choice of takes when we got back to the studio was more than I'd dreamed.

The next day we were back in the same grasslands for a scene with our main character, a man who lived during the Tang dynasty. If this was modern China, why were we depicting a poet who had died 1,200 years earlier? In my crisscrossing search for locales throughout the country, I'd come to the realization that the film would need a narrator but I feared anything he or she said would be taken as the direct words of the Communist Party, dismissed as mere propaganda. I could imagine someone in the theater shouting at the screens, "That's just what they want you to believe!"

America's perception of China in those days was colored by generational differences. Those who grew up during the Vietnam era had mental images of rice paddies and coolie hats. Their parents probably pictured the Red Army coming over the snow-covered hills of Korea's Yalu River Valley. An even earlier generation no doubt conjured up images of Charlie Chan movies or inscrutable Mandarins in pigtails. I was hoping a speaker who came out of distant history would negate current concerns for the politics and polemics of anyone within living memory, like William Shakespeare narrating a film about England.

I'd researched China's most revered poets looking for a candidate and settled on a Tang dynasty poet named Li Bai (701 – 762 A.D.), known in the West as Li Po. This beloved scholar had traveled extensively throughout China, creating over 1,000 imaginative poems celebrating simple pleasures and observations. The character's voice-over narration for the film would be inspired by his considerable poetic works, but I wanted audiences to also see Li Po, to feel comfortable with this real man who enjoyed life. If nothing else, maybe they'd get a sense of having connected with at least one person out of a billion Chinese.

As a filmmaker I knew there's an "itch" created every time a film cuts to a new location: "Where are we *now?*" While hardly anyone in the audience would recognize the answer Li Po gave them – "These are the hills of Guilin…" or "The magnificence of Huangshan…" – it didn't matter as long as that itch was immediately scratched. "Oh, I see…" they'd say, just before they'd forget the name. It was a simple solution but getting the great poet on film wasn't easy.

Weeks earlier I'd sent a telex to our hosts at China Film Co-Production Corporation and asked them to arrange a casting session in Beijing with a half-dozen local actors who also spoke English. When I arrived in the capital, China Co-Film threw the usual welcoming banquet and sitting across from me at the big table was "your new Li Po!" His name was Mister Du and he had a movie actor's stature and composure about him. I had to admit his deeply resonant voice was appealing. But where were the other candidates? It took me a jet-lagged moment to realize there was to be no casting session. This was it. I was looking at the one and only Li Po, done deal.

In a few days we were to begin a complex schedule of filming that would last through September and October. I was going to have to make the best of this situation simply because there was no time for anything else. The Chinese embraced the Western concept of "ducks in a row" and they'd pulled off their preparations with pride.

The following day we had gone out to the Beijing Film Studios for wardrobe fittings and make-up tests with Mister Du. When he was dressed in the full regalia of a Tang dynasty costume made by the studio, I took a few Polaroids. Someone commented, "Now he looks a bit like Shih Kuan."

They were referring to the lead negotiator for China Co-Film and our main government contact. The previous winter, Disney VP Bob Gibeaut and Randy Bright, a WED Enterprises creative executive, had accompanied me for a week of harried negotiations over each proposed location. We'd spent days slurping gallons of jasmine tea while sitting across from the stoic Shih Kuan who only spoke through translators. Every detail of our production would flow through Shih Kuan, the man responsible for lining up all those ducks. I personally liked him very much, a man caught between wanting to help us while at the same time responsible to his unseen government masters. After that formal January session, he'd revealed that he'd been a movie actor back in the 1940s and 50s. He'd proudly showed me photos taken during his short-lived career before he became a bureaucrat. He didn't yet realize that his current work, that fabled line-up of ducks, was about to be destroyed by the man in costume.

Mister Du announced in his resonant actor voice that he'd recently talked to his agent – a notion that caused my head to spin. "Your *agent*…?"

Even though he had already agreed to our modest fee, the two of them decided it wasn't going to be nearly enough. He wanted $10,000 for his role in such a significant American-Chinese co-production.

He was right about the importance of our project since we were to be fêted that very night at the Great Hall of the People, hosted by no less than the Chinese Minister of Culture. But I was aghast at his asking price, not to mention that Mister Du would try to extort us just as we were about to begin the shoot. He was demanding about 23 years' worth of his normal salary!

I went off to confront Shih Kuan and I'll admit I'd worked up a pretty good head of steam. By the time I arrived at his office, I realized it wasn't entirely his fault. This actor and his *agent* thought they'd stumbled upon a real meal ticket.

"I'm stopping the schedule," I'd told him. "Put everything on hold."

"No, no, that's not possible," said Shih Kuan. "It's all arranged!"

"Yes, but thanks to Mister Du, your schedule is now *un*-arranged. I'm going to get on a plane this afternoon and fly to Hong Kong. You'll have to wait while I set up a *real* casting session with local actors down there. I'll probably be back in a week."

I could see his color draining. Two months of his detailed preparations and scheduling would be delayed, not to mention he'd lose face with his superiors.

"Or..." I said.

"Or what?" he asked, looking desperate for any alternative.

"Or... *you* play the part of Li Po." I showed him the Polaroid of the character in costume and make-up. It really did look like him.

At that moment I didn't want to even contemplate what Bob and Randy might think about seeing Shih Kuan in this role. We had openly discussed strategy right in front of him during the negotiation meetings – kinda based on the man *not speaking English*.

Shih Kuan protested – he was too busy, he had responsibilities, he hadn't acted in a long time, and so on.

I let him squirm a bit and then reminded him, "But if you play the part, we can start on schedule." I promised I would work with him on his performance and give him as much time as he needed. Every actor is insecure at heart.

That was how the two of us found ourselves in the Inner Mongolian grasslands, walking through a rehearsal as the Circle-Vision cameras were set up on a dolly. It took only a couple of takes before I could see Shih Kuan falling back into the familiar rhythms of an actor, enhancing each run-through with more depth, nuance, confidence. By that afternoon, I had several good takes and knew we had our Li Po.

Charter flight to Beijing

Peking Hotel

Visiting Beijing Film Studios

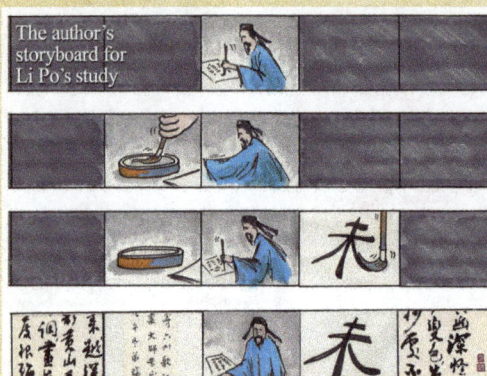
The author's storyboard for Li Po's study

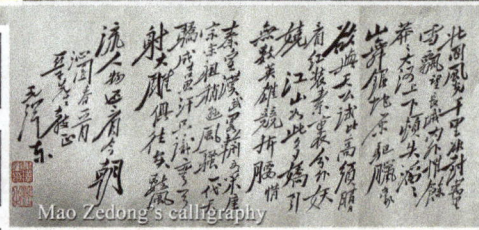
Mao Zedong's calligraphy

"China dolly"

Filming "The Peacock Princess"

Chinese studio dolly with metal wheels and balancing pedestal

Tan Shi Gui — Shen Zhi Hua

CHAPTER 2

The Chinese Way

We returned to Beijing on our chartered Russian plane with what I thought was a pretty good start to the production. We had one difficult location under our belts, and we were preparing to settle into a fairly straightforward and simple shoot at the Beijing Film Studios. It felt in a way like we were coming home to shoot in our own backyard after the exotic challenges of Inner Mongolia.

Camera tech Joe Nash and Guy Jones, our grip, appreciated returning to the now-familiar comforts of the Peking Hotel and its dual Chinese and Western menu. We even willingly put up with the hotel's sullen and uninspired service people. Lines of waiters would stand against a wall chatting and we'd have to wave a menu to get their attention before they'd wander over with a look of "What do you want now?" At the start Joe and Guy both found China not at all to their liking. Most Chinese men were heavy smokers who hacked and coughed up phlegm and spit on the streets. Joe in particular would weave his way around what he called fresh sidewalk goobers. Guy would flinch if he merely heard a Chinese smoker behind him start to clear his throat.

The Beijing Film Studios was located in a suburb of the city, in an aging *hutong* neighborhood filled with walled, compound-like homes that were designed with an inner courtyard and typically housed three generations of one family. The government had started tearing down what they considered these old, shameful homes for new apartment buildings, but the studio preserved some classic *hutongs* as a backlot for period film productions.

We checked in at the gate of the film studio where we were employing several departments and facilities, including their extensive scene dock to create a setting for Li Po's study. This scene was to be filmed with a single camera and later become part of a nine-screen montage. We arrived onstage to find the set already up and pre-lit by studio technicians. This is an area in which Chinese film crews were just as talented as any in Hollywood. Our local production designer and his small crew of art directors had furnished us with exactly what we needed. Overhead lighting was reminiscent of classic movie sets so there was little to adjust once we had Li Po in costume and make-up. Shih Kuan was back in a familiar place as an actor and knew many of the studio crew by name. What I discovered, however, was that his calligraphy left something to be desired.

The idea of the shot was that we would find Li Po writing out one of his poems on large scrolls of rice paper. We had a well-known calligrapher do all the prop set pieces that lay around his study and draped across his table, but we needed our actor to complete his writing on one poem before turning to camera to deliver his lines. I thought having eight of these nearly finished poems would be more than sufficient for filming because we were also providing Shih Kuan with plenty of practice paper. All we needed was for him to dip his brush into a carved Chinese ink tablet, make a few simple strokes, then set down the brush. At this point I'd been traveling in China for a couple of months and was familiar with a few of these techniques myself. I'd learned there's a real art even to the manner in which a calligraphy brush is held. A calligraphy student imagines gripping an egg in the palm while balancing a full wineglass on the back of the hand. This forces the student to not grip the brush so tightly that the theoretical egg would crack. Then they need to make slow, smooth movements forming characters while not spilling the wine.

Any good actor believes they can master any skill just long enough to appear competent for a few moments on camera. But even with practice Shih Kuan turned quite a few of the poems that our master calligrapher had provided into inkblots. After six botched takes, leaving us only two good ones left, I called for a little break. Time for another round of off-camera practice sessions on plain paper. Each Chinese crew member expressed their opinions about what he was doing wrong, adding to his distress. While penmanship is a lost art in America, in China there's a great deal of pride in having a "good hand."

Along with trying to imitate a skilled calligrapher, Shih Kuan was also having to recite his lines in English. He was doing well enough, but I knew we'd have to have another actor loop his words later for clarity and enunciation. I chose to distract him from his problems with the brush and focus instead on a particular line reading.

"What about my terrible writing?" he worried.

"*Mei guan xi,*" I said. "It doesn't matter in this shot." That was a complete lie and not the first ever told to an actor. "The camera doesn't see too much from this angle. I'll just cut to a close-up later."

"Oh, I see." He visibly relaxed and nodded. Of course, that made sense to him.

The next take was better, but still resulted in another Rorschach test. I told him the last one was great but why don't we do one more for safety? The final take with our last good poem was the one we ended up using in the film. Audiences would have to be looking closely to see the muddled character he created, but the polished finesse of his gesture with the brush spoke of the confidence of a master calligrapher and poet.

After lunch I checked out some equipment at the studio. I was particularly intrigued by their collapsible dolly system for location work. The entire rig folded up into a very small package that would be ideal for our needs because it could be reassembled quickly. Could we rent this dolly for the next several months of shooting? The technician who'd given us the demonstration was rather embarrassed to say it was one of a kind. He'd made it from scratch. We were about to leave, thinking maybe Walt Disney Studios could come up with a similar dolly, when my translators said the man would be willing to make us one of our own. Perfect!

That dolly was a lifesaver. We simply called it the "China dolly" and it became a regular part of the Circle-Vision package that I later used on other locations around the world. I'm surprised that rig wasn't used more effectively by the Chinese themselves. On our very first trip to this same studio back in January, Randy, Bob and I had been invited to see the ongoing production of one of their huge costume epics, "The Peacock Princess." We had been impressed with the scope and scale of the production in viewing dailies, but then we went onto the stage and saw the actual camera and dolly rig they were using. It looked like a little wooden flatcar with metal wheels on hard rails. A rigid metal post acted as a fulcrum for a home-built balancing arm. The camera, which looked like an Arriflex from a distance, on close inspection turned out to be a Chinese copy. This was part of their "Buy one, take it apart, make many more just like it" business philosophy. The cameraman sat on a little wooden chair, the kind you might expect in a kindergarten class, operating hand-held while balancing out this ersatz Arriflex camera with a box of lead weights. It was crude but it worked. During that set visit I'd also seen something we joke about in Hollywood: a so-called "Chinese light stand." Hiding behind a pillar of the elaborate castle set was a technician holding up a working light with his arms above his head. In another sign of their make-do innovation, Chinese technicians had come up with their own special effects facility which used an infrared screen for matting. Basically the screen was back-lit with heat lamps. They would do shots of a flying princess (a common theme) photographed hanging in an elaborate, jury-rigged contraption 15 feet tall made entirely out of bamboo. It looked more like a medieval torture device than state-of-the-art movie equipment.

We returned to our stage to finish the last piece of our studio shooting: Li Po in a cave, another single-camera shot to become part of a larger composite later. We had the prop department rig up a fake lantern that he could carry while approaching the camera out of the darkness, like a Chinese version of Diogenes. The wires for the battery-operated light ran through Li Po's voluminous sleeves. Compared to the scene in the study, this was very straightforward – no calligraphy required – and we were able to wrap quite early.

As we were leaving the stage midafternoon, I was stopped by a studio guard. I wasn't in trouble, he just wanted to make a comment after observing us from the stage door. He waved over one of our translators to explain that he was very impressed that we Americans had accomplished so much in one day. I wondered if he was joking. Seriously, two simple set-ups? He said he hoped Chinese filmmakers could learn from our efficiency. This had been the lightest day on our schedule and back home it would have barely qualified as a half day. But I eventually came to understand his comment. A year later his studio was still working on "The Peacock Princess." Time and budget weren't significant factors in their industry.

The reason for this was the Chinese economy of this era was still dominated by Mao Zedong's concept that came to be called the Iron Rice Bowl. This cradle-to-grave system ensured everyone had enough food, shelter, a job, and access to healthcare. The downside was that everyone made the same every month – in those days about $35. Everyone at the Beijing Film Studios made the same salary – the guard who complimented us, well-known actors, the lowliest technicians, even the head of production. But this raised in our minds the question of lack of incentive to work harder, to be more successful. It was clear the waiters at the Peking Hotel had no incentive to excel. We weren't allowed to tip them in encouragement because that was seen as fomenting "class differences." We didn't know it then, but the Iron Rice Bowl and this disparity between Chinese and American ways of working was going to create an enormous rift that would take us a very long time to overcome.

We packed our bags to fly to Chengdu in Sichuan Province, the jumping-off point for our trip into Tibet. We were going to film at the Potala Palace, one of the most iconic and memorable sights in the world. This would be my second time in Tibet as our film required a very thorough survey to pinpoint all camera positions before coming back to these same places with the film crew and equipment. To be as efficient and expedient as that studio guard had admired, we had to map out every move well in advance. I'd spent two full months scouting locations to determine precisely where our Circle-Vision cameras should be placed. In some ways, the most important decisions I'd be making on the film were already locked in.

That night we received a visit at our hotel from Tan, our Chinese location manager. We usually met every night to confirm plans for the next day, but tonight he was obviously anxious. He told us through our translators that there two problems. His assistant, Shen Zhi Hua, would have to immediately fly south to Guangzhou to negotiate with the People's Liberation Army (PLA), for permission to do helicopter photography. Leon, my volatile American production manager, did as he usually did in these instances and hit the ceiling. He reminded Tan these negotiations were supposed to have concluded months earlier. I tried to calm Leon down because we weren't scheduled to film helicopter shots for several weeks.

"What's the second problem?" I asked Tan, knowing it was a Chinese trait to hold back bad news as long as possible.

"The location you picked for the Potala Palace," he said. *"Bu hao!"* No good.

By this time, we had gone through months of on-again, off-again permissions for Tibet, stuck in a kind of bureaucratic revolving door. One day we'd be invited to visit but couldn't shoot, or later they'd say maybe we could, then a few days would pass and they'd say we couldn't even visit. When the door had finally swung open, we dashed in for a quick survey. Now Tan was saying circumstances had changed at a camera site we'd thought was approved. Tan wouldn't, or couldn't, tell me what had changed, but the PLA or their brethren at the PSB (Public Security Bureau) were usually in the middle of it.

After Tan and the rest of the Chinese crew left, I took stock of where we were and what it would mean for our success or failure. I'd been personally tasked with making a film about China, a place that most Americans would never visit, for a massive new Disney theme park that had a hard opening date and a theater being built for this film. We'd made plans to photograph one of the most far-off lands, the so-called Roof of the World, the Tibetan Autonomous Region of China, but that now looked doubtful. I kept thinking about what the studio guard had observed about our American style of working. I wondered if we really were more efficient and practical, or was I not yet seeing through Chinese eyes. Was one way better than another? Did I need to find a way to embrace both?

I felt a growing sense of the immense burden I was facing. Had self-delusion or ambition clouded my mind? Whatever made me think I alone should interpret China to the rest of the world? Self-doubt crept up slowly at first, like a rising tide, then the waves seemed to break over me all at once.

That night I was troubled by thoughts of *how exactly did I end up here?*

CHAPTER 3

Little Miss Pu

I was a long way from home.

Born in Canada but raised in the Detroit area, I would always think of myself as a Midwesterner. But Southern California made me feel like a displaced person where my ingrained values and work ethic were constantly being tested.

My wife Kathy and I had moved west from Michigan in 1975 after one brutal winter. Early one morning I'd shoveled snow to get out of our driveway to go to work at Omnicom Productions in Lansing. The small company made sales films, training films, medical films, documentaries, you name it. After a very long day I again had to shovel a foot of snow out of my driveway just to get my car in off the street. Then late that same night a third storm hit. I'd cleared about half of our driveway before I flung the shovel as far as I could, unleashing a primal yell. Not everyone can pinpoint the precise moment they were done with wintery climes forever.

I'd been making short personal films since junior high school and professional films since college with awards along the way, so it seemed a natural progression to head to the center of the film business. "Hollywood" had always pulled at me, like a deep gravity well. But make no mistake, the transition was only possible because Kathy has always been a willing and supportive partner.

On our long drive across the country I wrestled with how I would no longer be able to "do everything" on a film. Hollywood was highly compartmentalized, specialized, and unionized, that much I knew. I'd have to pick one job and then stick with it: writer, director, editor, cameraman, or even special effects. I'd enjoyed doing them all, but the idea I could continue that practice in the so-called big leagues was ridiculous.

Kathy and I rented a cramped little duplex in Burbank just a day before our furniture arrived. Our savings would only last a short while, so I called on my few contacts. Two friends I'd worked with at Michigan State University's film unit both recommended me for the same job: production manager on an IMAX film. Before "To Fly" was finished and premiered at the National Air and Space Museum in Washington, I'd been elevated to Associate Producer, contributed shots to the film as a cameraman, arranged props, did local casting, surveyed locations, and was pressed into playing two different characters in the film. Oh, and I built the spaceship for the finale in my spare time. I had landed at a place that actually wanted me to use my many skills.

But I also had to contend with the laid-back business practices of Greg MacGillivray and Jim Freeman. These two friendly and persuasive filmmakers got their start making surf movies and were part of a beach culture that was truly foreign to me. Suddenly it felt like I was living inside a Beach Boys' album. I remember my very first day at the Villa Bella, the beautiful offices of MacGillivray-Freeman Films in Laguna Beach. I was downstairs calculating the budget and scheduling locations for the ambitious "To Fly" and keeping an eye on the clock as we worked right past the dinner hour. Greg and Jim were still at it upstairs, nearing nine o'clock. I was thinking maybe I'd made a mistake in negotiating my daily rate. I've never been afraid of hard work but my stomach was growling and Kathy was waiting for me back in Burbank, about 60 miles away.

Finally, I went upstairs and said, "Uh, guys, is every night going to be like this?"

Jim said, "Oh God, no! We only stuck around because you were still working!" They both laughed in relief.

Greg added, "We didn't want you to get the wrong impression of us."

The next day I learned two key truths about beach culture: first, Greg and Jim would come into the office late if the surf was up. Second, they'd leave work early if the surf was up.

Eventually I adapted. But so did they.

I ended up full-time at MacGillivray-Freeman Films for several years, even after the company suffered a horrible tragedy. Greg had been in Washington installing the final print of our IMAX film at the National Air and Space Museum. Meanwhile, Jim and I were scouting locations in the mountains around Bishop, California, for a Kodak TV commercial. Jim Freeman, who'd won an Academy Award for his beautiful helicopter photography, died in a sudden crash along with an advertising executive. I had to call Greg with the worst news of his life. After a six-month hiatus when none of us even wanted to *think* about work, I added aerial photography to my growing list of other duties, along with editor, writer, and cameraman.

In the fall of 1980, Walt Disney Productions phoned our offices hoping that Greg, a filmmaker famous for stunning IMAX spectacles, would be interested in taking on a project for what was going to be called EPCOT Center. I was surprised Greg didn't come right out and say, "No." We were in the middle of scheduling a big IMAX production in Hawaii for the exact same time period. But Greg didn't like to turn down prestigious projects so his plan was to swap me out for him as the filmmaker. He just didn't inform Disney I'd be making their China project until we were well along into the approvals process.

During one of the preliminary meetings at WED, Greg introduced me to Randy Bright, the creative executive responsible for all EPCOT films, and Don Henderson, their executive production manager. Both Don and Randy looked me over with suspicion as a kind of usurper or wannabe filmmaker. I was already thinking of myself as the bait and switch. Greg assured them he would be on location in China every step of the way, even if I was the one writing and directing the film. I knew Greg's previous commitments in Hawaii would be in conflict but kept my mouth shut. Midwestern ethics be damned, I guess. Don and Randy asked for my résumé, saying they'd have to share it with Ron Miller, head of Walt Disney Studios. The son-in-law of Walt himself. Gulp!

I threw myself into China research but was severely limited to a few recent books, a handful of dense scholarly articles, and a couple of documentary films, all sources that were full of contemporary politics. Tell someone you're going to the People's Republic of China in 1980 and they'd automatically say, "You mean Red China?" The Cultural Revolution had slammed the doors so tightly to the West that getting a real sense of the country and people was difficult without being on the ground. I wanted the film to be truthful, but I also wanted it to be acceptable to both East and West without stirring up any trouble, meaning politics or ideology.

Randy and Don must have been impressed that I'd photographed the helicopter shots for Stanley Kubrick's "The Shining" because they handed my somewhat limited résumé on to Ron Miller. Within a few weeks Greg and I walked into the studio head's office. I admit I was only semiconscious with fear during my pitch. Miller, a former football player, had an imposing presence but the end result was that he said the project was a "go."

Randy handed me a recently published book entitled "China Scenes." It was full of beautiful images of fantastic locations taken by China's best photographers who'd probably waited months for the perfect light. But the book was mostly in Chinese.

Randy said, "Here, this is what we want. Make it into a film."

Well, sure… why not?

His simple comment turned out to be my one directive, my one instance of guidance from Disney, and it set in motion everything to come.

Only a couple of people on the whole planet had ever made a Circle-Vision film before. One of them was Ub Iwerks, the man who sketched Mickey Mouse for Walt and invented the nine-camera process. Ub had been gone for many years but his son Don ran the studio's machine shop which maintained the cameras. His shop was a fantastic technical resource but not so much a creative one. There existed no manual of what makes for a good 360 shot. My knowledge of the medium had to be extrapolated from several back-to-back-to-back viewings of "America the Beautiful" at Disneyland.

The original film had been shot primarily from the roof of a station wagon with the crew simply driving towards interesting subjects, like the United Nations building in New York. What they captured on the side cameras was somewhat incidental. Often it was pedestrians staring at the strange contraption motoring past. I was determined we were going to do better with our new film.

I spent the next few months tearing out images of Chinese scenics from picture books, buying every postcard in LA's Chinatown, roaming through library stacks at the University of California, Irvine. No ripping out images there. What could be done today in an hour on Google took me several weeks of nonstop research trying to correlate the images in "China Scenes" to specific locales I could track on a National Geographic map. I assembled my proposed locations into three thick photo albums in preparation for a face-to-face negotiation with Chinese government officials. Even then, I was hopelessly naïve about what we were attempting to do in such a vast and diverse country.

My anxieties at first were focused on traveling to China with Randy Bright and Bob Gibeaut. Bob was one of only six vice presidents at Disney in those days, so we went First Class and had sleeperette cabins on Japan Airlines. Bob made it clear that my crew and I would NOT be flying this way for the actual production.

We'd brought with us a newly struck print of "Fantasia" at the insistence of David Hayden, Disney's lawyer for the project. Despite only being in his forties, David was considered an "old China hand." He thought screening the film would be considered a cultural event since it hadn't been seen in China since it was released in 1940. Bob was particularly concerned about the print's safety because he had a sense of ownership: "Fantasia" was the first film he'd worked on at the studio. Everyone I met at Disney seemed to have these connections to such familiar touchstones.

Charles Randy Bright represented the classic Disney success story. He'd been hired while a political science student at Cal State Fullerton and worked his way up from a Jungle Cruise guide to senior special projects director for the company's theme parks. On the flight over, Randy's immediate concern was more mundane: that he would be forced to eat a Chinese preserved egg. The so-called Hundred-Year Eggs are wrapped in clay and straw, then buried. The yolks turn black with age and the whites become a sickly translucent green with a pungent smell. I thought we'd be okay to simply say, "No, thank you" without causing an international incident. Still, Randy fretted the Chinese might somehow sneak one of these disgusting delicacies onto his plate.

On the flight's last leg from Japan, we finally crossed China's border. I was glad I'd traded seats with another passenger for a window, even though I had to sit next to a smoker. China's terrain in January was a drab, monotone brown. As we descended lower, I could make out little communities of primitive brick and mortar buildings linked by narrow winding country roads. Actual communes! Closer to the ground I spotted a man in a fur cap and thick quilted coat peddling his bicycle between villages. As I became aware of other peasants and farmers, the reality of where we were finally hit me.

The January air was icy and dry as Randy, Bob, and I were met at the Beijing airport by Miss Pu, a diminutive young translator in a yellow head scarf, a thin coat, and brown baggy trousers. She efficiently whisked us away to Beijing in a chauffeured car. We weren't being accorded VIP treatment because, as we quickly learned, everyone in a car had their own driver. There were very few automobiles in China, and all were assigned to government units. Our driver smoked like a chimney and wore a shapeless blue tunic with four large pockets and kept his collar buttoned up against the cold. Like all government drivers, he wore white cotton gloves with one hand firmly on the horn. The man careened straight down the middle of a two-lane country road, only giving way to oncoming traffic at the last minute, like a game of chicken.

I glanced over at Randy who had a fearful look. He mouthed the words, "Are we going to die?"

The Peking Hotel (which still insisted on using the old designation for the city) had a sweeping elevated drive to a covered portico, impressive for its day. Government drivers waited around in the parking lot below, smoking while dusting their already spotless vehicles. At the front door someone from the Public Security Bureau stopped every Chinese visitor and asked for a government unit number. Foreigners could pass without questions, but Chinese people needed approval to enter, as if the hotel were a den of Western vices. I saw many locals turn away, rather than admit they weren't on official business.

We checked into large rooms with decor that seemed like Soviet vintage. The black-and-white TV only had one channel, mostly showing political recaps of the latest Communist Congress, interrupted occasionally by actual *commercials* for heavy industrial equipment. Who was watching this stuff, Capitalists? We ran into some British expatriates in the vast lobby who quietly warned us that the top floor of the 17-story hotel was given over to teams of Public Security Bureau personnel.

"They listen in on the conversations of Westerners, so watch what you say!"

I counted the hotel's floors from the outside and then made a note that the elevators stopped one floor short of the top. Just what we needed at the start of our trip – an added a sense of paranoia.

That same day, Miss Pu invited us to walk with her down to the impressive Tiananmen Square a few blocks away. She shocked us by freely speaking about the Cultural Revolution – the subject we were told never to bring up in conversation.

The massive upheaval from 1966 to 1976 killed millions, destroyed centuries-old monuments, buildings, and relics, and sent millions of its citizens to re-education camps. The national nightmare had only ended five years earlier with the death of Mao Zedong. His notorious wife, Jiang Qing, was about to go on trial for retaliation against her enemies while she was a member of the "Gang of Four." During this decade of terror, any family that had attained any sense of upward mobility was attacked and vilified by Red Guards and Miss Pu's family had been singled out. Her faint schoolgirl voice told us of the atrocities against her father in particular but she remained calm, measured, as if she were listing classes she'd taken at university. It was a stunner for the three of us that she could be so open about these personal calamities.

Still fighting jet lag, I was up at 5 the next morning to walk around the vicinity of the hotel. The normally bustling city was quiet, like a pall had descended. The only people I encountered were teams of female street sweepers. They were huddled against the cold in quilted coats, wore surgical face masks for the dust, and used long bundles of reeds to brush debris along the curbs. Very soon the sounds of *brinnng-brinnng* announced the first of the morning's bicycles. They would come in battalions.

After a breakfast of oily eggs made hours earlier, we again met Miss Pu. She led us on a tour of the Forbidden City, another fabled locale that humbles any visitor. We passed through the massive vermillion walls of the Meridian Gate, through expansive courtyards and into the most fantastic and ornate palaces and halls. I quickly spotted a couple of great locations for filming, such as the Hall of Heavenly Purity in the center of the Imperial Museum. We typically think of great skyscrapers as awe-inspiring, but in Chinese architecture the visual impact comes from scale and width, not height. Perfect horizontal symmetry represents balance and harmony.

The four of us entered one of the great palaces, crossing over a wooden threshold five inches high that been worn down and scraped of its red paint by countless visitors. Thresholds were used in China to protect a family's home from evil spirits as well as to control rainwater. Stepping over one was supposed to make the person entering more conscious of their physical acts.

As I was trying to get photographs of the Dragon Throne, a crowd of Chinese tourists shouldered their way in front of me, making it difficult to get a good angle. From behind came this loud commanding Chinese voice. The people suddenly moved back, making a path so I grabbed a couple of quick photos. When I turned around, standing there was little Miss Pu. She'd somehow made these civilians jump like they'd been zapped with a taser. I never learned what she'd said, but I was awed by the power that could be manifested by such a small lady with the right tone of voice. This incident also spoke of a rigid and unquestioning obedience among the populace. I recalled reading that during Mao's disastrous Great Leap Forward of the late 1950s, he'd put out a directive that every man, woman, and child was ordered to swat and kill five flies per day due to rampant outbreaks of disease. I don't know if the policy improved anyone's health or sanitation, but you could be certain 35 billion house flies died every week.

Wanfujing's only department store

The Great Wall at Badaling

Bob, Randy, and Miss Pu

A section in disrepair

A section under repair

China's official "One Child" policy

Miss Pu and Bob at the Ming Tombs

CHAPTER 4

No One Ever Says "Yes"

Randy, Bob, and I were ushered into a stuffy room at the Peking Hotel. For the first time, we were meeting with leaders of China Film Co-Production Corporation, an agency of the Ministry of Culture. Madame Li was the silent but polite figurehead while Shih Kuan, the true point man, appeared standoffish and aloof, slurping his jasmine tea noisily. Through a translator, he made brief remarks about the importance of "the spirit of cooperation between our two countries." Before I knew it, the spotlight was on me. It stayed there for the next few hours.

As I went through my photo albums, province by province, I felt I was being tested on my knowledge of Chinese geography, history, and culture. In a way I was because they wanted justification for every suggestion I made. Randy and Bob were unable to help. The Chinese side offered no commitments, other than the occasional flat-out "No" to certain places they considered off limits. It would take months of schmoozing with them during the surveys before we ever really understood what lay behind the negative responses. If we'd known we were never going to hear "Yes," we might have been able to offer better counterarguments or explanations. What seemed to be at the heart of their reticence was fear. They lacked any understanding of the capabilities of this bizarre camera system of ours. They somehow believed Circle-Vision could see around mountains or all the way across a province, so they wanted to make sure we never came within miles of a what they considered a sensitive locale. And that seemed to include all the places on my list I wanted to shoot.

My most effective rationale turned out to be describing how Americans of different generations saw them, such as the way my own father could only think of China as the wintry landscapes from the Korean War. My mission, I explained, was to show Western audiences the broadest diversity of landscapes and people from all corners of China.

They nodded and said they appreciated our needs but were adamant that certain areas had to remain off limits. I'd prepared materials on 150 locations, expecting that many would be eliminated, which meant we could sometimes barter, like trading one sacred mountain for another that was less problematic. Shih Kuan openly shared that there were military and strategic areas that we would not be allowed to approach. "Strategic" usually meant facilities or installations that the Soviets might find tempting, like bridges, tunnels, or trains. For years the Chinese had expected an imminent invasion from the north, so they'd moved military bases, powerplants, and resupply depots to remote areas. Unfortunately, those hard-to-reach areas were often right in the middle of beautiful scenic regions. The idea seemed sacrilegious to us, like building a coal-powered factory right in the middle of Yellowstone National Park. Sometimes when the Chinese said "No," it was quite wide-ranging and absolute, such as forget about the entirety of Fujian Province because it overlooks the strait of Taiwan. I was thinking if ground shots were going to be this difficult, then helicopter photography would be nearly impossible.

After I'd presented dozens and dozens of potential sites, Bob and Randy huddled with me during a break to ask if there was *anything* we had permission to film. Were we going to burn through 150 locales without ever hearing the word "Yes"? We finally settled on the strategy that a Chinese "No" was literal, but if they didn't actually reject a place outright, then perhaps it was possible. We hoped silence was their version of "Yes." Or at least "Maybe."

In the second half of the meeting, the Chinese found a way to gain an advantage. Somehow they persuaded Bob to hand over his preliminary budget for the film. The numbers would give them a great deal of leverage in negotiating the services and fees the studio would have to pay for. Minutes later someone from the China Co-Film office walked into the meeting and grabbed our metal film canisters. We protested but "Fantasia," which Bob had so carefully guarded, was gone. We were told they were just going to "check the print" but we later figured they were going to host a private screening for their bosses at the Ministry of Culture. So much for our cultural event.

Whenever we posed a question Shih Kuan couldn't immediately answer, they'd send us off to play tourists. We knew they were running the issue up the government flagpole. We left the meeting feeling somewhat dispirited, so Miss Pu offered to take us to Beijing's one main shopping street, Wangfujing. What we found was a single depressing department store with the charm of a 1950s

Woolworths, if most of the shelves were empty.

The next day while our hosts conferred once more with their bosses, Miss Pu took us to visit the Great Wall at Badaling, an hour's drive away. One section of the wall had been repaired and restored but much of the surrounding sections across the brown hillsides were crumbling and in ruins. Even this public section had been marred by Chinese graffiti scratched onto seemingly every brick.

Bob handed out Mickey Mouse stickers to many of the small kids we came across which seemed to be a big hit. I don't think the kids recognized Mickey but smiled because it was a gift from an American. Toddlers usually wore split trousers, which seemed odd to us. Then we found out it's so they can go to bathroom easily – which they did wherever they happened to be standing. Chinese parents of a single boy treated their son like a little prince. Having only one child was the official policy of the day and we saw this reflected in billboards and posters that proclaimed, "It Is Better To Have One Child Only." The implied threat on the billboard was real: there were severe ramifications for violations of this nationwide dictate.

Randy and I made the mistake of jogging along the Great Wall in parched winter air while dust from the Gobi Desert had drifted over the area. I came down with a fearsome chest cold that resisted even horrible-tasting Chinese herbal remedies. That night Bob confided that as far as he was concerned, Greg MacGillivray didn't need to come on location at all because I'd shown I could handle the project myself. As confirmation, he and Randy presented me with a gold Mickey Mouse watch as a full-fledged member of the team. While that made me feel a little better, that night I'd have traded the watch for some good ole American cold medicine.

It was the tradition of co-ventures that banquets were reciprocated. After China Co-Film hosted us at the fantastic Peking Duck Restaurant, Disney planned to host our own celebratory dinner at a pavilion in nearby Beihai Park. We had no idea how to do this but basically the Chinese would organize both banquets and we'd pick up the tab for the second one. For the obligatory toasts, usually Maotai was served, a fiery drink called *bai jiu*. The alcoholic content of this sorghum-based liquor is 180 proof, basically making it moonshine or hooch. I'd observed occasions when the stuff had been poured into an ashtray and ignited to burn with a bright blue flame. It was considered impolite to refuse a sip.

Randy was feeling in good spirits and began sampling dozens of dishes on a gigantic lazy susan in the middle of the round table. Before I could warn him, he'd popped a preserved egg into his mouth and had begun to chew. The ghastly look on his face was priceless. I gave him credit for not spitting it out. I noticed after the incident that he drank a lot more Maotai.

At the end of our week of meetings, it was time for the screening of "Fantasia." We'd been told we could expect the most prestigious audience of artists and cultural icons of Beijing that night, the cream of their artistic world. But we nervously paced the huge empty theater as showtime approached. Had there been a screw-up of some sort? Did notices not go out? Suddenly the doors opened, and streams of noisy rabble rushed in to grab the best seats. They were dressed in the muted blues and grays of ubiquitous Mao jackets and it looked for all the world as if our hosts had just directed traffic in off the streets. Where were the poets, opera singers, and famous filmmakers?

Our lawyer David Hayden arrived to reassure us these were, in fact, an audience of exceptional and influential people, as advertised. This wasn't so much an Oscars crowd as an example of the lingering uniformity of Mao's China. Then David went up to the podium to introduce our film and I saw a reaction I'll never forget.

The Chinese language is a powerful private bond between its people that creates a barrier of exclusion. They'd long been indoctrinated to believe Westerners cannot speak their unique and difficult language. If we attempt it, we just mangle the pronunciation and delicate tones, destroying any meaning. When David Hayden spoke his first few words, the entire crowd gasped simultaneously. I swear if this theater had curtains, they would have swayed at the sudden intake of breath. His Mandarin was so flawless that the audience was left stunned. He told us later that on his travels through China he'd sometimes stop to ask directions. Farmers and peasants would just stare at him slack-jawed. What language was coming out of the mouth of this "foreign devil," they wondered, because it couldn't possibly be Chinese.

Our night turned out to be a success, if not quite a cultural event. My private concerns that the audience would be offended by the movie's dancing mushrooms that looked like they were wearing coolie hats came to nothing. Miss Pu and our hosts gave us traditional bottles of Maotai to take back to America. On our flight out of China, Randy and Bob proclaimed that if they never saw another grain of rice they'd be just fine.

Well, good for you, I thought, but I'd be back in late April for the real test, the first of two month-long surveys of many far-flung locations, traveling with an all-Chinese crew. There was gonna be a helluva lot of rice in my future.

Ding, Bao, and Leon

He Bao Zhang

Ding Hai Hua

The Hall of Prayer for Good Harvests, the Temple of Heaven

Director's survey photos of the Forbidden City

Holiday crowds at the Summer Palace

A professional photographer takes tourist pictures

Bound feet

Second Class sleeping compartment

Entering Sichuan Province

Forgotten shoes in the Chongqing guesthouse

A river cruiser on the Yangtze

The Three Gorges

Anhui Province

The town of Huangshan

CHAPTER 5

OFF THE DEEP END

At Disney's suggestion, I began taking private Mandarin lessons from an instructor at a language center in Mission Viejo. There was no way to become proficient like David Hayden, but I saw the immediate value in picking up some skills. One particular word I learned very quickly was *tóngzhì* meaning "comrade." During the Cultural Revolution, the word was added to the end of sentences so often that it had almost lost its meaning. Years later, it was still favored by the older generations. Meanwhile, I was going to have to wedge my location surveys into and around MacGillivray-Freeman's upcoming IMAX shoot in Hawaii where I was expected to film second unit and helicopter shots.

As part of my frantic preparation, I interviewed Leon Chooluck, a 61-year-old production manager recommended by Fred Roos of American Zoetrope who'd worked with him on "Apocalypse Now." Leon had been around Hollywood a long time, going back to "High Noon," and had been location manager on the TV series "I Spy." In the late 1950s Leon had even directed a couple of episodes of "Highway Patrol" and reminded me of the show's star, Broderick Crawford, in both temperament and physique. What had once been a barrel chest had dropped below his belt, but Leon continued to display the brashness and confidence of a New Yorker. Leon promised that when we had enough free time in China, he would tell the hair-raising tale of Coppola's first day on his disastrous and epic production in the Philippines. I said I looked forward to it and figured with that kind of location experience he could certainly handle whatever China could throw at him.

Randy Bright gave the two of us a number of items to present on our surveys, much of it Disney memorabilia. We were to judge the relative importance of the people who helped us along the way and decide what would be an appropriate gift. We had a bunch of decals and stickers, a good handful of Mickey pins, a dozen Disney fountain pen sets, a few pairs of gold earrings, and just a couple of Mickey watches (not nearly as classy as mine).

When the two of us arrived in Beijing at the end of April 1981, our luggage (and all those gifts) didn't show up. Leon made quite a fuss at the airport, immediately demonstrating his short temper and dearth of diplomatic skills. No amount of yelling was going to make our bags appear, but I let him blow off steam. By the time we'd checked into the Peking Hotel I was desperate for a change of clothes. The hotel staff suggested I go to the local Friendship Store, a chain of foreigners-only establishments in major cities. When there, I bought a toothbrush and toothpaste, both of which were the local Seagull brand. The texture and flavor were like wallpaper paste. I wasn't surprised that the two pairs of Chinese underwear I bought were also Seagull brand as the company also made cigarettes. Probably bicycles and industrial machinery, too.

At China Co-Film, we had our first introduction to Tan Shi Gui, our 50-year-old Chinese production manager. Leon later confided his suspicions: he thought Tan was an Army plant whose real function was to spy on us and act as our minder. I preferred to withhold judgment until we saw Tan's organizational skills for ourselves.

Along with Tan, we were assigned our two young translators, He Bao Zhang and Ding Hai Hua. They would prove to be invaluable with more than their language skills. At this time there was still relatively little contact with Westerners, so students of English had to learn in a vacuum with no true speakers to correct pronunciation or give a sense of modern usage. That meant talking to these young people was like communicating through a time warp. Luckily Bao and Ding loved to hear our latest expressions and slang and they absorbed a lot. On a subsequent trip I brought a book of American idioms and they devoured it. These boys were able to supply a little sensibility to some of the more tired Communist ideals and notions. Their lives were going to be different as a result of mixing with an American crew and they seemed to sense that right away. Bao (who was called Shao He by the Chinese crew, meaning "Little River") was the more detail-oriented, the historian and scholar, while Ding had a broader conceptual view with a better sense of when diplomacy needed to prevail.

Very quickly Tan and the boys led us on a forced march through a number of Beijing locales, such as the Temple of Heaven complex. Its magnificent Hall of Prayer for Good Harvests was the model for the theater entrance at EPCOT's China Pavilion in Florida. The triple-gabled circular building rests on three levels of carved marble and was a sacred site visited twice a year by the Emperor. Unlike the Forbidden City's yellow-tiled roofs, these were colored blue to match the sky. Nearby was a main hall with huge wooden doors that opened onto a view of the circular temple. I thought this might be a great spot for a Circle-Vision shot, perhaps even the ending of the film. The only problem was the classic doors were in shabby condition with the red paint looking faded and chipped. I mentioned to Tan that they should ask the authorities if we could touch up the paint for filming. You'd think I'd suggested they burn the whole place down. That was simply NOT happening. The general state of disrepair of many sites we toured across China became an ongoing issue. To us it was simple: didn't they want the place to look its best for a film that would last for years? Did we care more than they did?

Our luggage finally turned up and we had a meeting with Shih Kuan. Unlike during our formal negotiation meeting, this time he was personable and warm. And he openly spoke English. He raved about our upcoming survey schedule which would have us rushing off to Inner Mongolia, to Tibet, and down the Yangtze River. All of this was good news, until he mentioned they'd be needing that $200,000 we'd promised them. In January Bob Gibeaut had agreed to $100,000 to cover the Chinese costs of production. With Bob back in Burbank, I felt like Leon and I were getting squeezed. Was this the way the Chinese did business? Worse, was the whole film going to unravel? Telexes, our only reliable form of communication with the studio, flew back and forth.

Meanwhile Tan continued to show us possible locations in the Beijing area. One day we were loaded into their car and their driver took us south out of the city. We came to a sudden screeching halt. A big billboard ahead proclaimed in multiple languages that no foreigners were allowed beyond this point without proper permission from the authorities. We made a quick U-turn back to the city. Tan never admitted that he'd forgotten our papers that day.

One lesson I learned in these early attempts to scout locations was that the special Disney equipment I'd been given was not very useful. Imagine two round, flat metal plates, one rotating horizontally over the other and mounted on a sturdy tripod. A still camera with a 32 mm lens was mounted on a bracket on the top plate to facilitate making 360-degree photos that more or less matched what the Circle-Vision rig would see. In theory it was fine, but I was terrifically frustrated using it, not because it didn't work as intended, but because it showed me how often a location in China was *not* going to work. A bubble level was attached to the top plate because Circle-Vision really works best when it takes a perfectly flat scene. Unfortunately for me, China was full of fantastic locales that were split-level, an object of great interest up at one height, then a matching object down at another. Using the analogy of a lighthouse: the beam of light arcs around in all directions, but there is *a lot* that it does not illuminate. Our camera rig may see in 360 degrees, but only 30 degrees vertically, missing a lot. I found it much easier and much faster to take my own photos, just keeping the horizon straight.

During our Beijing survey, the city was lit up with festive lights for the coming May Day celebrations. It also meant crowds of local tourists were overflowing at the Summer Palace and the Great Wall. Professional photographers set up their cameras at these sites. Their typical set-up was an elevated platform with the husband or boyfriend sitting at a table with a colorful tablecloth and vase of plastic flowers. The wife or girlfriend stood to one side trying for a look of pure domestication despite the Ming Tombs in the background.

While touring the grounds, I saw a sad legacy of China's past: an old woman hobbling along between two younger women who helped steady her. Foot binding was a horrific and archaic practice that reached its zenith during the Song dynasty but was outlawed in the early 20th century. Too late for this poor woman.

Our pace was exhausting and we were still jet-lagged. Leon mostly slept through the nightly entertainment of acrobat shows and a ballet performance of "Along the Silk Road."

We received official word through David Hayden that our Chinese partners understood we owed two payments of $100,000 each. But in the meeting I'd remembered Bob had written the number down on a yellow legal pad. He'd flashed me the amount he was going to offer, as if he'd needed my approval. It wasn't my money, so I'd nodded and Bob told the Chinese how much we'd pay for their services. In the end, I think Bob just had to bite the bullet and agreed. I'm sure he could hear the EPCOT Opening Day Countdown Clock ticking in his sleep. This double fee was no reason to shut down the film.

The five of us – Leon, Tan, Bao, Ding and I – set off on a whirlwind survey by planes, cars, minibuses, and old steam trains. Every time we'd come to a new town, there'd be welcoming ceremonies, banquets, speeches from the head of the local Communist Party, and an exchange of gifts. The Disney items were wildly appreciated, and we realized we should have been carrying twice as much loot with us.

Traveling in such close proximity taught us a lot about our Chinese team, especially when we were forced to get somewhere by train. There was no First Class (the notion itself was considered bourgeois) so Second Class was the best on offer. They called this "soft seat," as opposed to the Third Class hard wooden benches. One night we were on a train from Chengdu to Chongqing in Sichuan Province. That day we'd received upsetting news that we were once again being *dis*-invited to Tibet, putting us in a lousy mood. There was no escape from the blaring patriotic music and pronouncements played through the train's speaker system at all hours, so Leon and I took turns lowering the volume of that horrid racket. The conductor made sure the volume control stayed cranked up to the highest level. One time we turned it down while the conductor was in another rail car and Leon used a penknife to pop off the knob, then threw it out a train window.

That same evening the two of us had to share a sleeping compartment that was suffocating with Sichuan's heat and humidity. We couldn't imagine what it was going to be like in the summer. Our only relief came when the train was moving, and we could open a window for ventilation. After a few minutes, cinders and smoke from the old steam engine covered my pillow in a layer of dark ash and soot. I sweated like a pig through the night and was awakened by loud arguments on the platforms whenever the train stopped. Leon proved he could sleep through anything.

At dawn we enjoyed the mountainous Sichuan scenery despite a lingering fog and haze. This beautiful terrain has been notoriously unstable and an epicenter for many of China's most disastrous earthquakes. We were met at the Chongqing station by a woman from Cultural Affairs named Zhao, then taken in two Russian-made cars onto the landscaped grounds of an elaborate guesthouse once used during a visit by President Ford. Leon and I were each given a whole suite of rooms to ourselves. I took advantage of the relative luxury and spread out my personal effects in different rooms. I made the mistake of placing a new pair of running shoes under one of the many beds in my suite.

We were hustled off early in the morning for our cruise down the Yangtze despite a sky black with a fearsome storm. Lightning flashed every few seconds as we made our way through a downpour into our boat's Second Class cabins. Meals on board were segregated and we couldn't help but notice the Third Class passengers gathered at our windows, staring at us while we ate. Eventually the ship navigated up through the famous Three Gorges, an area that I could see would be target-rich for later filming with our Circle-Vision cameras. When we disembarked at Yicheng, I finally noticed I was missing the shoes that I'd specifically brought for the upcoming climb of Huangshan. Tan took me out to multiple stores in Yicheng looking for Chinese shoes that might fit. All they had were green canvas Army surplus and nothing in my size. I wear 9½, but seriously – my feet are bigger than those of the People's Liberation Army?

Our next stop was Wuhan, considered one of the "Three Furnaces of the Yangtze." It was treacherously hot already so we understood why Tan had set up our survey for spring and not summer. From there we flew to unspoiled

Anhui Province where lush green lowlands gave way to jagged mountains terraced with rice. Driving along the roads we saw faded remnants of Mao's famous Cultural Revolution slogans, like "The Factory is Small, the Aspirations High, Striving to make Great Contributions!" or "Hold High the Great Red Banner of Mao Zedong Thought!" During the 300-kilometer drive to Huangshan, we saw many changes in architecture from the mud huts and thatched roofs of the north to the curved roof corners, painted designs, and plastered brick buildings in the south.

Our hotel at the base of the mountain had no hot water, despite the town being famous for its natural hot springs and spas. Outside of major cities, lack of hot water was a regular problem. Power was also hit and miss wherever we went, and the 240-volt local current made us drag around a small step-down transformer to charge our batteries. As usual, Leon and I were supposed to be isolated during dinner because we were foreigners. We ate in the very same dining room as the rest of our crew, but restaurant management put up a folded screen between us. It became a running joke. Bao, Ding, and Tan would circumvent this silly separation whenever they could to join us. We'd kill time in the evenings playing cards or sometimes local students would gather around to practice their English on me.

Because Leon was overweight and out of shape, he'd rarely climb even a single flight of stairs to visit a pagoda. We both knew he wasn't going to attempt the rather strenuous ascent of a mile-high mountain. He'd stay below in our hotel while I climbed the 16,740 stone steps (I counted every one of them) while wearing my inappropriate leather-soled shoes. My guide was a very patient man named Fang who indicated well-known locations along the way, but they were easy to spot for myself. Huangshan (literally "Yellow Mountain") is considered one of China's five sacred mountains and every turn, every viewpoint feels like you've stepped into a classic landscape painting. The weather was quixotic, from fog so thick we could only see a dozen feet, to roaring winds, rain, and even brief snow flurries. All I could think about was how this was one of the most beautiful places I'd ever visited. But how would we ever find a way to get the cumbersome Circle-Vision cameras to the top of a mountain?

Rock formations on Huangshan

The sea of clouds

A Buddhist teahouse

The 16,740 steps

A narrow passage

Huangpu River, Shanghai

Shanghai's backstreets

A canal in Suzhou

The Humble Administrator's Garden

The town of Guilin

Li River

Houseboats on the Li River

Yangshuo

Elephant Trunk Rock

Step by Step, Brick by Brick

Halfway to the top of Huangshan we stopped to rest at a lovely teahouse run by a charming Buddhist monk. He'd been there for 50 years and when he welcomed us he showed off his strength by holding up a four-foot chunk of heavy steel rod with one hand. He could raise it level with his shoulder and travelers cheered his feat of strength. I was so whipped that I took a bamboo walking stick and held that out as if I was matching him. Best I could do. The monk had an infectious laugh.

On the way up we saw dozens of laborers who hauled stones, bricks, bags of cement, or foodstuffs in bamboo baskets balanced in dual loads across their shoulders. They were headed to the hotel at the top, a building assembled out of stone blocks, each of which had been carried up on laborers' backs. These men with their heavy burdens would blow right past us as we struggled up the stone steps. When we squeezed through a very narrow gap in the rocks, no more than 18 inches wide, I knew there'd be trouble getting our heaviest equipment through. The central pedestal traveled in a four-foot cubic shipping container that weighed about 300 pounds. Laborers were cheap, but how many would we need to get our entire camera rig, including two-dozen smaller boxes of equipment, to the summit? I didn't know how we'd manage, but it was going to be so worth it!

Along the twisting path we passed inscriptions carved directly into huge rocks with the calligraphy painted bright red. Craggy trees clung for dear life to spear-shaped chunks of granite as winds howled through them.

After we passed through a sea of clouds to reach the summit, I was shocked at the scale of the multistory hotel made out of stone blocks painted pink. Exposure to the elements had faded the paint which seemed to drip down the pillars and façade. The building's design was barely functional and utilitarian, yet the sight of it after an arduous climb was inspiring.

We were met by Mister Gee, a noted Chinese cameraman who had been arranged by China Co-Film to guide me to the most photogenic sites on the mountain. I was already pretty familiar from my photo research but okay, lead on. Mister Gee kept taking me to spots that were all wrong for Circle-Vision and I tried more than once to explain our needs. It was a frustrating day because he would lead us off on trails to places with very limited angles and views, pointing to some distant pagoda that could only be seen with a telephoto lens. Because he'd wasted our limited time on the mountain, I told Ding that Mister Gee would not be joining us when we came back to film.

Our survey led us down the mountain and brought us to Shanghai. It was a treat to stay in the famous Peace Hotel right on the waterfront of the Huangpu River. In the old days it was called the Cathay Hotel and Noël Coward hung out there while writing "Private Lives." As we walked into the classic art deco lobby, a band of six Chinese musicians dressed in white shirts and black ties were playing "As Time Goes By." The ensemble had been playing these old tunes over and over because they couldn't get their hands on any modern Western music during Mao's era. They were still stuck in a time warp, circa the 1930s and 40s.

Hotels with restaurant menus were rare so Leon and I usually found ourselves in a dining room at the mercy of whatever the chef had prepared. Food came out of the kitchen in waves of dishes. Sooner or later we'd find something we could eat. Because we were often isolated, we were on our own to identify the food. Leon was more adventuresome, never hesitant to dive in for a taste, but his guesses were wrong more often than not. When served whole fish, I made a point of bringing the head over to Tan, wherever he was sitting. At banquets some local official was always presenting me with the head of a duck or goose as a "great honor." The running joke was that I'd "honor" Tan with it instead. We had already begun to call him "Lao Tan," meaning "Old Tan," which was a sign of respect. We were starting to build some friendly relationships that would prove helpful when the production went off the rails, which it frequently did.

We made a short scouting excursion over to Suzhou, a city famous for its canals and waterways. We surveyed the intimate Humble Administrator's Garden as well as the elaborate Master of the Nets Garden. Afterwards, our contacts insisted on a banquet. Mister Mai from Cultural Affairs was a smooth diplomat and made us feel welcome with a feast of many courses. It's said by many that the culture, people, and even dialect of Suzhou is more refined and cultured than in the rest of China. We certainly couldn't disagree and really enjoyed the delicious local plum wine. The wonderful dishes just kept coming from the kitchen, more food than we could possibly eat. It seemed like a great waste but extravagance like that is considered the sign of a good host. I said a few words of gratitude to Mister Mai in Chinese and then he related a local saying, translated as "It is more pleasant to hear words of anger in Suzhou than words of praise in Guangzhou." In that moment, I realized my language instructor back in Mission Viejo had been deceiving me. She'd been teaching me Mandarin but had been unable to hide her own roots. All this time I'd been speaking Chinese with traces of her lingering Cantonese accent. Guangzhou has a harsh, guttural version of Chinese dialect that some have compared to ducks quacking. From then on, I never spoke another word of Chinese unless I was certain of its precise pronunciation in official Mandarin.

I wasn't the only one to be embarrassed at this banquet. We thanked our gracious hosts and the half-dozen pretty "Suzhou girls" who'd served us, then our crew retreated to our minibus for the drive back to Shanghai. We'd only gone down the driveway when I realized I'd left behind a shoulder bag with all my papers and maps. I shouted for the driver to stop and I jumped off the bus to run back. I didn't want my Chinese crew to fetch it since this was my mistake. I rushed back into the dining hall to find our hosts and waiters seated around the table eating our leftover banquet food. When they looked up and saw me, dozens of chopsticks stopped in midair. I mumbled an apology, grabbed my bag, and ran out. The last image I had of them, they were still frozen in their own utter humiliation.

Our team traveled south from Shanghai to Guilin on a commercial aircraft. Leon and I never quite got used to seeing condensation steaming out of the overhead luggage racks on some of our flights. Chinese air hostesses were there to hand out little gifts, like a paper fan or a pair of folding scissors, certainly not to reassure the flying public about what looks like billowing smoke.

The Guilin area was still an undiscovered scenic region to most Americans at this time. The local weather was overcast with intermittent rain, but the scenery still looked great, especially the aptly named Elephant Trunk Rock. We took a chartered boat down the Li River and I couldn't take photos fast enough. What an amazing experience as every bend in the river brought new landscapes and vistas. Somehow the fog and low clouds added to their majestic impact. Filming scenes slowly cruising down the Li River was not going to be a photographic problem, but I still had one other shot I was looking for. This one had to be on the ground.

I'd conceived what I wanted for the opening shot of the film: we're surrounded by classic Chinese paintings on scrolls, the kind that depict the fantastic shapes of mountains that could only come from an artist's wild imagination. I wanted the paintings to dissolve into a full Circle-Vision scene of this area and reveal the reality of the karst formations of Guilin. But seeking out the exact spot where I could get mountains to line up in a circle was quite challenging, especially in the near-constant rain and fog. I had been jumping off the minibus so often to climb yet another hill, that even the Chinese crew didn't bother to get out. They waited for me with Leon. I finally found what I thought was the ideal position in Yangshuo, at the southern end of the Li River cruise. It would be a half a year before I would be able to come back to this precise location to film the elements of my idea and several additional months before I'd see if it worked.

I had one rule of thumb that I developed over the course of this film about the suitability of a locale for a Circle-Vision shot. I would stand in a particular place – whether on a hill in Yangshuo, a farm in Tibet, or the courtyard of a Forbidden City palace – and ask myself one question: do I want to invite millions of people to come and stand *here*, right where I am in that moment? I had to use my best judgment to determine worthiness and saw this, "me first, then the audience," as my main responsibility.

We scouted a few other locales in the far south and then returned north on a very lengthy train ride back to Beijing. Leon finally had enough free time to tell me of the horrors of filming the first day of "Apocalypse Now" when the film's big stars were totally lost in a gunboat for most of a day in a swamp. Between that, Martin Sheen's heart attack, and a typhoon that knocked down all their sets, I wondered how that movie ever got made. The two-day train ride also gave Leon and I plenty of time to recap our first survey with Lao Tan, Bao, and Ding. We mapped out our next survey for the month of August, which would be followed immediately by two solid months of filming. We'd then have another month to capture winter scenes in January, and then a final month of shooting the following spring. Seeing a complete schedule confirmed that our goals were hugely ambitious, and I finally grasped the enormity of what I'd taken on.

By 5 a.m. the train's loudspeakers were playing awful martial music, announcing our return to Beijing. We'd traveled more than 2,200 kilometers by rail and arrived only two minutes off the scheduled time. Our little survey team had already overcome some setbacks and bureaucratic snafus, so we stepped off the train feeling rightfully optimistic.

But that was only because, like Francis Ford Coppola in the Philippines, we couldn't foresee the larger troubles that were headed our way.

CHAPTER 7

Chopsticks and Charred Birds

Back in the States, I was quickly immersed in filming second unit on MacGillivray-Freeman's IMAX film, "Behold Hawaii." I didn't get time to prepare for my next trip, which would be a solid three months in China, until the last few weeks of July. When we found out the Ministry of Culture was planning to host a huge banquet at the Great Hall of the People to celebrate the start of filming, I wanted Kathy to be able to attend this important event. My wife, a special education teacher, decided she would come for the entire August survey while her school was on vacation.

I had my first meeting with Joe Nash who'd been recommended by Rick Harper. When he was directing "Impressions de France" for EPCOT, Rick had chosen Joe as his camera tech. But when I discussed my China plans with Joe, he didn't seem impressed, like this was going to be just another job for him. He was already near retirement age but had recently married Gloria, a much younger woman. The assumption was that Gloria was the reason Joe kept on working. Joe seemed friendly enough, but I'd been warned that he could be a handful. He was said to be steady, a solid worker, very thorough, but don't get on his bad side. Hmmm, I wondered, how does one do that?

By the time Kathy and I flew off to Hong Kong, Leon was already there. We were met at the airport, not by Leon but a driver in a Mercedes limousine. We were whisked away to the fabulous Regent Hotel on the waterfront, one of the most spectacular places imaginable. I should have realized in that moment that allowing Leon to control the film's finances might lead to trouble, but I was blown away by the service and luxury. Leon had been ensconced at the Regent for days, having meals and drinks delivered to him poolside as if he were a movie mogul like Dino De Laurentiis. When we had a meeting with Madalena Chan, head of a local film equipment company, Leon referred to himself as the film's producer. I reminded him later that he was the production manager and Greg was the producer. Leon just laughed off the comment.

We headed the next day to the Chinese border by train. In those days the frontier was still a hard checkpoint with military guards and formal checking of papers. It reminded me of crossing into East Berlin in the 1960s. The gauge of the rail lines were different, too, so a Hong Kong train physically couldn't continue on into the mainland. All the passengers exited one train, walked through security, then boarded another train.

It felt like a reunion when I was met by Lao Tan, Bao, and Ding on the Chinese train. They were very welcoming of Kathy to the team, especially Tan's assistant, Shen Zhi Hua. His English was pretty decent so he could also act as a translator at times. When I would schedule events with Shen, he'd say, "That is Jeff Plan. What about Kathy Plan?"

I think he was particularly protective of Kathy since he'd discovered she loved Qingdao beer as much as he did. They'd always split the huge bottles served at meals.

But Kathy had an immediate problem in feeding herself. She's a leftie and couldn't quite get a good enough grasp of chopsticks. Unlike Chinese restaurants back home, no one was there to offer a fork. The train ride from Hong Kong to Yunnan Province was going to be a long nightmare for her if she couldn't find a way to eat. Ding took it upon himself to teach her the proper technique in the dining car. As soon as he explained how he did it, the rest of the crew started laughing. His was a completely different approach than seemingly everyone else in China so they made fun of Ding the rest of the trip. Kathy's eventual solution was mine. I suggested that since she was trying to pattern her brain with something new, she should start over and learn to eat with her other hand. She'd been fighting muscle memory, so when she switched hands she had no problem. To this day, eating with chopsticks is all she does right-handed.

Kunming, the provincial capital, was beautiful at that time of year. It's no wonder they call Yunnan Province the Land of Eternal Spring. It's located on the north shore of Dianchi Lake which has been called the "Sparkling Pearl Embedded in a Highland." Unfortunately, the lake's waters were fouled by thick green algae. We took a trip on it in a small boat and it felt like we were motoring through a giant bowl of split pea soup.

We drove south to survey the Shilin Stone Forest, an extensive formation of unique rocks. I found a few good spots to come back later to film, making note of what we'd need. We discovered a place nearby that was a so-called "free enterprise" restaurant, a rarity in China. This was the first inkling of change in their rigid top-down authority over all businesses. Here was an ambitious restaurateur in a remote province far from Beijing who'd been permitted to experiment with *Capitalism*. He just couldn't call it that and this could *never* have happened while Mao was alive. Leon and I insisted we give the guy a chance by having the crew lunch there, to encourage the flowering of free enterprise. The host was most grateful for our business and, as usual, we drew a curious crowd of onlookers around our outdoor table.

The chef came out of the kitchen with plates of… I'm not sure exactly what. Imagine a flock of small birds, maybe sparrows, that landed on high tension power lines then fell to earth in poses of terrified electrocution, crisped to a cinder. Chinese cuisine is about aesthetics as much as it is flavors and spices. Dishes have to be appealing to all the senses, and we were being handed blackened birds – charred, really – lying naked on the plates, without so much as a sprig of parsley. When we tried to slice them apart into manageable pieces, they crumbled, bones and all, into dust and ash. The chef was standing there with a big smile on his face, probably calculating how visiting Westerners were going to put his little restaurant on the map. I tried to munch on a little bit of wing to be polite, but it tasted like what it was: charcoal. Free enterprise in China was going to have to wait a wee bit longer.

The train ride from Kunming north to Chengdu in Sichuan Province was one of the most amazing rail experiences of my life. We'd settled in for a long trip of 1,100 kilometers through very steep mountainous terrain. We looked up from our books as our train started to go in and out of total darkness and bright sun at a rapid rate – sometimes three or four tunnels per minute. The cliffside views each time we emerged were spectacular drops to river valleys far below. Equally impressive were the viaducts, causeways, and trestles precariously constructed high up the sides of the mountains, as if they'd just bored effortlessly through the rock and stone with a laser. This engineering feat must have represented the hard labor of tens of thousands of peasants (and who knows how many deaths) to make the Kunming to Chengdu railway possible.

As we entered Sichuan Province, our train slowed and made an unplanned stop. We found out later that this was done so that Lao Tan could receive an important phone call! I suspected it was going to be about Tibet, which remained a revolving door of invitations and rejections. I was right, but the Tibetan authorities were only asking us to delay our visit by a few days. We used the time to divert from Chengdu to see another great wonder, the Giant Buddha of Leshan.

Carved into the side of a cliff over 1,000 years ago, this 233-foot-tall Buddha watches over the dangerous confluence of three rivers. The statue had been shaped from red sandstone in stages as funding became available. First his head and shoulders appeared, then years later he was completed down to his knees. By 803 A.D., the last workers revealed the statue's massive feet. So much stone had been removed and dumped into the river that the Buddha really did affect the currents. We thought the results spectacular, including staircases that snaked down the sides of the cliff. The surrounding walls were pockmarked by little grottos filled with hundreds of smaller Buddhas. I wanted to add it to my list of locales, but I had no idea how we could haul a Circle-Vision camera rig anywhere close to it, let alone get the enormous statue to fit within our circular frame.

While stalling for Tibet, we also went by train to see a location that fulfilled a request I'd apparently made back in January. We'd been told in the meetings that trains, tunnels, and bridges were considered "strategic targets" and therefore off limits. At the time I'd joked "Well, there goes my idea for a shot of a train coming out of a tunnel and crossing a bridge." The laughs in the meeting had been muted by translations, but it turned out they'd taken me seriously. We were now presented with the possibility of shooting the impossible, using our own dedicated train to cross a rail bridge that spanned a raging river, going from one tunnel and into another. I couldn't have designed a better shot. Of course, we didn't really have permission yet, but they'd allow us to have a look at the site. Lao Tan would have to get an official okay and have papers signed off by the PLA. That was his job. Mine was to dream about shots like this.

When we finally got our approval to visit Tibet, we flew from Chengdu to Lhasa. Technically our plane never descended because the airport is located in a valley at 12,000 feet. Another flight had just landed next to ours and, as we crossed the tarmac, I recognized Sir Edmund Hillary with a group of climbers. They'd come to explore the possibility of climbing Qomolangma Feng, the Chinese side of Everest.

We were packed into a minibus for a dusty ride of 70 kilometers on a dirt road through a treeless valley that looked like the desert around Palm Springs. The capital of Lhasa is dominated by the impressive white fortress of the Potala Palace, high on a hill. I couldn't wait to explore what had been the seat of Tibetan Buddhism for centuries. But first we checked into our hotel, the only one in town for foreigners. Our first impression was that this place could have been partnered with the Sheep Dip Hotel in Inner Mongolia. Did they have a chain of smelly and decrepit hotels? Instead of mare's milk tea, it was the smell of yak butter that permeated the wallpaper and furnishings. Walking up a single flight of stairs created instant headaches that felt like your head would explode. In the past, visitors to Tibet had come overland, taking a couple of weeks in order to acclimate to the altitude and lack of oxygen. They didn't step right out of a plane. Any exertion, like mounting the many steps to the top of the Potala, would set off waves of nausea and a pounding heart. Kathy and I realized *that's* why there were large bottles of oxygen in our hotel hallway. Until they changed the requirements in 1980, the government required visitors to pass a strenuous physical exam before being allowed into Tibet.

I was breathless and in pain but I found a very good location for a shot on the roof of the Potala, after we had been given tours of cramped bedrooms, elaborate antechambers with colorful murals, and dozens of alcoves crammed with miniature Buddhas. The palace was officially a museum and its curators normally charged 20 yuan for each interior photograph. The labyrinth of dungeons, dating to when the buildings were the center of Lhasa's political life, were not on our tour. We did see one chamber that was filled with displays of so many jewels it could have been a scene from "Pirates of the Caribbean." Our local guide showed us the Dalai Lama's old office which had inlaid gold patterns and a conspicuous bowl of pearls set out rather invitingly, like after-dinner mints. We must have seen literally tons of gold in the oversized sarcophagi of 14 previous Dalai Lamas interred within the Potala.

Life in the town of Lhasa must have been a hardscrabble existence. Buildings of three stories were made of large white bricks held together by crude mortar. They looked as if one good quake would level them. The streets were full of pilgrims who had devoted part of their lives traveling to this sacred place, some lying prostrate in the streets to pray. One man had fashioned leather pads for his hands so that he could lie down flat on his stomach, sliding his hands out in front of him until his face touched the roadway. Then he'd slide back up to his knees, move a foot or so to one side, then do it all again. He was circling the entirety of the Potala Palace in that manner. Other pilgrims made their way to the nearby Jokhang Temple, which had been one of Tibetan Buddhism's holiest shrines for the past 1,300 years.

Men wore shoulder cloaks and broad-brimmed straw hats. Women in colorful clothes were rosy-cheeked and their brown hands were cracked and leathery. Many walked while spinning their prayer wheels in continuous motion. Inside the cylinder was a written scripture and each revolution sent the prayer to Heaven. Overhead – on telephone lines and windowsills, in trees and bushes, hanging from ledges – were thousands of ragged prayer flags that fluttered in red, white, green, and blue. Their messages, invocations, and mantras were carried on the wind directly to Heaven. After burning prayers to carry them skyward, large Buddhist sacred ovens shaped like gigantic eggs were dusted with white ash like powdered sugar. It was easy to reach the conclusion that this town was built for one purpose. But religion wasn't the reason the authorities were withholding permission to shoot.

We couldn't film the palace from the streets below looking up. To capture a good wide image of the sprawling Potala Palace up on its massive hill, the Circle-Vision cameras needed to be at about the same height. As luck would have it, Lhasa had a matching hilltop a short distance away. I received permission to go up and at least have a look. As expected, the views of the Potala and the entire valley were fantastic, but also politically charged. A ruined stone fortress sat atop that hill, evidence of damage caused by Chinese artillery from when the military invaded Tibet in 1950. I found an old battle flag perched up there, its cloth fragments ripped by the winds. Even if the PLA gave us the go-ahead, I thought this would be way too sensitive for a Disney film. I settled for a possible location a little further down the hill so that we wouldn't see much of the ruins. I snapped a series of still images to represent the 360 view the Circle-Vision cameras would capture and then hiked down, believing I'd solved my problems.

Tibetan sunsets didn't begin until around 9 p.m. but they proved to be thermonuclear. Every color of the spectrum seemed to be glowing through majestic clouds. We were in such personal distress from the altitude that we could hardly enjoy the light show. We passed on the local food in the hotel and ate freeze-dried spaghetti we'd brought from a camping store back home. The meal wasn't bad, but our headaches, chest tightness, and labored breathing lasted through the evening. Kathy had such a bad night that she only found comfort by sleeping sitting up in our bathtub.

In the morning she said, "I'm so glad I don't have to come back here for the shoot."

Xinjiang Province

Hat shop in Ürümqi

An armed shopper

Bao buys grapes

A *shashlik* vendor

The western terminus of the Great Wall

The author and Kathy at the Jiayuguan Fort

Zhou Ge (China Joe)

Liu Be Xiang (Leo)

CHAPTER 8

A Train Ride from Hell

Airline routes in China were pretty much spokes of a wheel with the hub located in Beijing. We needed to return to the capital nearly every time there was a connecting flight anywhere. We had to travel from Lhasa in Tibet to Chengdu in Sichuan, then back to Beijing, and from there take another flight to the capital of Xinjiang Province, about twice the distance than if we'd been able to fly there directly.

Xinjiang is at the far western edge of China, bordering three of the 'stans: Kazakhstan, Kyrgyzstan, and Tajikistan. Four more 'stans could be found just a little further out: Pakistan, Afghanistan, Turkmenistan, and Uzbekistan. The people and culture of Xinjiang owe much to these neighbors, more so than to the rest of China. The Uyghur peoples, about half the region's population of 11 million, are a Turkic minority with Islamic cultural and ethnic ties to Central and Eastern Asia. Their wonderful music, clothing, lifestyles set them apart from the rest of China and that uniqueness is what had brought us to Ürümqi (pronounced Oo-roo-MOOCH-ee), a place of mosques and bazaars not found in Beijing. The province also seemed like the breadbasket of China, overflowing with many fruits and vegetables, especially the delicious *Hami* melons.

The locals who welcomed us were pleased for the attention their region was about to receive. They took us into the nearby Taishan Mountains to visit Heavenly Lake. The region was heavily touristic, but we hiked along the lake for a mile to find a pristine spot that would work for a shot when we came back with crew and equipment. On the return to Ürümqi, we checked out a local carpet-making factory. A large custom-made Persian rug would take four girls about four months to turn out, then the carpet would be carted across the border to one of the 'stans where the designs had originated.

Our little team mapped out the entire two-month fall shoot, then did what we said we'd never do: we split up. Leon, Bao, and Shen flew back to Beijing to meet the rest of the American film crew who'd be arriving within a week. Meanwhile, Kathy, Lao Tan, Ding, and I traveled by train to Jiayuguan, a fortress that was the gate at the western terminus of the Great Wall.

This section of wall couldn't have been more different from the other parts we'd seen so far: pounded earthen walls resembling eroded adobe. The old weathered fortress looked blasted by sun and wind. One had the feeling Marco Polo had passed through the gates just last week. Indeed, this place was a pivotal juncture on the Silk Road. The fort wasn't that far from the sand dunes of the Gobi Desert, so I added the location to my wish list. If we were planning to bring crew and equipment this far for the fort and wall, we could add a day or two for a camel caravan.

Then the rains came. Not out where we were, but between us and Beijing. Our train trip back was delayed as we endured one detour after another. We were told it was going to take three days and two nights which would put me behind schedule for the final prep of the coming shoot. Besides our camera tech and grip who'd be arriving soon, Greg MacGillivray was making his one trip to China. How could I not be there?

Lao Tan tried to find a charter flight for us through CAAC (China's Civil Aviation Authority). His plan for us was to jump off the train in Lanzhou, capital of Gansu Province, then rush by bus to the airport with no guarantee of seats. Meanwhile, our train was slowly passing through desert landscapes, pulling off the main line onto sidings while much faster freight trains roared by. Our train was considered lower priority and was operating off the normal schedule. Each day passed ever so slowly. I'd purchased a paperback when we were leaving Ürümqi, one of the few books I could find in English. It was an Agatha Christie mystery that was so badly written it made me angry. I was tearing out pages after I'd read them and tossing them out of our compartment window. Okay, maybe it wasn't the book that made me angry.

Our train was like a slow-moving prison and we'd regularly shuffle off to the dining car where desperate chefs served us chopped green peppers and shredded pork. That was the only menu item – breakfast, lunch, and dinner – every day of our endless trip. Kathy and I taught Lao Tan and Ding to play Hearts, which helped pass the time since they were sharing our compartment. My growing frustration with being stuck on a train while my American crew was about to land in Beijing had reached the breaking point.

Our train from Hell finally pulled into the station at Lanzhou in Gansu

Province but no one from the government came to the station to meet us. So much for Tan's plans to catch the CAAC flight. I suspected he'd never really arranged any connections and this charade had been to give us a little hope. Terribly disappointed, we reluctantly got back on the same train, feeling like prisoners denied parole. Lao Tan and Ding in turn taught us to play a Chinese card game they called "Up and Up" which passed a bit more time. I'd sleep when I could but would have preferred to have been in a coma. Wake me in Beijing!

We continued our frustrating stop-start-detour journey of 2,800 kilometers, supposedly avoiding flooded areas we never saw and watching the desert gradually transform to vegetation in Ningxia Province. I checked my watch constantly, knowing the time Greg was due to arrive in Beijing. Frankly, I was worried that he and Leon might deconstruct my plans for the shoot. After we finally chugged into the massive train station in Beijing, we rushed like mad to get back. I'd never been so happy to see that poor excuse for a hotel.

I hadn't previously interviewed Guy Jones, our company grip, but he'd been recommended to us because he'd worked on the Canada Circle-Vision film for EPCOT. Balding with a white Santa Claus beard, Guy was a mountain of a man who was really a big softie. His large size belied his gentle nature. Guy was modest about what I came to discover were his terrific skills at laying dolly track or making camera platforms under the most difficult circumstances. Given a bit of aluminum speed rail and a roll of gaffer tape, Guy could make whatever we needed. When I first met him after our exodus from the desert, he was giving the stink eye to the food Kathy and I were wolfing down in the hotel restaurant. I told him compared to what we'd found across the country, we looked forward to coming back to eat at this hotel, despite the dreadful service. I should have realized right then that Guy was going to be very anxious about Chinese food. If he found one item on a menu he liked and tolerated, he'd order it over and over.

Guy's partner on the technical side was Joe Nash from Disney's Camera Service Department. His fellow studio employees were grateful we were taking him off their hands for several months. They felt Joe could be a pedantic curmudgeon with few social graces, but I still wanted him on the team. We were going to be so far from any laboratory or support that I wanted Joe's head-down, ritualistic, and intense focus on loading magazines and his maternal hovering over the Circle-Vision rig. Joe Nash was the only reason we exposed over 150,000 feet of Kodak film and never had a single scratch, despite grinding away nine cameras at a time for months. For that alone, I was willing to put up with his antisocial shenanigans and outbursts of pique. I had to constantly make excuses for his behavior with our Chinese hosts and crew, but it was a successful trade-off, as far as I was concerned. I learned there were two rules for dealing with Joe: first, once a schedule was published for the next day, don't change it or Joe would freak out. Second, don't rush him when he's in the zone, meaning while he's changing our many film magazines. Joe would put up with a lot of personal hardship to get the job done, but we needed to give him the same wide margin as a caged tiger.

While Greg slept off his jet lag, I met with Lao Tan, Bao, Ding, and Shih Kuan to confirm our immediate schedule. Joe and Guy had to sort through our many boxes of equipment that had been released from customs. Hovering over them were the two Chinese camera assistants who'd been assigned to our show. Liu Be Xiang was the shorter of the two, with a dark complexion and fierce concentration. He was the one who'd jot down every step of camera procedure in a little notebook. He would also sneak about with a tape measure to transcribe all the details of our camera rig whenever he thought we weren't looking. Guy Jones quickly Americanized "Liu" to "Leo," a name that stuck, even among the Chinese. Zhou Ge was the taller of the two, fair, with a wide, open face, a broad forehead, and an artistic air about him. Which is a polite way of saying that Zhou sometimes lacked the focus of Leo. At times he seemed more interested in taking photos with his Chinese-made twin-lens reflex. A lot of his pictures turned out to be close-ups of our rig, again, when he thought we weren't looking. Since Zhou's name was pronounced a bit like "Joe," Guy thought that might be confusing. He started calling him "China Joe." Later, despite Guy's best efforts to *not* learn any of the language, he had translated the nickname into Zhōngguó Zhou (pronounced Jung-gwah Joe). Naturally enough, Joe Nash later became known to the Chinese as "Meiguó Joe" or "America Joe."

Our little American team was joined by our Chinese counterparts for the formal banquet at the Great Hall of the People. This prestigious honor was arranged to commemorate the official start of production. In attendance were many high-ranking Chinese leaders, including Zhou Weizhi, the 65-year-old Minister of Culture, the official host. Ours was the first American-Chinese co-production and it warranted an appropriate coming-out party. The hall was vast but surprisingly spartan, and the food was fantastic. Leon dug in with abandon while a nervous Joe and Guy, dressed in suits and ties, were very selective. Joe was just nibbling from a little bowl of rice with a bit of fish and ignoring dozens of exotic-looking dishes on display. Guy rubbed his bald head in frustration and sipped at a bottle of Chinese soda. I knew he'd be heading back to the Peking Hotel's restaurant at the first opportunity.

During the elaborate meal I found myself next to a curious young Chinese woman who spoke English well. I had mistakenly believed her language skills were why they'd seated her beside me. Her name was Wei Jia and she seemed fascinated by Disney's plans for EPCOT and had dozens of questions about our ambitious schedule. I gave her the full, highly polished and publicity-friendly account of how we'd found everything to be excellent throughout the country, even the food, (a bald-faced lie).

The next morning, I was told she was a reporter for Xinhua News Agency. Wei wrote a long article in the English-language *China Daily* with an embarrassing headline that proclaimed with some rightful incredulity:

How to Visit All of China in 20 Minutes!

CHAPTER 9

THE LONG MARCH

On September 7, 1981, Kathy left to return to teaching in the States after having stayed through our filming in Inner Mongolia and at the studio. I was losing my personal support system just as the joint American and Chinese crew was headed into the bulk of a two-month shoot.

Our first stop was the city of Chengdu in Sichuan Province, our previous jumping-off point for Tibet. We checked into the Jin Jiang Hotel but with half our luggage and equipment having missed the flight. Not a good start. We would struggle with this issue over several locations until we came up with a way to remedy the situation. We asked permission for China Joe and Leo to supervise the loading of our equipment and confirm it was properly loaded on every flight or train.

I've never liked early morning calls and I couldn't understand why we had to be up so early if our flight to Lhasa was a charter. Then I learned Leon had made a back-door deal with CAAC to sell several of our empty seats to offset some of our travel costs. After his extravagances playing big-shot producer in Hong Kong, Leon now appeared to be on top of his job to watch over the budget.

China Co-Film was responsible for our in-country hotel accommodations and domestic travel, so it was in their interests to also save money for themselves. When they asked us to double up in the same hotel rooms, we said, nope. Sorry. Not happening. I'll get up at 5 a.m. if I have to but I'm not going to share a room with Leon for six days. Not in a place like Tibet while we're trying to acclimate to the altitude again. We had the same hammering, vise-like headaches while our bodies struggled to get oxygenated blood. Greg was starting to feel flu-like symptoms and Lou, our Chinese grip (Guy's counterpart), had developed a fever. I knew Joe and Guy were never going to warm up to yak's milk so I figured the sooner we could film our scenes in Tibet and get out, the better.

Lao Tan finally admitted to me, with much coaxing, what had been wrong with the original plan to film from the hillside opposite the Potala Palace. I had taped together my earlier pictures into a crude 360 image. These paste-ups were a great way to educate the crew about what we were doing. Lao Tan delicately hinted there was "something" in the corner of one of my wide-angle images…

"Is that the source of our difficulty?" I asked.

Lao Tan nodded but couldn't bring himself to actually point it out.

I used a magnifier to inspect a tiny area of the photo. Way off in the distance across the city of Lhasa was the top of one particular building, its façade slightly taller than the rest. I recognized the yellow logo and red stars on the roof as that of the local PLA office. It was miles away, barely a speck in the photo, but that was enough.

"Got it," I said. Lao Tan smiled, relieved he'd never revealed a word.

Now that I knew the problem, there was no point arguing. I offered to shift our camera location a little further around the hill, so the view of that particular building was blocked. Lao Tan was happy, we had a new camera placement, but it was on a difficult slope. I asked if our local support could build a small wooden platform. They were embarrassed to admit they had no spare wood. This part of Tibet was treeless. Could they make one for us out of concrete? The diplomatic answer was sure, why not? Eventually I found a flat ridge on the hillside that fit everyone's requirements, Chinese and American.

We switched our schedule so we could begin our Tibetan filming on a farm. While traveling on the survey I'd seen a number of shaggy-coated yaks harnessed up as beasts of burden, so I asked for them to be part of our scene. We piled into a minibus, our equipment truck right behind us, and headed to the farm Lao Tan and his team had arranged for us a few miles out of town. Setting up our shot was fairly straightforward. We'd hired a wonderful old horse cart, loaded with straw and rosy-cheeked kids, to pass right in front of us down a bumpy dirt road among the farmers working the fields with their yaks. I came up with an innovation on the spot that became a technical innovation we've used many times on other films since.

The Circle-Vision rig is normally bolted down onto a stack of metal rings after I decide where to aim the nine cameras. "Aim" may seem like a misnomer, considering the unit photographs in all directions at the same time. The reality is there's a hard line – splits – between each image so where the separation falls is very important. I didn't want to have some key element of the scene split by these separations. On a whim I asked Joe to loosen the support bolts. As the horse cart passed us, I reached up from my hiding spot under the cameras and twisted the rig in a panning motion to follow the cart. I couldn't see exactly what the cameras were getting (video assist was still a long way off for us). During postproduction, I would refer to this as my "pan shot" and was surprised how many otherwise sophisticated studio viewers never even noticed. Their focus was on the passing kids in the cart so that even though the entire image was rotating in the theater, they didn't experience it as such. This was an important lesson that would carry forward for years. I later had Don Iwerks, the son of Ub Iwerks, build a special panhead so we could continue to do shots like that.

Just when I thought we'd accomplished a really good scene, trouble broke out. It could have been Guy setting off Joe or the other way around, but suddenly there were angry words. The next thing I know, Guy is storming away down the road.

I asked Joe, "Where does he think he's going?"

"Beats me," he shrugged. "Maybe he's walking home."

Home to our hotel in Lhasa, which was miles away? Home to Beijing? Or to somewhere more serious? We loaded up our equipment in the truck. I rode in the minibus and let Guy walk for the better part of a mile before we slowly came up behind him. I got out and accompanied him in silence.

Finally, "You have every right to be angry," I said. "Joe can piss me off, too."

Guy just kept trudging along.

"My problem," I said, lowering my voice, "is the Chinese are looking at this as me losing face as a director, as the leader of the team." I was making that up, but it was true enough.

Guy barely went a few more steps before he stopped and got back on the bus. The incident was never mentioned again.

The next day I felt awful, like I'd been punched in the stomach, probably the effects of altitude. I couldn't eat or drink anything, but we carried on. During the survey we'd been on the lookout for a common vehicle that could be found all over China. Guy would only have to build a rig for it once, then we'd know that it would work wherever we went. That vehicle turned out to be what the Chinese called a Beijing Jeep-o, as familiar as an American Jeep, but a convertible, probably military surplus and pretty rugged. Guy's arrangement would position the cameras just high enough to not show the vehicle. We harnessed some Tibetan ponies in front, and stuffed hay in and around the cameras to make it look like we were now on the horse cart from the previous shot. This set off nervous clucking from Joe about getting dust on the lenses and mirrors. The cart driver sat on the hood of the car holding the reins. The whole contraption looked ridiculous from any angle – except the one that mattered: from the camera viewpoint. The rig was rather heavy for the little ponies so Guy slowly drove the Jeep-o but it looked on film like we were being pulled. Meanwhile, I had rehearsed a bunch of school kids whose job was to come running out of a building to greet us and run alongside. We fought clouds and sun in and out all day, but Guy's set-up worked great.

About this time, I discovered we were not getting the proper sound recording from our Chinese audio man. Circle-Vision has a very particular requirement that we capture sounds in monaural, not stereo. With mono we can later move a particular sound to the appropriate speaker during the mix. I'd asked the soundman to record the squeals of happy kids, for example, but isolated from the jingling bells of the pony. Or the creaking of the old cart, separate from other background effects. Our man just wasn't getting it, thinking that what we really wanted was what *he* really wanted: beautiful stereo sound that captured every sonic element at once. I tried to explain, through Bao and Ding's limited technical vocabulary, but my words were falling (ironically enough) on deaf ears. After I reviewed his tapes, we had to come back the next day to record better sound, directing the man to capture individual elements, hoping that would educate him on what I needed.

We suffered through more local Tibetan food issues and then decided to boycott the hotel's dining room because every dish tasted and smelled like it had been doused in yak butter. For my dinner I tried making a dried mix of dehydrated chicken and rice in a thermos of boiling water. It was as unappetizing as it sounds.

The next day was scheduled for the wide shot encompassing the Potala Palace and Lhasa Valley from our newly approved position on the opposite hillside. What I'd conceived for this shot had never done before in a Circle-Vision film: I wanted to zoom in on the palace. The nine cameras have 32 mm fixed focal length lenses and even changing focus on them is a complex process that can't be done during photography. Each lens is designed to capture an image precisely 40 degrees wide and 30 degrees in height. So how to do a zoom on one of the cameras? Well, you don't. We were far enough away from the Potala Palace that we could set up a separate Arriflex 35 mm camera with a zoom lens and capture almost exactly the same view. We'd start with a focal length that matched our rig's and then slowly zoom in. The idea was that when we returned to the studio, we would replace the footage from camera number one, which had been aimed at the Potala, with the Arriflex footage. In effect, we were making an eight-camera shot plus one.

While we were setting up in the morning, Leon was focused on his latest scheme. Coca-Cola was just about to enter into a distribution deal in China but finding the real thing in the country was pretty rare. Chinese soda (their word for it translated as "air water") contained unappetizing floating bits of *I don't know what*. Laoshan bottled sparkling water, with a distinctive red label, didn't exactly pair with high altitude. Their green label, plain flat water, was much harder to find. But Leon had somehow finagled an entire case of bottled Cokes from the would-be distributor and was taking photos of the crew, the camera rig, and the Potala Palace, all with what he thought was a well-placed product in the foreground. We just shook our heads and went about our work. As if Tibetan Buddhism needed to be associated with commercialism…

The rest of us were stuck up on that hillside for much of the day. Whenever I thought the light looked great for a vista, I'd call for Joe to roll on the Circle-Vision rig while Greg would shoot the single-camera zoom so we'd have matching light, exposure, and time of day for both. By the time we packed up our gear and returned to our hotel, Leon was in a rage. He was upset with CAAC, the Bank of China, and Lao Tan because we still didn't have tickets for our Yangtze cruise. After another thermos-made dinner and a hot shower, he settled down. Leon was placated because Lao Tan had brought on a new member of the team to help Shen with travel arrangements. Our new assistant production manager was named Zhang, but Leon had already dubbed him "John," which was close enough. He turned out to be a tireless worker and a decent guy who would later make a great sacrifice for us. I wished Zhang/John had been on from the beginning.

The next day was scheduled for filming on the roof of the Potala Palace itself and we were blessed with decent weather and dramatic clouds. I'd already decided on the survey where I wanted to place the cameras and I walked through the shot with Greg. I asked him to shoot this one because I was leaving to find a new location for the following day's shoot.

I broke away from the crew, taking Ding and a local man named Guo. I was looking for a setting that better represented the Roof of the World and we couldn't do that while stuck in Lhasa's valley, even at 3,600 meters. I needed a place much higher with a wider view. So, *we took off* out of town in a Toyota Land Cruiser. I mean that literally: we took off. Our driver attacked the dirt roads and steep switchbacks as if he were in a sports car climbing Pike's Peak. It was a terrifying ride. He would blare his horn while passing slow-moving vehicles on the outside where there were no barriers, just a steep drop-off of thousands of feet. At one point I actually made him stop so I could get out to catch my breath.

"We are never using this driver again," I told Ding. The young man was frightened enough to agree.

We soldiered on to a height of 16,000 feet where we found an amazing vista overlooking a ring of mountains surrounding a crystalline Alpine lake. Okay, it was worth it, but seriously, why the rush?

We shared a boxed lunch from the hotel on top of the mountain. Since we'd be back to this same place the next day, I buried a couple of bottles of Laoshan greens to chill overnight. At that altitude, I got light-headed a few times just walking a short distance. Nearby we found Tibetan relics of platforms with the remnants of Buddhist prayer flags whipping in the wind. Guo said they were built during funeral processions. Bodies would be wrapped, blessed, and then left out for the vultures to feast on and carry away the dead to Heaven. Rest in pieces, I guess.

Back at the Potala, the shoot with Greg had gone smoothly. I briefed our crew on what to expect at the new locale the next day.

We all wore dust masks in the minibus, which didn't help us get much oxygen. Our speedster driver was back again, despite my warnings about his death wish. Somehow everyone made it to the top alive. We captured scenes of the lake and mountains in beautiful light with puffy cumulous clouds. The only problem was deciding which filters to use: polarizing, graded or straight neutral density. This discussion with Greg went on for some time and we ended up shooting way too many combinations for the studio's taste. I heard about it later from Bob Gibeaut, who also privately complained Greg had shot too many single-camera scenes of the Mongolian horsemen as well. I have never blamed Greg or said a word to him about it because film was the cheapest part of our production. Besides, his photographic eye was a huge asset for us.

When we wrapped at the Roof of the World, we discovered another problem that was going to linger for weeks without a solution. It was an old problem, rising again.

Part of our deal with China Co-Film was that we'd always have the same nucleus of a Chinese crew for the duration of all shooting periods. We needed to be able to count on them and not have to re-educate new members. By now we had an idea of what to expect, we knew their limitations, and they seemed to work hard enough. But the supplementary local laborers, those men and women China Co-Film was obligated to arrange at each location to help move equipment, turned out to be uniformly lazy. I use that word advisedly because in general I don't think I've ever been to a country with harder workers than I've seen across China. But there we were at 16,000 feet, having to haul our own heavy boxes back to the truck while our hired local people, who were built for this altitude, stood around watching. We had to rest every ten feet or so to catch our breath or wait until our heads stopped spinning. I recalled how many times friends in America would ask about China, "Hey, you gonna need somebody to carry your bags?" My jokey response was always, "Thanks, but I'll have a billion people to choose from."

Why were these locals we'd hired not offering to lift a hand to help while we struggled to breathe? We wouldn't get a truthful answer to that looming question for a long time.

On the drive back to Lhasa, I wanted our driver to stay behind the equipment truck, just in case it broke down on these twisty mountain roads. But China's Mario Andretti didn't like eating the dust of any vehicles in front of him, so he took off again, laying on the horn. That night I put diplomacy on the back burner and dressed him down. He ended up apologizing to me and the crew, which was a huge deal in Chinese culture.

I only knew that we needed to get out of this place where shortness of breath can lead to shortness of temper.

The Giant Buddha of Leshan

Chartered equipment boat

The Buddha's right foot

Street corner vegetable sellers

A thatched roof in Sichuan

CHAPTER 10

A Wastebasket Story

By September 15, we were done, done, done with Tibet. The place may be one of the greatest cultural and historic centers on the planet, and we had a fondness for the warm people who struggle mightily to live in those harsh conditions, but our working there even briefly was quite a trial.

We were driven in our minibus through 70 kilometers of dust to the airport. It took two hours to get all of our equipment onto the chartered plane, especially since Leo and China Joe were now taking responsibility for loading. When we were finally allowed to board our charter, Leon and I found two French guys sitting in our seats. Were they that desperate to get out? It required some airline authority and eventual insults to get them to move.

We arrived back in Chengdu and checked into the very familiar Jin Jiang Hotel. Our nickname for the place was the Housefly Inn. You couldn't walk through the lobby without passing through a swarm of files buzzing in a cloud and you could only get through that cloud with your mouth closed. Where was Mao's one billion flyswatters when we needed them?

When I opened my suitcase at this lower altitude, it seemed to explosively decompress. We repacked into smaller bags because we would be temporarily moving on again the same day. We drove for a couple of hours to Leshan and checked into a very comfortable guesthouse for a one-night stay. After a late dinner we had a quick meeting about the next day's shoot. Lao Tan liked to pontificate in Chinese to the members of his crew and we Americans would have to sit there listening, waiting several minutes before we'd get a translation.

This night Lao Tan was going on and on, and I could only understand the occasional word, maybe one in 20 at most. What I could comprehend from his lengthy rambling were the words for "tomorrow morning" and the number "eight."

Before Bao and Ding could translate, I said to Lao Tan (in Chinese): "I agree, comrade. Let's start at eight."

I passed this information on in English to my crew. When we gathered up to leave, I caught a glimpse of the look on Lao Tan's face. I don't know whether it was respect or fear, but I think he believed I'd understood *way* more of his speech than I did. From then on, when I was around and he wanted a private conversation with his crew, he'd lean in and whisper.

The next day we found ourselves standing on a shore at the intersection of three rivers with the Giant Buddha staring at us across the churning water. The Buddha was supposed to guard passing ships and boats from the treacherous currents and whirlpools where the Minjiang, Qingyi, and Dadu Rivers converged. Lao Tan and Shen were supposed to arrange for a boat to ferry our equipment across to the landing at the Buddha's enormous feet. We were shocked at what showed up: a huge double-decker river cruiser capable of hauling hundreds of passengers and tons of cargo. It was massive overkill, but we couldn't complain.

Again, our hired local laborers were useless. Most of the loading onto the cruiser was done by our own crew. The ship's captain navigated to the other side, next to the Buddha, but it wasn't easy unloading across a gangway. The ship had to keep its engines running while maintaining its place along the river. Leon, who'd taken to smoking a pipe, stood around leaning on the upper-story balcony, looking like this was all his domain. He was as immune to helping as our laborers.

The giant statue was almost unrecognizable when standing at its feet because of its massive scale. Ten adults could stand on the big toenail of one foot. To get the giant to fit into our limited view, we were going to rely on a piece of equipment I hadn't used before. It was a studio-built tilt plate that allowed the whole Circle-Vision rig to be inclined up to 60 degrees. The problem with this kind of shot is that as the front cameras tip up, those at the back face the ground. Side cameras are also problematic as the image is twisted at an odd angle, so this tilt plate only works in very limited situations. In this case I wanted the effect to be a reveal. We started the shot with the cameras level to see various extras walking around on what looks like a stone platform. As the scene tilts upwards, we see the legs, then knees and hands, and finally the face of the enormous Buddha. The rear cameras, numbers five and six, end up looking down at the rushing waters which I felt was appropriate since that's exactly what he's guarding.

I hadn't counted on the extras I'd asked for to be quite so brain dead. My specific directions for acting like typical tourists just weren't getting through to them via my translators. I acted out their parts for them, but that didn't help. Even the normally patient and diplomatic Ding commented to me that he thought they were just plain stupid.

On top of the technical challenges of Guy and Joe setting up the rig on the tilt plate, we had to clear out every single shipping case for our equipment. Sometimes we were able to leave a few smaller boxes hidden under the cameras, but with this set-up we'd see the ground behind us. We hoped we had what we needed because the boat was sent away to park downriver until we wrapped the shoot. The sun dodged in and out of clouds throughout the day, but I finally got a couple of excellent takes where the tilt, and the not-too-bright extras, were working in sync.

We were fed an enormous lunch by the local authorities, a banquet really, with 15 courses, including one of duck, three of chicken, and two of soup. We appreciated the hearty meal because we still had to get all the equipment back on the boat, across the river, then loaded into our truck, and finally travel four more hours back to Chengdu. All during a heavy rain. The local laborers were no more help than they had been earlier.

At the Housefly Inn, the dinner was pretty crummy as usual. It wasn't just that Sichuan food was way spicier than Sichuan food in America. I found the dishes not very appetizing. I settled for some simple noodles in the snack bar. I was physically exhausted, so I was glad Leon had built an actual day off into our schedule.

Sichuanese towns and villages could be rather primitive. The homes in one village had thatched roofs, but not in any picturesque sense, like in Britain. These felt more like the locals had to make do with whatever materials were at hand. Even in Chengdu, there were sections of the town that were run down with crumbling and patched ceramic tile roofs. Repairs stood out because the tiles were different colors. In so many cities, even Beijing, heating and cooking was typically done over crude braziers, often homemade. The *hutongs* had stovepipe stacks that belched black smoke from fires made from charcoal bricks.

One side effect of centralized economic planning was that village farmers in each region were mandated to grow the same vegetable. They'd all come to market at the same time, resulting in every street corner displaying uniform piles of cabbage, or radishes, or whatever was ordered by Beijing. I couldn't imagine what that meant for variety in a family's dinner recipes during turnip season.

I wandered the streets looking for some stationery for letter writing but kept hearing *"mei yo"* from shopkeepers, a common refrain that means "don't have." This was supposed to be a relaxing day, or at least a half day. The plan was to catch the train to Chongqing after dinner. I hoped I'd given Joe ample warning about what would be required of him. Every night Joe worked on dozens of camera reports, updated studio paperwork, and prepared exposed film for shipment by our customs broker back to the United States for processing. He rarely had free time but that was the way he liked it. Joe had his own secret stash of canned tuna and would get a bowl of rice from the restaurant, dump the tuna over it, then drench the works in soy sauce. None of that local Chinese soy, mind you. He'd brought his own from home. The concoction kept him going most nights, so I had no qualms or ever questioned his habits. I'd remind him every now and then that he'd have to occasionally join us for a banquet when we arrived in a new locale, for diplomatic reasons. He understood and would make an appearance, but then he'd be off to his room with his canned tuna and rice.

But all didn't go well that night. We were packed up and had bags ready to travel, but before we were ready (and by "we" I mean "Joe"), the equipment truck took off without supervision. Seeing Joe get upset, Leon hit the roof and took it out on Lao Tan. Our Chinese production manager was so embarrassed by the incident that as penance he rode the entire way to Chongqing in the baggage car to personally watch over our equipment. Meanwhile, I had to share a compartment with Greg, Joe, and Guy. The weather wasn't as hot as the previous time I made this trip, so we didn't have to open the train window for ventilation. We'd be breathing the fumes and ash from a different train soon enough.

When we arrived the next morning in Chongqing, we were put up in a real hotel, not the President Ford guesthouse I'd been lodged in last time. I joked that we should drive past the expansive grounds of that guesthouse to see if some gardener was wearing my new American running shoes. In those days it was common to hear visitors tell what was called a "wastebasket story." Typically, a Western tourist would throw out an item that had lost its usefulness, like a dried-out ballpoint pen. They'd drop it in their hotel wastebasket. When the tourist was getting on the bus to leave, a well-meaning hotel employee would come rushing out with the pen, as if it were some valuable artifact accidentally left behind. They'd present the empty pen back to the visitor with great fanfare. These apocryphal stories circulated as an example of how the Chinese went to great lengths to demonstrate both honesty and frugality, not to mention Western waste. But where was my own wastebasket story? I used to complain I was due for one after all this time traveling in China. At the very least, I fantasized an employee from the fancy guesthouse in this town rushing up to bring me my missing shoes.

Chongqing was an old city on the banks of a broad intersection where the

Jialing River merges with the Yangtze. During World War II the Japanese bombed the city 200 times from 1939 through 1941 because it was the seat of the Nationalist government. Many of the citizens took shelter in nearby caves and there were still visible scars from the war, but the city was buzzing with industrious people and the sounds of commerce. Women pulled two-wheel horse carts overloaded with cargo, struggling up and down the narrow streets and steep hills. The wide harbor was full of commercial traffic chugging along, blasting their air horns, navigating the muddy waters. We had come to find a barge that was suitable for filming.

I wanted to depict the busy harbor traffic in an area where the river's steep slopes were lined with dozens of wide stairways leading down to precarious gangways on loading docks and shanties. We found the right kind of boat after lunch and loaded it up with fake cargo. I had Guy Jones mount the Circle-Vision rig near the front of the barge, hoping audiences wouldn't notice we were actually being towed by a second craft about 30 yards in front. Leon, Bao, and anyone else not needed were on the front boat, out of sight. I still needed someone to play the part of our barge's tillerman, even though the steering of the camera boat was irrelevant. I selected Lao Tan. He was about as far removed from the real boatman as imaginable: pasty white skin, no upper body strength, looking more like an office worker. I wanted to make up to him for his baggage car ride, to say no hard feelings. He rolled up his pant legs and took off his shirt, revealing the Chinese equivalent of a wife-beater undershirt. Good enough. The owner was a cranky old man who refused to leave his boat, so he stayed in the open cabin right behind the hapless Lao Tan. As our barge steered through traffic, it looked more like the tiller was steering *him*. This business was limited to the back panels anyway, a little Easter egg for viewers who turn around to look at screens five and six. Through the various takes, the angry old boatman was either yelling directions or telling Lao Tan he was doing it all wrong. At least our production manager was game and the shot, while not great, worked well enough within the context of the film as a connective narrative device.

The next day we traveled to a remote railroad station, our staging area for the train-bridge-tunnel shot. I was very pleased we were finally doing this. Steam engine number 4038 looked freshly painted, jet black with bright red trim. Two flags had been painted on the nose, but six more real flags were displayed on the sides. Even the cowcatcher was a brilliant red lacquer. The engine was perhaps outfitted the way a special train carrying Mao might have looked and I loved it.

I'd also asked for an empty flatcar to be coupled in front of the engine. We'd be filming from the platform at a height where the cameras couldn't see what we were on, just the train behind us, pushing us along with a clear view of the tracks ahead. On a siding off the main rail lines, we assembled the rig on the train. Our soundman, still on probation as far as I was concerned, was told to ride in the cab of the engine and record various sounds. Meanwhile Joe, Greg, Guy, and I would huddle under the cameras for a thrilling ride. Or that was the plan, anyway.

The main line would be open to us from exactly 11 a.m. to noon, so if we didn't get the shot during that window, there would not be another chance. The main line was otherwise busy with freight and passenger traffic. When the appointed hour approached, I radioed directions to Ding and Bao riding in the engine that I wanted to motor down the main line into the first tunnel entrance, then proceed cautiously ahead. When we came out onto the large iron trestle bridge over the river, I wanted the train to stop. We needed to remove a protective tarp in order to check the cameras' alignment and framing. A light reading in the area of the river canyon between the tunnels was required. I was also calculating when to start rolling cameras. I had to budget our film because one full load (9 times 400 feet), only lasts about three and a half minutes. There'd be no time in our short window to reload, which usually took Joe about 45 minutes to an hour. I was counting on enough film for three long takes at the most.

The engine pushed us ahead and Guy made some adjustments to his support rig and cables. Now that we were moving on the tracks, he could see there was quite a bit of vibration from the old flatcar. We wore surgical masks in the tunnel and really needed them. What I wasn't prepared for as we chugged along in the blackness was the thundering roar of the steam engine echoing and reinforcing itself. My first thought was that we should have brought earplugs instead of masks. We came out of the tunnel into bright sunlight and the train stopped in the middle of the bridge, halfway across, about 50 feet above the river. We pulled off the tarp and I checked the cameras for final framing and alignment. Greg read the light on the bridge with a meter and gave Joe an f/stop for exposure. We were ready so I radioed Bao and Ding and told them we could back up and the next time we would shoot.

The train got up a little steam and started to chug backwards off the bridge and back into the first tunnel. The engine had been behind us the first time through but, as we reversed to our starting position, it was filling the tunnel ahead with thick smoke we'd have to eat. By the time we came back out to the start, we were choking and light-headed. Who knows what toxic residues we had taken in? I was certain there was a lot of carbon monoxide remaining in that tunnel. Joe circled the cameras in a last look for ash and grit on the filters or mirrors. I was very aware the clock was ticking on our access to the main line. but I didn't give the signal to start the train for two minutes in hopes some of the poisonous fumes would clear out.

We'd already lost a good chunk of our window in lining up the shot. It was time to roll. I gave the signal to Bao and Ding and the engine lurched forward. Joe was huddled under the cameras, hand on switch, waiting in the blackness of the first tunnel for my signal to roll cameras. We were clipping along at a good rate. It was noisy, dark, smoky, we were coughing, but I patted Joe's hand at what I thought was the right time. He flipped the switch while we were still in the tunnel. Our cameras required a few seconds to come up to the proper speed and, after about ten seconds of black, we came roaring out into sunlight. It was perfect – and then the train came to a stop right in the middle of the bridge! The engineer thought we were practicing again. *Cut!*

We backed up once more, eating even more smoke and fumes. We tried lying down on the flatcar to get as low as possible but that didn't help. As soon as we'd returned to the start by the station, I immediately gave the go-ahead, no time to waste. Once more the train made a run at the tunnel. In the darkness I gave Joe the signal and he rolled cameras. This time, as we emerged into sudden daylight, the engineer kept the train going. We charged right across the trestle bridge, between the canyons of the narrow river, and then barreled into the tunnel on the other side. We were in the dark when I yelled cut, but Joe couldn't hear me. I patted him on the hand again and he shut it down. I was grateful we got a good take. We were still in the second tunnel when the train stopped, then started to back up again. We were now in a hurry to get off the main line.

Using flashlights, Joe and Greg quickly put covers over the mirrors. We'd have to traverse two smoke-filled tunnels while being pelted with grit from the stack. I don't think we could have taken much more.

When we were safely back on our rail siding, I discovered our soundman hadn't recorded what I'd wanted. I relieved him of duty on the spot, in effect firing him, without even knowing if that were allowed. He got angry and then started throwing things. Not at me, just slamming our equipment around and yelling. That was a very un-Chinese reaction. Leon wanted to strangle him which was a very American reaction. Apart from the histrionics, we were pretty proud of what we accomplished this day: three "strategic targets" initially designated forbidden to film – all in one shot.

We were ready to begin our journey down the Yangtze.

A river cruiser on the Yangtze

Second Class cabin

Joe and Guy set up amidships

The Qutang Gorge

The tow-rope footpath

The Wu Gorge

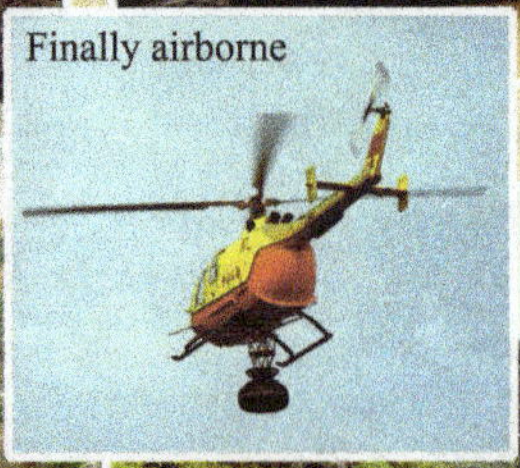

Finally airborne

Entering the town of Yicheng

Approaching the helicopter landing tables

CHAPTER 11

Porcelain Footprints

Really early morning calls we used to call "Zero Dark Hundred." Our crew would stumble around with flashlights in a murky fog to load equipment onto our truck because the Yangtze cruiser was scheduled to cast off at 7 a.m. At least we weren't contending with the explosive lightning storm Leon and I had experienced on the survey.

We arrived at the dock on time, unlike a handful of European tourists who'd lost some of their baggage. The captain patiently waited for the stragglers, so we weren't able to sail until closer to 10 a.m. We checked into our individual compartments on the ship which were cramped but comfortable. Meals would again have to be endured in the dining room under the watchful eyes of Third Class passengers at the portholes.

I informed Joe, Guy, and Greg that we'd made a little discovery on the survey that they might find useful. Chinese toilets for men were typically a standard urinal and just a hole in the floor. On either side of the foul-smelling opening were two raised footprints of porcelain, apparently to help one find the right position to squat. Our Yangtze river cruiser was no exception and the male and female facilities were communal, of course. But Leon and I had discovered that the ladies had Western-style sit-down toilets. In order to do our business with a bit more comfort, we just needed to station a friend outside to temporarily fend off female intruders. I was hoping my crew would keep it secret and also cover for each other.

The green-and-white cruiser, nicknamed "The East is Red," was the same style we'd had on the survey. About 150 feet long, the ship had three full-length decks and a raised area farther forward. The second deck was reserved for a total of 16 foreigners in Second Class. Below that was Third Class which stuffed six passengers to a cabin, and at the bottom were wall-to-wall bunkbeds in Fourth.

Lao Tan and Shen had made arrangements with the shipping line for us to be able to film from two positions: the roof of the third deck and the bow. Guy didn't wait until we'd cruised very far before constructing a rig for us out of speed rail. Five curious young Chinese women hung around watching every move that this "foreign devil" made. Guy also pre-rigged another set-up for the bow where the winds were fearsome enough to make us hang on to railings or risk being blown right off the ship.

The Yangtze has been a historic, political, and geographic barrier that divides China neatly into north and south. Our cruiser shared this mighty river with a variety of craft: cargo ships, tugs, barges, junks, sampans, and smaller boats, some little more than bamboo rafts. We hadn't traveled far down swirling brown waters before terraced farmland gave way to steeper hills and valleys. Our boat made a scheduled stop in the town of Wanxian to be ready for the next morning's sail into the Three Gorges. Taking advantage of the break, we jumped off for a quick tour of a local silk factory and an antiques shop. There was already talk that the coming Three Gorges Dam would inundate two-thirds of this city.

The scenic region of the gorges is almost 200 miles long, so I knew we'd have a lot of opportunities along the way, but I wanted to make sure we captured the feeling at the entrance where the walls begin to close in. We had a production meeting on the ship that night to make sure everyone was ready for our 9 a.m. arrival at the start of Qutang Gorge.

In the dining room, we were informed the captain was now saying we'd reach Qutang an hour early. That was just the kind of rushed change of schedule to put Joe into a funk for the rest of the day. We had to stop eating mid-breakfast and scramble to the upper decks. Joe hurried to mount the nine cameras on the pedestal and check all the lenses. China Joe and Leo would follow along behind him as he circled the rig, backstopping him to make sure all f/stops were set the same. We knew that once we entered Qutang there'd be no take two. As it turned out, the information from the captain was erroneous, and not for the first time. The ship arrived just before 9 anyway, so Joe had been upset for no reason.

The first gorge was pretty impressive, and the ship skillfully passed between the ragged cliffs. I hoped our soundman was recording the cruiser's honking blasts which echoed back and forth off the cliffs. I had Joe run the cameras a couple of times – decent takes, I thought – reserving some film for later. Part of my job was to budget the timing of my film, knowing it would take the better part of an hour to reload all the magazines and get set for another round of shooting. If I burned too much on the first gorge, we might be in the middle of a reload when we arrived at the second. While Joe had a specific footage counter on his control box, I also referred to a stopwatch of my own just to be sure. There were times when I'd hold off shouting "Roll cameras!" until the very last moment because I knew there'd be just enough film for one more take.

As we approached the Wu Gorge the weather became quite variable. If the sun happened to pop in or out right at the moment I wanted to shoot, it could mean a quick run around the rig by Joe to adjust the nine lenses again. One significant feature of the gorges I wanted to capture was a narrow footpath carved along the rockface. These tracks ran the length of the gorges and were a holdover from a time when boats had to be hauled upstream against the strong currents. According to the stories we heard, sometimes 400 *qian fu* (tow-rope workers) were needed to pull a large boat with 1,200-foot-long hawsers. The men coordinated their strenuous efforts by chanting work songs to the accompaniment of gongs and drums. These trackers performed the backbreaking work nude because clothing was deemed too restrictive. I have a pretty good imagination, but I couldn't picture the chaos and confusion of so many peasant boatmen on that narrow ledge struggling to pull the boats with long lines. Uncountable numbers of naked men must have died falling off the cliff every season, chalked up to the cost of commerce on the mighty Yangtze.

Our crew came out of hiding to join us when I told them we were done with the position amidships. After successfully getting five good takes on the first load of film, Joe set about reloading. Each camera had to come off, one at a time, in the proper order. Joe meticulously unthreaded then rethreaded the cameras in a ritualistic way while China Joe and Leo, who were more than capable of doing this task themselves, would patiently stand by, acting as a shield against the wind or as a shade against the sun. If Joe was the priest, they were his acolytes. As Joe finished one camera, Leo would mount it back on the pedestal while China Joe would hand him another, neither rushed nor out of numerical sequence. No one spoke to Joe or distracted him in any way during these rites. His work required an obsessive-compulsive personality and he was perfect for the job – social skills (and eating habits) be damned.

Only when Joe was ready and the rig fully reassembled, did I call for lunch. Had we sent some of the crew off early, that would have added to his funky mood. The irony is that Joe didn't really want to eat with us, of course. He just didn't want to be taken for granted.

During the meal we heard that the captain's timetable was off again – we would arrive at Xiling Gorge a half-hour early. There was no panic this time. The rig was ready. The weather was much better and I got the kinds of shots

I wanted. My idea for the sequence was that we would establish our location amidships, clearly showing the cameras were riding on a cruiser. But the next shot of the sequence was to be from the bow where there was no evidence of the ship in the front five cameras. We were deliberately far enough forward that the ship "disappeared," even though it was still seen in the back panels. Then, as I'd mapped out the sequence months ago, the third shot would be from a helicopter, taken from this same height. What I was hoping for was a "gotcha" moment where the audience thinks this third shot was just another "front of the boat" shot until the cameras soar up and fly over the scenery. Of course, that would require our oft-delayed permission to film from a helicopter.

We completed the journey through Xiling Gorge which ends at the Nanjing Pass in Hubei Province. Our ship had to navigate locks to get to the town of Yicheng where we were checked into another guesthouse. This one had terrific accommodations because it was where the premier of China stayed. I doubt he ever had to put up with porcelain footprints around a hole in the floor.

The newest American member of our team was waiting for us in Yicheng. Ernie Gustavson was our helicopter mount mechanic who'd flown in from the States. I was especially glad to see Ernie because he brought along a care package and letter for me from Kathy. At that evening's production meeting we were introduced to our newest Chinese crew members, the aerial team.

One of the great mysteries of the entire shoot, from my perspective, was that the Chinese finally gave us permission to film from the air with our Circle-Vision cameras but wouldn't let me be in the helicopter. This despite aerial photography being my old job back at MacGillivray-Freeman Films. What wasn't I supposed to see – which the cameras were photographing for the rest of the world? It didn't make a lot of sense, but the only solution was to bring in a Chinese cameraman specifically for these shots. His name was Han Jian Wen, a gentle soul, quiet and unassuming, unlike the two Chinese pilots.

I took my time explaining, through Bao, what was involved in filming aerials with Circle-Vision. It was particularly hazardous task because the helicopter has to first land on two large wooden platforms which we'd had shipped in from the U.S. Then a specially built mount is slung underneath the Messerschmitt BO-105. The Circle-Vision rig is bolted to the mount and various wiring has to be fed up to the control box in the helicopter's back seat. That's where Han would fly and turn the cameras on and off.

I made a little presentation and had a map of the area, but the main pilot seemed distracted and not paying attention, even when Bao translated my words. I suggested that this was going to be very new to them since landings and takeoffs from these platforms are quite risky. The pilot is unable to see the rig hanging beneath him and has to rely on his ground crew to make sure he's lined up straight. It's their job to guide his approach with great care to ensure he doesn't ram into the tables – or worse.

I took Bao aside to find out why the pilot seemed so disinterested and was told, "He says he's done this before."

Well, that would be *impossible*. As I pressed for answers, the pilot told Bao he'd flown a rig like this before – in the Soviet Union. That made it even more unlikely.

Circle-Vision is a system invented and patented by Disney and, to my knowledge, had never been used in the Soviet Union. The short version of the answer, which took the better part of an hour to find out, is that long ago, when the system still used 16 mm cameras, there had been a demonstration that Disney put together and traveled through Europe. The film was presented in a blow-up tent with portable projectors and sound system. Joe Nash had even worked on the equipment preparation. Somewhere along the line, the Soviets caught the demo, decided to rip off Disney's designs, and built their own rig from scratch. Apparently, they'd been making their own 360 films since then and at some point, way back when the Soviets were still close allies with the Chinese, our pilot had been invited to come to Russia to do some helicopter shots.

As incredulous as I was at hearing this, I thought perhaps this might be a stroke of luck and we wouldn't need to endure a steep learning curve. I handed out my shot list to Han and went to bed feeling strangely optimistic.

The next day was not good. Not good at all. The aerial crew shot two complete loads (7,200 feet of film) and none of it was usable. Between Han and the Chinese pilot, they hadn't followed any of my directions. I could see from a video recorder Ernie Gustavson had mounted on the rig that they were at the wrong altitude, flying at the wrong speed, and they weren't even in the right location. So much for my map and shot list. At least there were no incidents with takeoffs and landing on the platforms. I was thankful the pilots had brought along an experienced team of military ground crew who were very cautious and knew what they were doing.

Almost fittingly, our truck broke down and we had to offload equipment into the minibus. Joe had to get back to the hotel to download all the magazines and package up all this unusable film for shipment to our customs broker in Beijing. I held a production meeting that night to reconstruct what went wrong so we could do better the next day. Greg wasn't able to join us because he'd become quite ill, suspecting he'd eaten bad shrimp during the river cruise. On the Chinese side, our two pilots didn't even bother to show up, sending their "representatives" from the ground crew.

Leon hit the roof because that's what Leon does. But this time Lao Tan got just as angry, not at the flight team but at Leon who had embarrassed the Chinese crew by displaying temper. Lao Tan even went so far as to say we were not respecting that old "spirit of cooperation between our two countries." Yeah, Lao Tan went there, making the gathering a rough go for a while.

I called off the meeting after the representatives told us the pilots weren't coming because they needed their rest for "safety's sake." I didn't call them prima donnas, but I sure was thinking it. Instead, Leon and I arranged for Tan, Shen, and Bao to join us later in a "crisis meeting" when tempers had cooled. Everyone promised to try harder the next day.

I started out the morning by soothing the ruffled feathers of Han, our aerial cameraman, by relating my own experiences doing the same job. Meanwhile Joe and Guy had the cameras loaded and the rig had been attached with cables hooked up – but the helicopter just sat there. We had located our base of flight operations on a high bluff because it gave us an unobstructed view in all directions. But this morning our pilots refused to fly because there was a "breeze." One of the ground crew held up a portable anemometer to check the strength of the wind and the dial barely moved. I've flown safely in much stronger winds, but our pilots were adamant. The sky, of course, was beautiful, the river far below us was serene, and we had to just sit there on the bluff, impotently waiting. We wasted the entire morning trying to coax our Chinese flight crew to take off. They had numbers on their side, claiming the military wouldn't let the pilot fly with this size load until the faint whisper of a breeze died down.

I suggested we remove the camera mount and have them do a safety flight check, just so they weren't sitting around. They agreed and we had to completely disconnect and un-cable the cameras. Joe wasn't happy with being jerked around and quickly got into a snit, lashing out at China Joe for no reason. The helicopter took off and I spent my downtime putting out fires among the crew. Meanwhile, Greg was laid out in the back of the equipment truck groaning and barely able to move. He looked pale, feverish, but kept saying he was fine, that it was just bad seafood.

The pilots came back from their test flight and landed on the tables, proclaiming that all was now well and we could proceed with shooting. I had to wonder if there was an element of what I'd gone through with the Mongolian horsemen at work. The pilots obviously felt confident that the power had shifted back to them.

Joe and Guy set to work reconnecting the camera system. There was no room between the platforms for anyone else, so we just stayed out of their way. I gave Han last-minute directions on what I was hoping he'd shoot. We were in a bit of a rush because, as I'd stated to everyone in the previous meeting, we had a train to catch that evening. I'd already told Joe once and didn't want to mention it to him again. He might think I was piling on. I reminded the pilots they'd have to get airborne no later than 1 p.m. if we were to be successful and still make the train.

The helicopter lifted off at precisely 12:53 p.m. and had no issues with the breeze. I swear it was windier than it had been all morning, but I wasn't the one guarding the anemometer. When they came back about a half-hour later, the report from Han was that they got a pretty good shot. I checked the video and, while it could have been improved, it was superior to what we'd filmed the day before. I gave them some encouraging words, then glanced at my watch and the footage counter. They had enough footage for a few more shots so I sent them back up again. That paid off in an even better take, closer to what I'd been looking for, plus one more in which Han grabbed a scene with one of the river cruisers passing by. All in all, a more successful ending to the day than I'd expected.

We stripped off the cameras and hustled to pack them into their shipping boxes, calling it a day at this location about 3 p.m. We had just enough time to check out of our hotel and rush to the station for another night train, this time to Wuhan.

Chang'an Boulevard

The hydraulic lift in the Peking Hotel

Badaling

Trying to control the crowds

Tourists along the Great Wall

CHAPTER 12

A Renovation in Bamboo

On the train ride, I thought about Greg's illness. Earlier in the summer, when we were filming in Hawaii, we'd staged a Makahiki festival with a large crowd of extras and a boxed lunch was provided. Shooting ran long that day and by the time we could eat the sandwiches, the boxes had been sitting in the hot sun. I had to leave very early the next morning for a meeting with Disney in LA and I was sick as a dog on the plane. I thought it was just me and didn't realize until I called Kathy that almost everyone in the cast and crew was just as sick, some violently ill.

Riding on the train, I did the math. That incident happened almost exactly 90 days earlier, the gestation period for hepatitis. Greg didn't want to hear of it, still insisting it was Chinese seafood, but now he was looking like a ghost.

The next afternoon we connected from Wuhan back to Beijing. As often as we checked into the Peking Hotel, the front desk staff would have to process our papers before assigning us to a room. The sprawling hotel was divided into three sections. During negotiations we'd stayed in the more "Modern" wing, renovated in 1979 but feeling like 1959. On the west end was the much older unit done in the grand "Soviet-style" which was gloomy, dusty, overheated, and in need of serious upgrading. Wedged between the two was an intermediate section generally reserved for "Overseas Chinese," their term for anyone of even remote Chinese ancestry who returns to visit the homeland. The three lobbies were linked with gift stores, snack shops, and a foreign language bookstore. Ever since our earliest surveys, Leon and I had been given rooms in the old Soviet section and we were used to it, never the same room twice. On this day the front desk handed me my key. I went up the creaking old staircase to open the door to find a bundle wrapped in brown paper and twine sitting on the bed. My name was written on it – no address, even in Chinese. I certainly hadn't been expecting a package. Besides, who knew which room I would end up in?

I tore open the paper to discover... my missing shoes! At the front desk no one could tell me how the package got into my room. Neither could anyone at China Co-Film. Those shoes would have to remain a mystery – but at least I finally had my own wastebasket story!

We were scheduled to begin filming the following day at the entrance to the Forbidden City, the gate made famous when Mao declared the beginning of the People's Republic from its balcony. I walked down the few blocks from the hotel to check it out and was shocked to discover the Gate of Heavenly Peace was completely enclosed in bamboo scaffolding. The entire façade would be under intensive renovation for some time in order to prepare for China's National Day, the first of October. Our shooting schedule had been knocked sideways.

Our original plan for this day was to use a Chinese Hongqi ("Red Flag") limousine convertible for travel shots through Beijing streets with the vehicle turning into the entrance directly under Mao's portrait. This kind of limo, initially designed with Soviet help and financing, was built to regularly carry political dignitaries into the Forbidden City through the same entrance. But, due to the renovations at the gate, we had to change plans. I decided to improvise a brand-new scene. Improvisation and Circle-Vision, I painfully learned, don't go together very well.

What I had in mind was to get a bicyclist's view of Beijing streets, the kind seen every day by tens of thousands of bike riders. Government cars were pretty rare, while public buses and taxis were limited. Even Shih Kuan used to ride his bike to the office. Standing on any corner and watching the bikes hypnotically whir past was like witnessing a great migration. I wanted to find a way to share that experience with an audience. I thought we might mount our heavy camera rig on the back of a three-wheeled bicycle cart. I'd seen them toting huge loads of cargo in cities across China. I'd even seen one toting a dead body wrapped in blankets on the way to the morgue. This type of vehicle has a flat wooden cargo space over the back two wheels, like a table mounted right behind the driver. From the perspective of our cameras, I thought it would look like we were hitching a ride on a bike, since we would not see the platform, just the rider's back and head on the front camera as he steers us through traffic.

Once we'd secured a sturdy bicycle cart, we found there was barely enough room on the table to hold the camera rig along with one of our heavy-duty truck batteries and the large control box. Guy Jones worked with Joe Nash to lock everything down. It had a weird beauty, stacked and lashed together on the back of the bike. I really thought it would work – until the poor bike rider tried to move it. The rig wouldn't budge so we would need to give it a lengthy push to get him going. Once underway, I wanted the rider to pull out into the flowing stream of bike traffic. But I could see it would take forever for us to get out of the shot once we'd set it in motion. I couldn't just turn on the cameras and waste nine rolls of film while the rider was laboriously peddling away from us. I decided I could run alongside the rig and turn it on and off when it seemed right. What made this a terrible idea was that I'd have to double over to stay out of the shot. While still running. In traffic. Unable to see because I had my head down. After less than 50 yards I thought I was going to have a heart attack. I was gasping for breath and the driver had little ability to steer because the heavy weight in back cantilevered his front wheel up off the ground.

We packed that in and decided we'd do the camera car shot after all. We'd just have to avoid the bamboo at the Forbidden City entrance. Guy had already inspected the floor of the Red Flag limousine and had prepared it for the camera's base plate. We arranged the height of the rig to just miss seeing any of the limo. That meant we could drive down the streets as if the cameras were floating along. The design had been based loosely on a 1958 Chrysler Imperial. The resulting limo weighed nearly three tons (including armor plating and our heavy rig), but that made for a smooth ride.

We did a few rehearsals that went pretty well, then rolled cameras while driving along side streets dappled with the shade of trees. I noticed bike riders would become very curious about us, staring as we drove by, and I worried we might cause an accident. We pulled out onto the much broader Chang'an Boulevard which was considered a *Da Ma Lu* (literally "Big Horse Road"). This main thoroughfare runs past the Peking Hotel and down through Tiananmen Square. Some visiting head of state happened to be in town so there were lots of flags lining the boulevard, adding some color. We got a couple of takes but the sun was getting low and coming into our shot. A number of curious policemen showed up, too – exactly what I'd always worried about in filming in China. With so many people staring at our cameras, we'd have to wait for much more controlled conditions.

I worked on revising the schedule with Leon at the hotel. In a few days we were supposed to be filming right in the middle of Tiananmen Square for National Day: October 1. Huge crowds were expected. I still hadn't determined an exact placement for our camera rig because I didn't really know how that would impact us. There wasn't going to be a way to control the masses, but

I thought we'd be okay if we could get a higher angle than usual. Back home we'd have simply rented a high-lift, a cherry picker. I had been told weeks earlier that none would be available at this time because they were assigned to construction projects. So far, I hadn't found a suitable substitute that could hold our heavy rig, especially after my bicycle cart idea fell through. While Leon and I were meeting in the hotel's dining room, I happened to look up and see a rolling rig that hotel staff used to change the light bulbs in the 20-foot ceilings. On top was a platform at least the size of the bicycle cart's table and it could be hydraulically pumped up to the height we needed. Leon wasn't optimistic that it could be arranged in time, but I offered to roll it all the way down to the square myself, if needed. At first hotel staff refused, as they did to almost all requests (because no one ever says "Yes"). Authorization would have to run all the way up the Ministry of Culture's flagpole, but there was still time.

The next morning had been scheduled for the *de rigueur* shot of the entire production: putting the cameras right on the Great Wall. To make it work, we'd have to haul coals to Newcastle.

In 221 B.C., Emperor Qin Shi Huang ordered the consolidation of many short sections of wall, used for centuries as defensive barriers and fortresses against nomads from the north. These sections, actually a series of fortification systems, were scattered in all directions and varied widely in local construction materials, from quarried rock cut into blocks to tamped and compressed earth. It was Qin's act of unification that made his name synonymous with "China." During the Ming dynasty (14th to 17th century), the wall was strengthened and developed on a larger scale reaching 6,000 kilometers. The battlement walls rise at least 20 feet above the terrain with watchtowers built at irregular intervals. The biggest challenge for the builders was maintaining these dimensions across rugged mountain ridges and valleys, from deserts to grassy plains, to the sea in the east. The structure had been fabricated over the centuries by soldiers, peasants, and convicts, several hundred thousand of whom died during the work and were buried within the wall itself.

At Badaling, a site made famous by visits of foreign dignitaries like President Nixon, the reconstructed wall runs about 16 feet wide. On any given day thousands come to visit this section. A large bus parking lot, a building with restrooms, and a few snack bars were about the only accommodations for so much traffic. A small team of Americans and Chinese trying to set up an elaborate camera system on the wall would have drawn a massive crowd of curious spectators. People could have been hurt trying to get a better look at us in the chaos. All we could have filmed would be faces. Rather than even attempt the impossible, we tried for the possible.

We brought a busload of our own "tourists." They were Chinese extras hired in Beijing wearing their most colorful clothes. We also invited along a few of our expatriate friends to make a mix of people. The idea was to close off regular foot traffic between two designated watchtowers where narrow doorways afforded natural pinch points for control. We had a handful of uniformed security people at each end, working with our crew on walkie-talkies. Once the area was stripped of curious tourists, our crew would come in to set up the cameras without the interruptions of gawkers. Then the people we'd bussed in would be asked to follow one simple direction: act like tourists but ignore the cameras. That was the plan. *In principle.*

In reality, it took hours to clear out the section and make room for our many cases of equipment. Simply because the area was now "off limits" made it even more attractive to hundreds of visitors who were starting to stack up at each watchtower. Security had their hands full as younger men tried to climb up and over. The Ming dynasty probably had similar problems with Mongolian hordes swarming the battlements. At least no one wanted to kill us. That I know of.

Joe, Guy, Leo, and China Joe set up the camera rig fairly quickly on our dolly. Meanwhile I rushed around spotting our imported extras at various distances from the cameras, all waiting for me to yell action! Our American friends Joe and Ellen Irish, in China on a building project (appropriately named the Great Wall Hotel), were given some business to do up on top of the second watchtower. I asked Bao to play a tour guide leading our customs broker (Klaus) and his wife past the cameras. As usual, I wasn't asking for complex behaviors, just for them to act like typical tourists: walking, talking, smiling, taking pictures, and pointing anywhere but at our cameras.

This was key to what we were forced to do at almost every location in China. We'd have to use hidden security to control a large area around the cameras, then replace any regular people with hired extras who would follow directions. I was trying to create a sense of what a particular place looked like *as if we weren't there,* as if this incredibly noisy and complex machine with mirrors being pushed along by Americans on their hands and knees didn't exist at all. In effect, our job was to go to unnatural lengths to make the scene look natural. But we only had to do it for about 30 seconds at a time.

Even after we got the shot with a few fast takes, we still had to maintain tight security a little longer, just to get our shipping cases back up on the wall. The team tore down the cameras and removed our equipment in record time, but the seas would no longer stay parted. We were awash in those curious tourists we'd kept out for so long and it was a madhouse escaping the Great Wall.

Just when it seemed we were gaining a little momentum, we stumbled into another crisis.

National Day celebrations

Coal Hill from the Forbidden City

The Meridian Gate illuminated

Peking Hotel

More than one child

The Monument to the People's Heroes

The borrowed hydraulic lift

Police "crowd control"

National Day crowds

Joe adjusts the lenses

The final set-up

CHAPTER 13

Iron Rice Bowl

We were already on the minibus headed back out to Badaling for helicopter photography of the Great Wall when we discovered the People's Liberation Army had moved our base of operations. The PLA didn't bother to inform us, even though the new site would require the helicopter to dodge some power lines. Shih Kuan was with us on the bus and I told him this situation was completely unacceptable. He would have to renegotiate with the PLA and postpone this section of helicopter photography for our spring shoot. Greg had gone out to the airport that morning to pick up his wife, Barbara. They arrived at the location just in time to see me cancel the plans for the day.

The next morning was very clear, especially for Beijing, a city that sometimes choked on the bitter smoke from its own charcoal fires. Our schedule took the crew to Jingshan Park. The Imperial Gardens there dated back almost a thousand years and were sited according to the principles of *feng shui*. In the center is an artificial hill made from the soil excavated from the moats surrounding the Forbidden City. The 150-foot-tall mound was known as Jingshan, then Feng Shui Hill, but more recently Coal Hill, after rumors the Emperors had used it to store reserves of the fuel. Atop the hill is a beautiful pagoda with a fantastic 360-degree view of Beijing and the northern entrance to the Forbidden City.

We climbed to the top, everyone but Leon who doesn't do hills, and I lined up the shot. This was a fairly straightforward set-up: laying track for the China dolly and placing and directing a dozen extras. Down below, Leon was getting upset that Ding's radio was off. We only found this out when Leon huffed and puffed all the way up to the pagoda, just to let everyone know how angry he was he couldn't talk to anyone.

After I got a shot I liked, we called it a wrap. The crew, who'd been hiding out of sight, came up to clear the cameras and equipment. But once again the local laborers refused to work – a literal sit-down strike. This labor action underscored the nagging problem that had plagued us from the beginning. Coal Hill was the shot that brought the issue out into the open and led to a barely satisfactory solution.

At every location we needed to bring on laborers for tasks like hauling our many crates and cases of equipment. Because this was Circle-Vision, it was never that simple. The boxes had to be taken down off our truck, hand-carried up the hill to the site, unloaded, then the empty boxes had to be moved out of the shot. When we wrapped, the boxes had to be brought back in again to be loaded, and finally carried back down to our truck again. That's a lot of heavy lifting. Usually the laborers stood around smoking, squabbling over who'd get to carry the smallest or lightest crates, but Coal Hill was the first time they'd refused to work at all.

China Co-Film had arranged for these men and women the way they did on all locations: they'd approach some relevant local government unit who would in turn assign workers otherwise unemployed that day. The going price we'd negotiated for each laborer was $5 a day. That's dirt cheap in the U.S., but in those days, when everyone in China received a monthly salary of $35, that's a pretty substantial bump in wages. We thought workers would be wildly grateful for that much money for a few hours of schlepping boxes, but that's not how they saw it.

The unemployed people we got from these labor offices had been quite happy sitting around reading the *People's Daily* and slurping their tea. What did they care? The Iron Rice Bowl guaranteed them the same pay whether they worked or didn't work. When we had Bao and Ding talk to the laborers directly, they were told, "Who do these Americans think they are, asking us to do heavy labor for nothing?"

Wait, what? That's when we realized the individual laborers weren't getting that $5 – their government unit was. No wonder they resisted picking up boxes and struggling on the hill. No wonder we ended up doing the heavy lifting ourselves. But this revelation brought forth an even bigger and more important issue.

Back in January, Bob Gibeaut had negotiated deals for our Beijing crew members as well. A camera assistant in the U.S. would have cost about $250 a day. But our deal was for $125 a day each for the services of China Joe and

Leo. So we were shocked to discover they weren't getting a penny above their normal monthly salary. In effect, working for us put them in the same situation as the local laborers.

As was his normal reaction, Leon hit the roof. Those fees we were paying were going straight into government coffers. Leon and I approached Shih Kuan to demand more money for our loyal crew. We begged to be allowed to pay them more, but his hands were tied. In the end, after weeks of pleading, the government decreed that we would be allowed to give each member of our crew a per diem of $1 a day whenever they were out of town, meaning in any location other than Beijing. Leon and I thought this proposed solution was pathetically inadequate. But when we broke the news to our crew, they were thrilled. An extra dollar a day for a film that mainly shot on location meant they were nearly doubling their salary! As for those future local hires we counted on, especially for climbing Huangshan, Leon found a way to slip them a few bucks under the table, now that we knew their motivation problem. For all his gruff manner, Leon had a big heart.

We had a small get-together with friends and crew that night to celebrate my 35th birthday with chili and hot dogs, which I'm sure seemed strange to our Chinese friends. Barbara had brought along $100 worth of canned tuna to refresh Joe's supply. At our party, Bao and Ding tried to recall a specific local expression for the occasion. Ding finally remembered and blurted out the translation: "Thirty-five means you're half in the ground!" I'm sure it sounds less ominous in Chinese.

Greg was still feeling poorly and, now that Barbara was there to encourage and support him, he decided to see a doctor at a local hospital. They wanted him to have X-rays and blood tests, which meant they thought his condition serious.

That night I went out with Joe to do some single-camera shooting with the Arriflex. Twice a year, the city's government buildings are outlined with strings of small white bulbs giving the train station and museums a very festive look. I wanted nine images like this to pay off a sequence that would start with the Circle-Vision shots we were due to capture next: National Day celebrations.

The Imperial Palace complex had been home to China's Emperors from the mid-Ming dynasty (1420) to the end of the Qing dynasty (1912) so the symbolism of Mao Zedong's speech from the balcony of the Gate of Heavenly Peace on October 1, 1949, was significant to all Chinese people.

Floral arrangements and large posters of Karl Marx, Friedrich Engels, Vladimir Lenin, and Sun Yat-sen had been displayed in massive Tiananmen Square for years but recently the CCP (Chinese Communist Party) had stopped including Joseph Stalin. These large portraits had been painted by Ge Xiaoguang, the same painter whose image of Mao remains hanging over the entrance at the Gate of Heavenly Peace.

Near the center of the square stands the Monument to the People's Heroes, a ten-story obelisk on a raised marble platform, surrounded by statues carved in dramatic poses. Flanking this monument to the east and west were the National Museum of China and the Great Hall of the People with the Mausoleum of Mao Zedong to the south. For special occasions, including National Day and Labor Day (May 1), public and government buildings like these are bedecked with hundreds of large red flags in addition to the outline of white lights at night. In the past, there'd been impressive military parades which had been cut back since the disaster of Mao's Great Leap Forward. The Cultural Revolution had made everyone nervous about mass displays so at this time the tradition was for local residents to simply converge on the square in a low-key gathering. It was more like a holiday, a chance for common folks to a hang out in Tiananmen Square.

Our team assembled next to the huge motorized crane that had been required to bring our hydraulic lift down the street from the Peking Hotel. No one would be changing light bulbs in the dining room that day. We quickly became the central focus of an enormous crowd, mainly because there were no other activities planned to divert them. Today we were the parade, as we cranked up the platform with the Circle-Vision camera rig mounted on it. My plan was to shoot at various times, right on through to night, in order for the viewer to get a feel for the ebb and flow of people on this important day. But there was no ebb. And nobody was flowing. The citizens, many of them soldiers in uniform, were stacked around us in a ring about 20 deep. They were silent, staring, smoking cigarettes, curious.

Once I had the cameras lined up with the framing I wanted, we had to deal with all these people standing around who wouldn't leave us alone. I was reminded that Leon had expressed concern the night before that we weren't going to get *any* crowds. At first, we tried using the half-dozen uniformed police who'd been assigned to us but they were fairly ineffective in breaking up the crowd. They only asked them to move back which just widened the circle and brought them even more into our shot. Where was Miss Pu with her authoritative voice when I needed her? Needless to say, my plan to capture a natural-looking environment wasn't working. The police brought out megaphones and that energized a few of the gawkers. But once people realized there was no real consequence, they'd just swarm back around the base of our platform. The police had been instructed to ask people to keep moving, but once the crowd settled into a counterclockwise movement, the result was just a huge circle of people shuffling around us like a human gyre. All of them staring right at us, of course. Eventually, with the help of some plainclothes cops, the police got the crowd dispersed enough that I could grab a shot or two. But sharp-eyed viewers will spot uniformed police shambling along like everyone else.

We simply outlasted the curious and ignored the handful who came in so close to the base that they weren't even seen by the cameras. When I was happy with a number of takes, I asked Joe to switch magazines and load up with high-speed stock. The only film available in those days was Fujifilm, rated about ASA 250. We shot through magic hour when the sky still had some post-sunset light and the building outline lights had come on. The Fuji made for a decent night image of the square but, in the final film, the color differences between this and our normal Kodak stock for the daytime shots was noticeable and aggravating. At least to my eye.

Later I went out to shoot a few more single-camera night scenes of the festivities. Greg, despite his illness, was a real trooper and came along to help out. We filmed the little lights outlining the TV tower and even the Peking Hotel. After an exhausting day, late dinner was simply noodles in the hotel after-hours bar.

And there was still another month to go on this first shooting trip.

The town of Guilin

Part of the Yangshuo "painting" vista

Yangshuo rain

The Circle-Vision set-up on a hill

Joe and Leo

Yangshuo

Reed Flute Cave

A single-camera set-up

Tourists loading

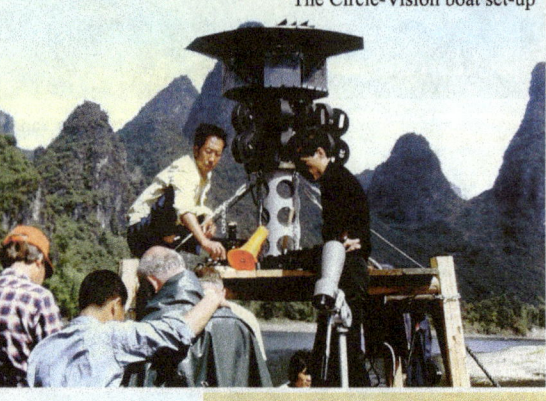
The Circle-Vision boat set-up

Typical tour boat

Fishermen on the Li River

A raft with a sail

Motoring down the Li River

Chapter 14

Scattered Dragon's Teeth

As we began October, the start of our second month of shooting, Greg decided he wouldn't join us as we traveled south to Guilin. He felt he needed a few more days to recuperate and we should go on without him. Barbara would keep him company in Beijing.

The weather on arrival in Guilin was dreadful as a heavy, oppressive overcast shrouded a wide region of Guangxi Province with frequent rain. Those wispy puffs of mist between jagged mountains that I'd found so artistic on the survey were long gone. But Guilin itself was a remarkable sight, in any weather. City buildings had been tucked in among the sharp, craggy peaks with green vegetation tumbling down the steep slopes. Roads circumnavigated around the spires, weaving in and out of the serrated formations that marched to the horizon. But despite the beautiful scenery, no one on our crew really wanted to go out in the rain.

I'd complained about inadequacies of the 700-bed Lijiang Hotel that we'd stayed in last time. The dining room had been set up for large tour groups, mostly Japanese for whom the Chinese still nursed a longstanding hatred. The food seemed appropriate to serve an enemy who had bombed them during WWII. This trip, Lao Tan and Shen made more of an effort to find us better accommodations. The Ronghu Hotel was marginally better since it was a 100-bed guesthouse.

I was concerned that we needed to keep up the momentum of our production schedule because very soon our crew was going to increase in size.

Leon had arranged for a fairly expensive team to drive up from Guangzhou with lights and a generator we would need to shoot inside the very large Reed Flute Cave. Their drive was only 500 kilometers, but they were making slow progress over two-lane country roads. I wanted to already have a few shots lined up in the cave but found we wouldn't be allowed inside until four in the afternoon. We'd have to face this same restriction even on the shoot days we'd been planning for months. So even though we were paying for the privilege, the local authorities had no interest in closing down their money-making tourist site early for an American crew. Our papers from the Minister of Culture didn't seem to carry much weight this far from Beijing.

Instead of waiting all day to get into the cave, I thought we should get a jump on the river cruise. Unfortunately, the boat we were renting for the shoot wasn't in town. It was 40 kilometers away. Then the situation worsened. We'd planned to film while we traversed the Li River from Guilin all the way down to Yangshuo, the usual end of the cruise. Our local contacts told us the river was drying up, restricting travel. We'd have to drive south for a few hours to get to our boat and then we'd only have a 17-kilometer stretch for filming because the water level was so low. I couldn't believe the locals were telling us this with a straight face while a biblical rain poured down outside.

One last insult was that our previously planned helicopter landing site had been moved farther south on us. No consultation, no collaboration, none of Shih Kuan's "spirit of cooperation between our two countries," just a unilateral decision. The new site was closer to Yangshuo, hours away from where we were housed in Guilin. That would complicate our ability to respond quickly and get airborne if conditions changed. How could we take advantage if the sun suddenly popped out? I called for a production meeting that night in Leon's room. We were bursting at the seams as our Guangzhou lighting crew had just arrived. We discussed contingencies for the weather, what we'd do should the river rise or not, how our plans would change if we could get into the caves earlier, and what we'd do if the helicopter never arrived. Afterwards, I called Greg back in Beijing and told him he wasn't missing anything.

The next day we were out of luck at our boat site because of the continuing bad weather. My alternative location was to drive down to Yangshuo to try for the opening shot of the film, the one in which I'd envisioned fantastic Chinese landscape paintings turning into real mountains. Thankfully, the hilltop I'd found on the survey wasn't reliant on anyone else's cooperation, just some decent weather. We set up quickly as squalls blew through and left us with overcast skies. It took time to line up this shot because each of the nine cameras had to be aimed at a mountain or mountainside that would lend itself to being turned into a painting. After a fair amount of compromise, panning a few degrees right or left to adjust nine compositions at the same time, we shot off a few takes that I thought were pretty good for a safety. I made sure everyone knew this was an important scene, so they knew we'd come back to this very spot and do it again if we got a real break in the clouds. While in Yangshuo, we took the time to check out the new helicopter landing site. I wasn't crazy about the locale and spotted a number of much more suitable sites while on the road back to Guilin.

We used the afternoon to load into Reed Flute Cave after they closed their doors to the public. In the film business we often plan what we call interior "cover sets," for scenes we can shoot during inclement weather. Both the pinnacles above ground and the caverns below were karst formations. The area around Guilin is full of caves, many of which were used by the populace to shelter from local bandits. Some were even strongholds of resistance during the war. What they didn't resist was water.

I hadn't expected the caves to leak like a sieve. Limestone is highly porous and, while it wasn't exactly raining, the cave was constantly dripping so we had to take care to keep cables and lights dry. While the Arriflex could be set up on a tripod very quickly, our team from Guangzhou needed hours to lay heavy cable from the generator that remained outside at the entrance. The team was efficient, but the cave was narrow and very uneven in places so getting around and communicating was difficult. It wasn't a matter of simply saying "More green light over there in that corner, please." Because of the late start and dodging the puddles, we were only able to get three complete takes. I'd need a minimum of eight separate images to be combined with our shot of Li Po on the stage with his lantern. We finally broke at 8:30 p.m. and would have to come back to shoot more underground formations another day. The cave managers allowed us to keep our cables in place as long as the lines wouldn't interfere with the walkways and ramps used by tourists.

My day didn't end any better. I ate some canned beef stew heated up on a Coleman stove in Leon's room, then went to the lobby to make an international call home. In those days long before cell phones, the call had to be scheduled and arranged by the hotel operator while you waited. Then it was put through, sometimes to a special phone booth. Connections were always hit or miss, even in Beijing, which is why most of my communication with the studio was by telex. At the hotel in Guilin there'd be no privacy because they had to put the call through on their lobby phone. I had called the U.S. before and knew the difficulties of getting through, but I had one of the worst connections at the worst possible time.

Kathy answered, already crying because she'd just been in a bad car accident. At least that's what it sounded like through intermittent static and dropout. The line then went dead. I begged the hotel staff to call back immediately. It took them another half-hour and what I got was an even worse connection.

After a few seconds, it went dead again. I was so upset I couldn't comfort my wife when she needed me most that I ripped the damned phone off the desk and threw the offending instrument across the lobby. As I stormed off to my room, I caught a glimpse of the horrified faces of a couple of young clerks behind the desk. I was furious that I felt so helpless and, at the same time, I was upset with myself for losing my temper. After an hour I'd calmed down enough to try again – from a phone in a different building. Kathy was also calmer and informed me her car was totaled, but she was physically okay. We both were distraught by the fact that I couldn't be there.

I thought I might use the physical comfort of a relaxing bath but discovered there was no hot water in my room. In other words, a perfect ending to the day.

Karma then swung its pendulum in the other direction. Morning clouds opened up somewhat, so the crew jumped into our two minibuses and we quickly motored south to our boat launch facility. Our cruiser was a double-decker, about 90 feet long, with a low railing on the top deck and bench seats below in the cabin. Some river cruisers were even bigger, like triple-deckers, for large Japanese tour groups. We'd asked for a wooden support to be built on the roof of the upper deck. Guy had calculated very specific dimensions for it so the Circle-Vision cameras would not see the cruiser at all, and we'd be able to sail "invisibly" down the Li River. It was a pleasant surprise to find the local boat crew had done the work precisely as we'd asked. On the one hand, that felt refreshing. On the other, it reminded us how infrequently it happened. The platform, made of crude timbers, was quite serviceable. By the time we'd mounted up the cameras and were ready to shoot, the light was still good. The river remained smooth and we were underway.

We avoided the tourist cruisers and made plans to shoot among the more natural Li River traffic. Some fishermen had bamboo rafts 30 feet long that were only two poles wide, seeming like an invitation to fall in the water. Other low rafts were three or four feet wide, some with canvas sails jury-rigged on the front. Some rafts had cramped living quarters covered over with woven mats with small cook fires tended right on the deck. We passed clusters of rafts tied together along the shoreline. These were no doubt family-based groupings which gave us the impression of a kind of trailer park.

We cranked off a number of pretty good takes of the traveling river scenery and then had to change magazines. The boat dropped anchor for the better part of an hour. By the time Joe had us reloaded and ready to cast off again, the skies were darkening. We got one more shot before we had to call it a day. I wasn't sure if we'd need to get more cruise shots later or if we'd be able to make up for it with our aerial photography.

When we'd regrouped back at the hotel, we found out our helicopter pilot still hadn't left Wuhan, 800 kilometers away. Our Russian-trained pilot informed Lao Tan by phone that the weather in Wuhan was "unpleasant." By this time, Bao and Ding had been unduly influenced in their choice of English phrases by Joe and Guy. Their comment on the helicopter pilot: "He's just being chickenshit."

I called Greg to keep him up to date using a newly installed phone in the lobby. No surprise, the connection was excellent this time. I saw the clerks huddled in the opposite side of the lobby, so I smiled and apologized again in Chinese for my rude behavior. Greg informed us he was having night sweats and was waiting on the results of a test for hepatitis. Leon thought that sounded serious and wanted to send him back to the States as a precaution. That night my bathwater had made it up to lukewarm, which was an improvement, but I could feel the karmic pendulum once more changing direction.

A huge rain system moved in the next morning and seemed planted right over Guilin. Leon tried calling Disney Studios to get an accurate report for this part of China. These were the days long before satellite weather imagery could be called up on a personal phone. We found the worst of it was stationary right over Wuhan where our pilot was hanging out, of course.

We couldn't get back into the cave until late afternoon and I needed us to keep shooting while we were waiting on the helicopter. I decided we'd do a contingency shot I'd been holding in reserve. Ever since I'd assembled my photo albums of potential locales, I'd wanted to get one of those classic shots of terraced rice fields from the south of China. Sadly, these are mostly located in hard-to-reach areas. My back-up was a beautiful field of water chestnuts growing among the same limestone formations that made Guilin famous. The surprising part of this locale, one that still shocks me all these years later, was that it was right in the middle of a People's Liberation Army base.

The PLA helps unload

Farmer extras with water buffaloes

Filming on an Army base

Gathering crowds

"Helicopter Town"

Parked on the landing tables

Preparing for an aerial survey

Images from the film

Mayor of Helicopter Town

Leon had been right all along.

I had also come to believe Lao Tan was a kind of government minder for our crew, assigned to report our movements and operations. Still, I always showed him respect even though he hadn't displayed much savvy as a production manager, foisting the real work onto Shen and later John. But over time we'd been slowly earning some personal points with our Chinese crew and even wearing down Lao Tan's autocratic demeanor. Maybe all those fish heads I'd presented him paid off. I believe he was the one who'd put in a good word for us with the PLA and that's how we got into an otherwise-inaccessible military base.

Our little company was given permission to travel onto the location, which had the same karst formations as the rest of the Guilin area. The night before, when I'd heard we were given access, I'd requested a couple of water buffaloes to be used as beasts of burden by our peasant farmer extras working in the fields. How the crew acquired them in time for our filming I do not know. We set up our China dolly on a narrow strip of land bordering wet fields of water chestnuts. The plants looked a lot like rice and have naturally been misidentified as such by most viewers of the film.

The set-up went without problems, other than the crew having to drive a very long way to get our equipment truck – and themselves – out of the shot. On these occasions we relied on walkie-talkies so that I could inform Leon when it's safe to return for wrap. On this day they were beyond our radios so

Joe and I, with Guy pushing the dolly, were on our own. I had given the extras their start and end marks and told them what they needed to do. By now I could do most of this in my crude Chinese, including the famous "Everybody back to one" for the next take. Pantomime filled in the gaps. But we were stalled for the longest time because a low layer of broken clouds was alternately throwing us into and out of shade so quickly that we couldn't get a shot. If it was all sun or all overcast, we'd just set the appropriate f/stop and get underway, but the contrasting light levels as the clouds roared overhead was like watching a time-lapse movie. We rehearsed the shot anyway, over and over, so the action was smooth and natural. The extras instinctively knew to go back to their first positions, and everyone had their jobs down. We finally spotted a patch of sunlight headed our way that looked like it might be long enough for a take. I had Joe roll cameras at the instant the cloud was starting to open up. We got a perfect shot, the one that made it into the final film, and I cut just as the clouds were closing up again. There never was a take two.

We drove back to Reed Flute Cave to find our Guangzhou crew was moving much more efficiently than the day before. Perhaps they'd worn down the cave supervisors to allow an earlier start to the work. We accomplished seven more single-camera set-ups in the cave and wrapped by 9 p.m. I had a late dinner at Chez Leon on his Coleman stove again. He'd called Beijing to discover there was a problem with Greg's liver. That was it. Greg and Barbara were headed back to the U.S. on the next available flight.

Rain poured down the next day and we made a command decision to change hotels. We moved the company down to the Yangshuo area so that we could respond quickly if we got any good weather. I went out in the rain to check possible locations for our fisherman shot but none of them seemed suitable. In the midst of what seemed like a complete washout, we learned that our helicopter had arrived in Guilin. I would never have guessed our pilots would brave this dreadful weather to fly that distance. Despite this good news (the bad news of this day was the shocking assassination of Anwar Sadat), Leon was in a foul mood at dinner in the new hotel. While Joe was upstairs logging camera shots and eating his soy-tuna-rice, Guy and I were interested in the food which kept coming out of the kitchen in waves. Leon could normally eat whatever the Chinese threw at him, but tonight he just wanted the food to stop. It was too much, so he stormed off, but then what did he do? He had Dinty Moore beef stew on his little stove. Sometimes I just couldn't figure him out, but I knew the long survey followed by a long shoot was fraying everyone's nerves.

The next day, despite the rain, Ernie Gustavson was able to test the helicopter mount with a vibration test. If the blades aren't balanced, the vibration travels down through the rigid mount and shakes the far end of the chain: the cameras. But his test was all the flying we were able to manage. Local weather reports were not encouraging. Out of total frustration I created a new card game called "Guilin Solitaire."

When we awoke on October 9, we found sunlight streaming in. Unfortunately, the CAAC ground crew wasn't ready with our landing tables. We'd shipped these very heavy platforms airfreight from the U.S. and they had to be carted around by truck wherever we wanted to film Circle-Vision helicopter shots. The CAAC crew started bolting them together in an area of rice fields. The two tables stood five feet high, 12 feet long, but each of them was only two feet wide, not a lot of room on which to land a helicopter. Before they'd finished, we'd started to draw in the locals. Among the rural crowd were old barefoot women and peasant farmers, many of whom wore pants with several patches. Within a short time, we needed uniformed police to hold back hordes of school-aged kids who had nothing better to do than wait around to watch the spectacle of a helicopter taking off and landing, a most unusual occurrence in these parts. We'd even attracted several enterprising types who wandered the crowds selling candy and cigarettes from trays. I joked to Leon that he had a good chance to be elected mayor of Helicopter Town.

We probably missed a good hour of flying time because our cameras couldn't be assembled until the helicopter had been moved up on top of the tables. By the time the rig was mounted and Han was airborne, it was about noon. That's the least interesting overhead light but I'd take it. When they came back after the first flight, we found the video recorder was dead. But this turned out to be good news in a way.

The Chinese continued to have an unwillingness to allow me in the helicopter to film. I understood that initially they might be fearful of the Circle-Vision cameras but were they really worried I'd go rogue and shoot unauthorized footage with their own military pilots doing the flying? In any case, we now had a situation that I saw as an opportunity. Without a video record to know what was being photographed, I suggested that they let me go up on a survey flight with the two pilots – no cameras attached. Bao would come along to translate. I wanted a chance to "walk them" through the shots so they'd know what I wanted. I had maps of the area and could draw out diagrams while we were in the air. I thought for sure the obstinate chief pilot might object (perhaps because this isn't the way they did things in Russia) but he agreed.

As expected, this was Bao's first helicopter flight. He was nervous but he felt better once he could focus on translating my words to the pilots. I was able to line up a half-dozen shots very quickly as the region is absolutely ripe for aerial photography. With so many options, the question was always about making the right selections for the 360 process. I had Bao make note of sun angle, altitudes, and flight direction as I instructed the pilots to fly the routes I thought best, including suggestions for shots with sweeping turns. I was also able to call out precisely where I wanted cameras to roll or to cut. We numbered the shots like menu items so Han and I would have a common reference for later. Once I felt certain the pilots understood, I signaled that we should head back for the tricky landing on the platforms. I thought Bao was going to faint from anxiety. The pilot requires remarkable skill to set the helicopter down on such small areas. His crew had stretched out a white string as a ground marker for his approach. Missing the line-up by even a few degrees of angle could put the helicopter in a precarious position where it might tip over if the aircraft suddenly lost lift. Typically, the pilot would set it down within a couple of inches and then members of the ground crew would grab the skids and help physically maneuver it to the very center of each platform. They were subject to shocks when they first touched the skids as the blades generated a lot of static electricity.

By the time Han came back from his first flying trip using my maps and notes, we thought we had a good chance of success. The issue that faced us was one that has long-plagued Circle-Vision filming: bugs. Flying insects splatter on the front surface mirrors and make an out-of-focus blob that ruins a shot. These subtropical agricultural fields were full of bugs and the helicopter stirred them up on both landing and takeoff. But it makes a huge difference *when* they splattered. Joe would scrupulously clean the mirrors, so we knew they were spotless at the moment of lift-off. The helicopter always came back with bugs. Without fail. But were those splatters picked up right after takeoff, meaning the entire roll of film was ruined? Or did they get picked up much later as the helicopter was coming in for a landing, meaning all the earlier footage was clean? There was no way for us to know while we were in China. That meant our only option was to keep cleaning, keep shooting, and keep hoping *somewhere* in the footage was a section that wasn't damaged by dead insects.

After a very late lunch from our hotel that was served picnic-style on the ground by girls with waist-length pigtails, I kept an eye on the movement of the sun. The old adage about only shooting between 10 and 2 had come about because direct sunlight striking one of the mirrors causes it to flare to such an extent that it ruins the shot. Yet afternoon is the time when the light becomes more interesting, the shadows longer, the contours of the land more pronounced. The key is to wait until the sun is blocked behind some object or is diffused by a layer of clouds. I saw that we were going to have a little of both so I asked Han to go up once more for some late in the day shots, reminding him of the angles that would work best.

The helicopter team took off and I watched them through binoculars, monitoring the flight angles and speed, fingers crossed. "Ah, good, they're lined up to do shot number five…" When he landed, Han said he thought the footage should be good. But there were dead insects all over the front mirrors, of course. We would just have to keep shooting for safety.

As it turned out, a shot grabbed at sunset was great and that scene has survived two versions of the film at EPCOT. The sharp-edged mountains were rimmed by the last light of day and were characterized by Li Po's poetic narration as "…scattered dragon's teeth. Whoever looks on this, loses himself in eternity."

Morning brought total overcast so I decided to take a trip down to Xingping to see yet another proposed location for a ground shot of fishermen. The area looked ideal – for about six of the nine cameras. The back panels weren't bad, no powerplants or garbage dumps, simply naked without much of interest. Because we'd be shooting at sunset when those areas were dark, it would actually help keep the audience's attention on the fishermen. The view looking forward was terrific with a natural place to launch the rafts, so I marked this location as approved.

The ride down to Xingping and back took a couple of hours. What a trip, first a flat tire which our driver seemed ill-equipped to repair, then our vehicle struck a small dog in a village. There was, as we used to say in West Africa, quite a palaver over responsibility. Luckily there were no lawyers lurking about with an inkling of Disney's deep pockets.

When we finally returned in the afternoon, the weather had improved enough to send Han and the pilots back up again in the helicopter. The clouds opened a little and we got a total of four afternoon shots on one load of film. As usual, there were bugs on the mirrors, so we could only hope…

By late afternoon, we'd downloaded the cameras from the helicopter and set off for Xingping. This turned out to be a relatively easy set-up as there was no dolly move. The five fishermen we'd hired took direction well because I only wanted them to do what I'd seen them do in their daily routines. It's always surprising how people asked to just "be themselves" on film can suddenly choke. I was trying to fill out the front cameras which meant timing the placement of these moving pieces, sending them off in certain directions so that at the key moment they'd be at the right spot in the composition. My only concern was exposure. We were filming after the sun had dropped behind the ragged mountains and I was hoping the kerosene lanterns hanging off the bamboo rafts would read properly, but they weren't very bright. Under normal circumstances, we would have replaced them with more powerful battery-operated lights. Tonight, we had to make do with what we had.

These fishermen were famous for using cormorants to do their fishing for them. Birds wearing a leash would dive into the water to catch a fish. Metal rings around the cormorants' necks prevented them from swallowing. The fishermen would then make them cough up the whole fish and would occasionally share their catch with the birds as reward. No surprise, Guy thought the whole process off-putting. That night at dinner we were served a whole fish with the head still on it and he bolted right out of the dining room. Joe, an avid fisherman, just laughed at Guy's squeamishness, then retreated to his room with a bowl of rice.

Huangshan (Yellow Mountain)

Exposed peaks

Guest Greeting Tree

Fall colors on Huangshan

Fang, Ding, Tan, and Mu

The hotel annex

The hotel at the summit

Annex hotel room

Our equipment heading up the mountain

Thick fog at the summit

CHAPTER 16

Above the Clouds and Off a Cliff

It took a whole day of travel to get from the Guilin area to Hangzhou, a city and region that I'd always found to be rather more civilized than other parts of China. At least we could order food off a hotel menu again, a real luxury. The next day was another Zero Dark Hundred call time. Ding and I were driven by car for six hours to the spa town at the foot of Huangshan. I was still impressed by the gorgeous scenery of Anhui Province, only now it had an overlay of spectacular fall colors. We enjoyed a box breakfast from our hotel along the way which even included a small piece of cheese, a rarity. At this time the Chinese had a real aversion to any dairy and used to say Westerners always smelled to them of milk products, and not in any admirable way. Today they love pizza, so go figure.

At the base of the mountain Ding and I were met by John, our assistant location manager. He'd brought along our original guide, Fang, the man who'd accompanied me up Huangshan on the survey trip. The four of us started for the summit and this time we were going to get there a lot faster. I didn't have to stop every hundred yards or so to take photographs of the beautiful vistas or look for camera locations. After a couple of hours of ascent, we passed through the sea of clouds and then broke out into sunlight. One of the great sights I remembered from the survey was called Guest Greeting Tree. This marvelously gnarled pine, bent by constant winds, is estimated to be over 800 years old. It grows from a crack in the granite and branches seem to reach out in welcome. Painted reproductions of that tree are found near the entrance of many traditional Chinese restaurants. After this spirited climb, experience told me that for the next few days my calf muscles were going to feel like the gnarled wood of Guest in Agony Tree.

At the top, I was greeted by someone I didn't want to see again – Mister Gee, the still photographer who'd wasted so much of our time during the survey. I was beginning to comprehend how hard it is to actually fire someone in China or at least relieve them of their duties. I wasn't in a mood to argue. As long as he didn't interfere in our plans, Mister Gee's inappropriate suggestions could be ignored.

The management of the Beihai Hotel (which translated as the "North Sea" Hotel for the nearby sea of clouds) treated me a little better this trip by assigning me to what they called the annex, separate quarters from the starkly austere main building. My rooms were on the second floor of a building made of stone with a Chinese pagoda roof. The views, in those brief moments when the clouds cleared, were amazing. I just wish there'd been glass in all the windows. One was broken and the wind whistled through a fist-sized hole keeping the temperature of my room in the forties. The twin beds were so short my feet hung over the end. Between the beds lay a large writing desk where I could spread out my papers and notes. I ate a mediocre dinner next door at the hotel, then tried stuffing a blanket into the broken glass, but it didn't warm my room. There seemed to be no heat in the stone structure and the windows were all single pane, but at least the hotel provided plenty of hot water. I took a long soaking bath to relieve the deep aches in my legs. As the mist swirled, I got the idea to fill the tub again to the brim, let the bathroom steam up, then open the door to circulate warm air into the bedroom. The sheets remained like ice so, before climbing into bed, I lay on top for a while to transfer some body heat. During the night I climbed out of bed to fill and refill that tub three more times. I might as well have just pulled the covers off and slept in the bathroom. To top off a miserable night, I could hear something scratching around in the darkness, then the patter of little feet on the desk not far from my head.

The morning brought thick flog with visibility less than 50 feet. Leon was down at the base organizing the flow of equipment and crew coming up. I worried how Shih Kuan was going to make it since he didn't appear to be in great shape for his age. Leon and I had briefly considered a sedan chair with four bearers for him, but the steepness of the steps would have made for a horribly bouncy ride. I gave Shih Kuan credit for wanting to attempt the climb. Perhaps he was inspired by seeing Chinese tourists even older than himself who'd made the pilgrimage to this special mountain.

Individual boxes of cameras and film were not a problem for our hired laborers, as long as they could sling two equal loads across their shoulders with a split bamboo pole. The camera pedestal that I'd been so worried about wasn't really an issue. My plan had been to have four carriers bring up the heavy and awkward contraption with four more laborers as "spares" to relieve them along the way. But that morning the head carrier, a little wiry fellow who smoked cigarettes like a Mongolian horseman, walked around the pedestal and eyed it carefully. He roped one thick bamboo rod across the top and two guys just hoisted it on their shoulders and headed up. The two of them left at 10 a.m. and made it to the summit by 2:30 in the afternoon without additional help. I guess if these men were capable of carrying an entire hotel to the top, our camera rig wasn't nearly the problem for them I'd feared. Shih Kuan arrived, huffing and puffing, a half-hour after the last of the equipment.

Meanwhile I re-scouted our mountaintop locations with Fang, Ding, and Guy Jones. The locales were fairly close to our hotel so I figured all we'd need would be some decent light and visibility to get our shots. That night Guy and Joe didn't join me in the hotel dining room. I ate alone at my table which, awkwardly enough, was right next to the table with my growing Chinese crew. We'd added Mu, a make-up and wardrobe artist from Beijing. This had to be quite an adventure for many of them so far from the studio. Plus, we were out of town, so they got an extra $1 a day – woo-hoo.

In the early 1980s, there wasn't really much personal travel in China. One went to another city strictly on government business. This policy was reinforced by a two-tiered system of money. There was *renminbi* (literally "The People's Money"), and Foreign Exchange Certificates which was a different form of paper currency used exclusively by Westerners. Trains, planes, and hotels rooms all had to be paid for in Foreign Exchange Certificates, effectively limiting and keeping local Chinese in their place. The kind of travel we were exposing our crew to was a unique opportunity to see their own country in ways that wouldn't happen for other Chinese citizens until years later.

The next morning was the strangest and most unexpected weather I'd seen on Huangshan: absolutely clear skies and naked mountains. Not even a wisp of cloud. We mounted our cameras with the China dolly on a stone lookout, the equivalent of a Kodak viewpoint. We could finally see the entire pattern of jagged peaks that make up the summit of Huangshan laid out before us. Shih Kuan was fitted by the wardrobe man into a special costume for Li Po, a yellow tunic with a green sash and flowing burgundy pants. Mu had added a lovely red tassel onto a ceremonial sword. This time Li Po did not wear a traditional headpiece, just the usual wig and long beard. I got a couple of good takes of him practicing his sword routine, then turning to admire the mountains and valley below. We waited awhile to see if some of the characteristic clouds that define this region might roll back in. When it was obvious we weren't getting a version of the shot with clouds, I called for a move to a second location.

We scrambled to set up on the stone steps, a short distance down the backside of the mountain. I had arranged for a few painters and artists to be extras because they were a common sight at the summit. You couldn't go very far before running into someone in the woods with an easel trying to render the fleeting atmosphere of Huangshan in paint, ink, or charcoal. The set-up was going smoothly until either Joe or Guy (this argument was never settled) dropped one of the polarizing filters and it broke on the stone steps. We had to borrow the one from Guy's still camera to fill in. I asked Joe to use this on a back screen, just in case there was a little mismatch in coloration. Despite the altitude and after a fairly grueling climb, getting two Circle-Vision set-ups in one day had to be considered a success. A new record for me.

After work, Joe and Guy crashed and burned very early, heading to their rooms after first sharing canned beef stew on Leon's Coleman stove. My side of the hotel property, the annex, had a blackout that night and no one could find the fuse box. I played cards with my Chinese crew in the main hotel just to put off going back to my dark freezing room until I had to.

The weather socked in again the next morning with solid fog and visibility of less than 20 feet. We never managed to get a shot. We had a new member of the Chinese crew come up that day, another young man named Zhou, a tall good-looking kid who was basically the office go-fer at China Co-Film. This was his big trip out of Beijing and he came up the mountain bringing us more canned food. Guy dubbed him "Little Joe" to distinguish him from all our other "Joes."

The next day we still couldn't see more than a few feet, but I had Guy and Joe set up the cameras on the edge of a cliff. I had to assure them there really was a spectacular view out there. The cameras were tilted down about 30 degrees towards the drop-off so Guy cabled the rig to a tree in back for safety. We waited for hours looking into a white void, sometimes tantalized by churning mists that looked like they were going to lift. We'd get faint hints of how great the shot would be, but had to wrap late in the day, still in fog, never running the cameras. I was determined we were not leaving the mountain until we accomplished this shot which had the potential to be really wonderful.

That evening another blackout made the situation in my room more interesting. In the middle of the night I thought I heard the familiar sounds of scratching nearby. Were they eating my papers? As I was lying there shivering, unable to see, I heard little feet starting to scramble. They're getting louder, faster – as if coming right for me. I swear they ran right up to the edge of the desk just above my face! I leapt out of bed, swinging my arms to avoid the certain leaping attack. I slept bundled up on the bathroom floor that night.

Joe and I spent the entire next day sitting with our feet hanging over the cliff, eating peanuts from a big bag, watching empty shells drift down and disappear into the foggy abyss. The swirling clouds opened up at one point for a few brief seconds and we found ourselves staring across at shrouded peaks and windblown trees. It took our breath away, as spectacular as I'd dreamed. But by the time we could reach the control box, the view filled in and was gone. After that Joe and I agreed that one of us would always keep a hand on the switch. If we even *thought* a break in the clouds might come, we had permission to roll.

That afternoon, we were able to grab a few really wonderful takes that had a ghostly, almost painterly, quality. What we'd shot was good, but I wanted better. By 4 p.m., I'd called a wrap due to darkness. We left the pedestal, minus cameras, in place for the next day.

We were greeted by solid rain all morning, just cold and miserable, and no one wanted to move. I insisted that rain like this might break up the system of clouds that surrounded us, but I sensed the crew were dragging their feet as we returned the camera boxes to the cliff. Leo and China Joe seemed more interested in snapping photos for themselves than in getting the rig assembled. Joe and I were back and ready to shoot, feet dangling over the edge, hand on switch by 1 p.m. The two of us skipped lunch in favor of more peanuts. Our efforts paid off as we were able to film another couple of really solid takes when the clouds lifted for a few glorious moments.

I changed my room in the annex, but it was just as cold as the one with the broken window. I was hoping for fewer rats or mice, or whatever. The nightly blackout came almost on schedule, and I was filling the tub with the usual scalding water by 9 p.m.

Leon expected us to come down the mountain the next day, but the mercurial weather turned out to be really great. I had everyone rush to set up the cameras again on the stone steps and we reshot the scene with the artists. This time I pressed Little Joe into service in the back panels and he really threw himself into the part. He had me convinced he was actually making charcoal sketches on a pad, but he was just faking it.

That evening I came across a soccer match on the hotel TV. I sat around with my Chinese crew as they yelled and screamed for their national team. China was up 2-0 over Kuwait. As my crew went crazy, I teased them.

"Wasn't it Mao who said the spirit of competition between nations should 'inspire the collective work spirit necessary for the national unity?'"

Bao glared at me, then responded with a dismissive, "Yeah, right!"

They yelled again as China won 3-0 and I'll admit I was just as excited.

By early the next morning, the laborers began to take our equipment down the mountain using the back route. I preferred to descend via the front which is four times longer but much more scenic. I could take my time to enjoy the views without the pressure of finding or making new shots. Joe and Guy took the more straightforward route down the back and finished the 4,750 steps in one hour (this time I'd asked Guy to count every one of them). At the bottom, I handed out gifts to the crew which I'd had made in California, T-shirts that read: "I climbed Huangshan!"

CHAPTER 17

Ernie Haller's Hat

Leon, Bao, and I crowded into a government car with a chauffeur who drove us from the town of Huangshan towards Hangzhou, about six hours away. We had a planned stop about halfway along the route. On the survey I'd spotted a classic and unspoiled little roadside village named Chah Sheh. The place didn't even show on most maps. Lao Tan and Shen had arranged for us to be met on the road there by a Beijing Jeep-o for a driving shot past this picturesque town. I was adamant about using this shot in the film, but Leon had always been skeptical because we'd be working without a net. There was little around for miles, no resources or facilities to call upon if any kind of emergency came up. The only reason he'd agreed to let me attempt the shot was because I promised it wouldn't take long. We wouldn't be dealing with actors or extras, so we could just load up the Circle-Vision rig on the vehicle and do a drive-by. Done. We were expected in Hangzhou that night, so I promised Leon we'd leave the locale no later than noon, even if I didn't have the shot. For some reason, that promise made Leon more skeptical, not less.

The weather had improved somewhat by the time we arrived at the locale. The little town would have been easy to miss but during the survey I'd insisted we take a good odometer reading so we could find it again. I was very pleased to see the Jeep-o parked alongside the road as advertised. Guy knew what to expect for this kind of rigging, so he and Joe had the cameras up and ready in short order. The crew and their vehicles were driven back down the highway and around a little bend in order to be out of sight during the shot. Local authorities provided traffic control but there was hardly anyone on this remote road.

I grabbed one quick take in hazy overcast as my insurance policy, then planned to wait for an improvement in the sky and better lighting on the village. Leon and I kept in touch by walkie-talkie. While we'd been gathering our forces, the weather had changed rapidly. Three distinct layers of clouds had rolled in, driven by unusual winds aloft. We could see the middle layer of cumulus blowing in one direction, the upper stratus moving in the opposite, and the lowest layer of patchy clouds rocketing along in still another. Leon had been keeping an eye on these patterns for nearly a half-hour and kept calling, wanting me to move on. I believed the clouds would part long enough for a really good shot and he insisted I didn't know what I was talking about. I walked down the highway to the bend in the road to talk with him directly, instead of airing our differences over the radio.

I assured him I'd stick to my promise, we'd finish our shot by noon. I'm not sure what was really bothering him, but I could see he was growing angry. Leon stood in the middle of the dirt highway and pointed at the sky. "It's not going to happen, you have to believe me." Leon was absolutely certain from his lengthy experience that he could tell the clouds racing overhead were never going to open up in time. Leon claimed he'd been taught to "read the clouds" by Ernie Haller. I was amused that Leon had called in such a big gun to make his argument. Cinematographer Ernest Haller only had seven Oscar nominations including one win for a little picture called "Gone with the Wind." I remained confident in my own assessment, which only provoked Leon more. Finally, in frustration, Leon said he'd eat his hat if I managed to get another shot before noon.

Glancing at his dark brown fedora, I said, "If you need soy sauce with that, check with Joe."

I walked back up the highway and climbed into my position in the Jeep-o with Joe and Guy. Leon announced over the radio that he'd had it and was leaving for Hangzhou. A moment later, as scudding clouds continued to darken the landscape, Leon's car and driver motored around the corner and drove right past us, heading down the highway. I noticed he'd taken Bao with him as the vehicle disappeared in the opposite direction. I kept my eyes on the skies as I said to Joe and Guy, "Leon's finally gone round the bend."

We waited for several minutes and then, like magic, the three layers of clouds synchronized their movements just long enough to allow sunlight to stream down onto the little village. We were ready and filmed a really smooth take in beautiful light. I announced over the radios to the rest of the waiting crew that we had the shot. We drove the Jeep-o a little farther to the bend at the other end of the road. Standing there was Leon, head hung in shame, his fedora clutched in his teeth. As we pulled up beside him, I looked at my watch. It was three minutes to noon. He gave me a big smile.

I said, "You know, Ernie Haller would be in Hangzhou already."

When we returned to Beijing, we finally had a video playback machine. We had mounted a small video camera on the rig to give us a recorded view similar to what camera number one was seeing. It wasn't very accurate, not like through the lens monitoring, but it was good enough to check the action of some of our dailies, if only for one screen. Reviewing the record, I grew quite enthusiastic about what we'd accomplished – with the exception of helicopter footage, but that was no surprise. I was getting infrequent reports from the studio where they were looking at my developed footage by projecting five screens at a time. Everyone said they loved the material, other than Bob, who'd complained about shooting too many identical takes at the Roof of the World in Tibet. I could live with that.

The next day was very cold but very clear in Beijing. Typical mid-October weather. A recent dust storm that had been blowing in grit and sand from the Gobi had settled down. I decided we'd go back up to Coal Hill and get an even better view of the city, Forbidden and otherwise. The seasons had changed since we'd shot there the first time, so it was freezing cold at the top. Joe was in a lousy mood all morning, perhaps because he felt we'd already finished this shot, but it spilled over and put Guy in a funk, too.

By the time we moved on to Qianhai Lake in Beihai Park, Guy had mellowed. I wanted to familiarize him with the location. He would have to lash together two of the rental rowboats, then build a level platform on top strong enough to support the Circle-Vision cameras. When we got to the park, the man who ran the rental facility acted like a real jerk and wouldn't let us in just to have a look at his boats. It was frustrating and I wondered for a moment if he was the helicopter pilot's brother. I walked away without too much concern because I had a lot of confidence Guy could find a way to get the job done. I didn't know then how this one shot would affect Guy for some time to come.

The next day we went to the offices of China Co-Film to use their facilities while setting up the camera car. In a nearby alleyway, I then grouped our bicyclist extras, giving them assigned positions where they'd be most effective across the nine screens. The idea of the shot was to have these bikers act like a barrier around the camera car as we negotiated the traffic on Beijing streets. I wanted the riders to stick with our car in a kind of formation while at the same time "ignoring" us. I hoped their blasé behavior might prove infectious enough so civilian bikers wouldn't look because staring crowds were a constant issue wherever we went.

As if to prove this point, we drove out onto a street and then pulled over to a curb to get a light meter reading and make final adjustments to the lenses. Within seconds, we'd started to draw a crowd of the curious, the bored, the indifferent. After a minute, it was ten people deep and we'd become a traffic hazard. I always thought this phenomenon was because Chinese working people had such regimented and structured lives that witnessing events beyond the ordinary, especially where "foreign devils" were concerned, sent them home to report to their families: "You're not gonna believe what I saw today!"

We got our formation together and set off, filming some takes on shaded side streets and getting a few good ones without too many gawkers. I asked Leo and China Joe to shoot behind the scenes with the Arriflex, as our camera car and bikers passed by. When I saw their footage of Joe, Guy, and me in the black limo convertible driving slowly along the avenue, it was unfortunately reminiscent of the Zapruder film. With growing confidence that our plan was working, we drove our little caravan over to Tiananmen Square where the citizenry was more rowdy. Someone on the street yelled at us, accusing us of being spies, but we were never threatened.

When we learned the Gate of Heavenly Peace had been freed from its renovation bamboo, we arranged to try our shot entering the Forbidden City. We had at our disposal 14 undercover police officers who would help clear the path. Our limo negotiated Chang'an and turned right, went up the curved marble bridge over the moat, then slid under Mao's portrait and through the main gate. The center archway was just big enough for our wide vehicle, but the driver laid on the horn anyway to make sure no spectators were caught in a tight squeeze. We turned around and tried the same shot a few more times at different speeds, not knowing which would look the smoothest. My only concern was that the police seemed to be quite visible in their efforts to hold back the curious, especially in the side screens as we passed. Hopefully the film's viewers would be more interested in *where* we were going than *how* we got there.

Later I showed our video dailies to the Chinese crew which they found encouraging, but even Shih Kuan admitted the helicopter footage wasn't that great. He promised they'd do better when we tried again in the spring. For now, our focus was on packing up for the far western province of Xinjiang.

Xinjiang Province

A street in Ürümqi

Uyghur National Minorities

One of Ürümqi's many markets

Winning a bet

Guy Jones samples *shashlik*

Street vendors

Meat sellers in the snow

A mobile butcher shop

The delivery of our Beijing Jeep-o

CHAPTER 18

DISTANT LANDS

We left Beijing at 9:30 a.m. *local time.* That's kind of a misnomer since the government of China insists there is only one time zone in the whole country. It's all local, officially if not practically. The CCP wants all regional governments to be responsive to Beijing and be available to them on the same schedule. But China is so enormous geographically, it actually covers five zones (Zhongyuan, Longshu, Tibet, Kunlun, and Changbai). When it's high noon in the capital, way out west in Ürümqi it's still dark. Regional governments accede to the central dictate of one official time nationally, while still honoring local traditions and practices. For the sake of clarity and uniformity in setting our production's call times, I asked that we always use Beijing time, even if it wasn't the most logical. That directive didn't eliminate confusion, however.

The flight to Ürümqi was quite comfortable since China Co-Film arranged for us to fly First Class. What had happened to Communist doctrine about class struggle and the bourgeoisie? We didn't care. Joining us on the trip was our expatriate friend, Ellen Irish, who probably thought we traveled like this all the time. For some reason, there was a large Chinese military delegation on our flight and, in retrospect, their presence had ominous implications for the current state of affairs in Xinjiang.

We were met at the airport by Han Chinese government officials as well as representatives from the Uyghur National Minority. Our contacts provided us with thick green Chinese Army greatcoats for the crew, double-breasted with brown fur collars, long enough to reach mid-calf. They also handed out hats, the sort that have fur-lined earflaps. I slipped mine over my Dodgers baseball cap, so I also had a brim to keep falling snow out of my eyes.

During our earlier survey, Leon and I had grown fond of the ethnic culture, cuisine, and music of Xinjiang. I'd even purchased an authentic long-necked *tambur* after attending a wonderfully spirited performance one night. I'd been promising Guy that he'd find the food more to his liking, especially traditional *shashlik*, which is barbequed cubes of meat on skewers served with fresh pita bread. We'd even made a friendly bet, with me insisting he'd love lamb *shashlik*. I saw his growing doubts as we were driven into town past mosques, minarets, and horse-drawn carts. I pointed out several Muslim vendors with their metal troughs and smoky charcoal burners on the dusty street corners. The idea they were handling raw meat made Guy a little queasy. We had a production meeting at which the head of the Cultural Bureau served delicious *Hami* melons, but Guy was turned off because he'd seen the same fruit piled up for sale on the streets.

The scents and sights of this exotic capital, the furthest from any ocean, was a wonder to Ellen. She was thrilled to visit the noisy and colorful bazaar near our hotel. Ellen enjoyed their Turkish coffee that was black as mud and wanted to sample their regional tobacco as well. She rather prided herself on smoking unfiltered American cigarettes, so how bad could it be? Pretty bad, as it turns out and she had a coughing fit on the street, to the delight of the crowd.

At this same marketplace, I invited Guy to finally try *shashlik*. Smoke wafted up from the charcoal into our faces, while the smell of spices was mouth-watering. To most of us, at any rate. We drew a gathering of spectators as they sensed this was some kind of wager. The vendor enjoyed all the attention that had singled him out from so many other *shashlik* sellers. He was expert at turning the sharp metal skewers and shifting their positions over the coals to get an even cook. The man handed a kebab to Guy who handed it right back. He said he'd prefer one with more of a char. When he got the one that seemed the least threatening to his palate and sensibility, Guy took a bite of the top chunk of meat. I wolfed down my own which was tasty and well-spiced with cumin, ginger, chili peppers, coriander, and a little bit of nutmeg. A little natural grease from cooking flavored the pita bread, too.

I looked over at Guy and he smiled as he chewed and chewed. And chewed. I thought he was happy that he'd won the bet. That night he told me that the meat on his skewer was mostly gristle and fat. He'd spit it out when I wasn't looking. I was sorry to have put him through that in such a public place, but Guy was always a good sport.

The morning of October 25 we woke up to snow on the ground. My plan had been to film in a marketplace located on a twisty backstreet.

Arrangements had been made with dozens of vendors that lined both sides of the road and operated from crude wooden displays with canvas covers. They sold meat, spices, leather goods, Persian rugs, big bags of nuts, fruit – you name it – from two-wheeled horse carts parked at odd angles. These carts had long handles so they could be maneuvered like a big wheelbarrow. The sellers had agreed to be filmed and were paid a small fee, but that wasn't the case for the regular citizens wandering through the marketplace haggling for the best deals. Ever since I'd seen this place on the survey, I'd had concerns about drawing a surly crowd who would only stare. In the same way in which we'd brought along our own bike riders to not look at the cameras, we'd hired a half-dozen extras to wander about and appear natural.

In the garage of a government building a couple of blocks away, we assembled the Circle-Vision rig on a Beijing Jeep-o, a fairly easy set-up for us now. My idea was to prepare the cameras away from the public and then, when the timing and light seemed good, we'd just drive out and slowly roll through the market and grab our shot. By the time they'd really noticed us, we'd be done and heading back to our hidey-hole to wait for another take. *In principle*.

We were keeping warm in our unheated garage by drinking gallons of tea and munching on delicious *Hami* melons which are like an especially sweet cantaloupe. We'd left our camera assistants down at the market with light meters and walkie-talkies. They called in to say the sky was looking good and gave us the f/stop. We sent our extras out to take their positions with a final reminder about ignoring the cameras. A few minutes later we drove down the street and into a kind of chaos.

A few people walked right in front of the Jeep despite our Chinese driver laying on the horn – which caused everyone to turn and glare at us, even our paid extras. Well, *that* didn't work. We hurried back to the garage to regroup and get warm. No one had any better ideas other than to try again and hope the shoppers grew bored with us. That and let's lay off the horn, please.

We tried three more times with similar unusable results. Then it started snowing again. At least our Uyghur extras were figuring out what we wanted from them and were consistent. I would have liked to have had three-dozen more just like them but that wasn't possible at this late stage. I should have taken my own advice from the Great Wall shoot and just stripped the place of everyone but our people. Instead, I suggested maybe some of our Chinese crew might try to engage in conversations with any civilians who might be inclined to stop and stare at us. They'd only have to distract them for a moment or two as the camera rig passed by. The next time we heard that the light was actually improving and the sun was coming out, we decided to go for it. Joe had already changed all the f/stops. We could feel this was going to be the take, the one.

We rolled out of the garage and headed to the market. No horn honking by our admonished driver. The scene was looking as good as it was ever going to look. But just as we reached the center of the market, I saw a Chinese man in a long Army greatcoat step right out in front of the Jeep to take a photo of us. He was holding a distinctive twin-lens reflex camera and I realized this was Zhou – China Joe!

Back at the garage I was upset – our one good take was ruined. Joe was already reloading, and we'd have to try again after lunch. China Joe sat there in silence taking all the verbal abuse from me, Leon, Lao Tan, and even his friend Leo. His only defense was that he thought we were "rehearsing." The weirdest part of the entire fiasco happened weeks later when I was back at Disney Studios looking at dailies. In the heat of the moment, I could've sworn I'd seen a flashbulb go off, somehow making China Joe's sin even worse. But on film I discovered there was no burst of light. His camera wasn't even set up for a flash attachment!

Back in the garage, China Joe never contradicted me when I was going on about his folly. What I saw had only happened in my mind, a trick of my imagination in that moment of distress. My personal apology to China Joe would have to wait for months, until we came back for our winter shoot. The final take we photographed of the market after lunch wasn't nearly as good as the one he'd spoiled. I sent Han out with the Arriflex to grab some single-camera images that I thought we might be able use to "fix" any less-than-stellar moments by editing them into the master take.

We'd deliberately left our soundman behind in Beijing, so I went out with a recorder to pick up effects and voices that would help enhance the sequence. Later we filmed samples of calligraphy with the Arriflex in a large room in our hotel, the Kunlun Guest House. I needed eight images of poems and famous sayings to accompany Li Po's study scene. This sort of tabletop photography would have been very easy on a stage, but we were only able to get local access to these samples. In fact, these were considered works of art, some of them antiques, so an improvised solution was called for. We had to borrow extension cords and struggled to light the broad scrolls evenly with the small lighting kit we'd brought from the States, even blowing some fuses.

The weather looked awful the next morning, but we stayed on schedule by heading up into the Taishan Mountains, 60 miles away. We had no way of knowing in advance what the conditions were like at Heavenly Lake at 6,000 feet, other than to simply go there. The twisty road reaches the summit from a northerly approach that follows a narrow river. Our minibus driver, for reasons we never quite understood, stopped a kilometer from the top and refused to go any farther. We had to walk from there while the driver retreated to the bottom of the hill to wait for us. At least the equipment truck driver did not face a similar lack of courage.

The area around the parking lot at the top was overdeveloped with rather ugly tourist facilities which I'd seen on the survey. We hiked about a mile along the lake to get to a clear view, showing just the beautiful alpine lake ringed by rugged snowy mountains. This is the singular curse of the Circle-Vision filmmaker: some otherwise wonderful locations have to be passed up because of distracting visual elements that can't be hidden. Countless times on the survey I would find a spectacular spot that would only work in five or six cameras, sometimes even seven or eight, but not a full nine. It was usually a random construction site, power lines, a poorly situated apartment complex, or sewage treatment plants that partially ruined the view. The regular filmmaker would simply crop these eyesores out of their shots. In moments like this, I envied my friend Rick Harper. He'd shot "Impressions de France" with this same Circle-Vision rig, but he'd only had to deal with five cameras, 200 degrees. Oh, to be able to hide four cameras' worth of unsightly problems in China!

Once we'd turned a corner on the lakeside path and could hide the tourist areas, the set-up was pretty straightforward. No dolly, just a lock-off shot. I sent away our crew with all our equipment boxes. We got lucky when some young boys came along the path with a flock of black and white goats, so I pressed them into service as extras. A herd of feral cats might have been easier to control, but after two takes with the snow falling and the mountains reflecting on the lake, we had what we'd come for, a natural-looking scene.

Now we had to do the same process in reverse: bring back the empty boxes, break down the cameras, haul the boxes back to the parking lot, then load the truck. It took four hearty laborers just to haul the biggest camera box. We were starving by then and Leon provided an interesting lunch for us with a variety of local foods. We jammed ourselves into the back of the equipment truck to get a lift down the mountain and reconnect with our wary minibus driver. By the time we'd made it back to the city, the sunset over Ürümqi was buried in a layer of haze and smog.

Leon and I had *shashlik* for dinner, but Guy and Joe reverted to their tuna and rice standby, then we watched a local film. Most Chinese movies of this era featured wooden acting that veered towards posturing, especially when there was an overt political point to be hammered home. Some of these dramatic poses and iconography can be found on posters from the Cultural Revolution. The photography of the films always looked professional, except for a reliance on snap zooms. The film this night was about an "Overseas Chinese" woman who leaves America to come back to visit relatives in her homeland. The problem for the producers was that they needed to depict a scene at San Francisco airport for her departure but had to fake the scene by filming at the old Beijing airport. American tourists were still a rarity, so the producers rounded up some Western tourists from countries like England, Norway, Germany, and Switzerland who were already traveling with tour groups in China. The producers needed them to make the airport look a little more Western but never bothered to give them directions or dialogue. As a result, these extras were saying whatever came to mind, their words recorded directly on the soundtrack. Filmmakers call meaningless background chatter "walla." But it's supposed to be more of a sound effect, not meant to be intelligible. To an English-speaking audience, the opening sequence was hilarious:

"God, this is taking forever! How much longer are they keeping us here?"

"I'm starving. I don't think anyone on the crew knows what they're doing."

And the classic:

"I don't know why I ever agreed to be in this stupid film!"

The next day we headed to White Goat Valley, a scenic region deep in the mountains about fifty miles south of Ürümqi. We had decided to boycott our cowardly minibus driver. Guy, Bao, and I took one car, while Joe, Leon, and Ding went in another. The rest of the team rode in the equipment truck. Joe started the day in a bad mood for unknown reasons and then passed it on to Leon. My production manager usually stayed out of my way when I was directing, even though he had no shortage of opinions, loudly expressed on other occasions. This day he was certain I was staging a scene all wrong.

For this shot, we'd asked for several local ethnic mountain people, some rustic yurts, and the various farm animals that these people normally tended. We even had a Kazakh man riding a steer like a horse. I wanted to have a central fire where they might be roasting a lamb carcass on a long pole. Whatever I asked for in the way of added production value I had seen examples of during the survey, so I wasn't just making up these requests. I left it to the locals to arrange the fire and meat traditionally, but Leon kept butting in. He claimed he knew the way a *real* Kazakh would build a fire and cook meat. I tried to be patient (at least I didn't say, "Is this another skill Ernie Haller taught you?") and listen to his suggestions. In the end I preferred to let the locals do it however they felt comfortable, rather than rely on Leon's vague assertion of traces of Kazakh blood in his veins. He flared up anyway and I relegated him to staying inside the biggest yurt while we shot. I filmed a total of four takes: the first two were no good as we needed to sort out the actions of the extras and wayward animals, and the third was spoiled when Leon stepped out of the yurt while we were filming. Even if he'd missed my loud call for action in Chinese, after all this time he couldn't tell when our noisy cameras were grinding away?

That night we shared a big banquet with some of the locals to celebrate the conclusion of filming in Xinjiang. The feast included an entire roast lamb

(I had to assure Guy that it was *not* the one we'd used as a prop) which the restaurant staff wheeled around on a cart, parading it for other diners to see. The bright red ribbon trussed around the lamb's neck was a nice touch, in a macabre sort of way. Lots of Maotai flowed that night.

On our flight back to Beijing, again First Class, our Chinese crew showed off their purchases: shopping bags full of fruits and vegetables not available in Beijing, like *Hami* melons, raisins, and almonds. Commerce in China relied heavily on trucks traveling two-lane roads so almost all cuisine was local.

When we landed back at Beijing airport, we made a terrible discovery. We always traveled with two heavy-duty truck batteries with enough amperage to power the Circle-Vision cameras. The local crews had built wooden carrying cases for the batteries and had marked them very clearly with signs in English and Chinese that said, "This Way Up!" The danger was that if they tipped over, they might leak acid. Today there is probably no airline on earth that would allow this to happen. We were especially careful, making China Joe and Leo supervise the loading, and inspecting for themselves that the batteries were safely and properly stowed. But this day they found someone must have turned both batteries upside down in the cargo hold. Even though they found no leak, we informed the airport authorities right away. I was only half joking when I told Lao Tan to write down our aircraft's registration number. We wouldn't be flying on that plane anymore.

Three archways, Beihai Park

Rowboats on Qianhai Lake

The White Dagoba

Guy goes in the drink

Guy takes a drink

Chapter 19

Polishing the Dragons

Back in Beijing, I heard from Bob at the studio. The report on dailies from Guilin was very good which was reassuring. The crew sensed the end of a long marathon of shooting. We had only two scenes left for this trip and both were within Beijing city limits. We'd come down to the end of October and had less than a year to finish the film and have it installed and running at EPCOT.

Our Chinese friends were back in the comfort of their home. Joe, Guy, Leon, and I were checked into the newer wing of the Peking Hotel instead of the creaky old Soviet section. We'd almost forgotten the rumors about surveillance from the top floor. One night I talked with Leon in his room to strategize how we might deal with the recalcitrant soundman. The next day Lao Tan made comments that indicated my private remarks had been passed along directly to him. We never said a word to our Chinese crew about this incident, but it certainly seemed to confirm that the suspicions were more than rumors.

One of our last scenes for this marathon shoot was inside the Forbidden City at the Nine-Dragon Wall. This screen, 90 feet long, 21 feet high, and several feet thick, is one of the oldest in China, although it only dates to the relatively recent 1771. Under a sloping, tiled pagoda roof, nine huge coiled dragons are depicted in relief in colorful glazed tile, playing with giant pearls among swirling clouds. Imperial architecture was heavily influenced by numerology, which is why the Imperial Palace supposedly has 9,999 rooms, one shy of the 10,000 in Heaven. Dragons were the symbol of the Emperor and nine was a significant number to the court. However, many little dragons had been worked into the tile details, so the wall actually contains 635 of them.

My plan was to film a shot with the Circle-Vision rig showing the wall's full extent while we dolly in towards the large middle dragon on camera number one. Then I'd edit in single-camera close-ups of the other eight main dragons so that, in effect, the entire wall would bend around the theater.

To make the shot, the camera rig had to be raised up several feet so that it could appear level with the dragons. Guy arranged this by using risers on our China dolly. At the same time, I worked with my extras, placing them in various positions for maximum effect. I never seemed to have as many as I'd have liked. The rule of thumb was to divide the total by nine and that's what the average per screen would be. Eighteen is only two per screen which can be pretty sketchy, depending on the location. We had security arranged at a number of access points so that we could shut down foot traffic long enough to film with only our extras visible.

When our equipment was nearly ready, I told Ding, "Please find me a bucket of water and some rags."

My translator thought he'd misunderstood me, so I explained. Because of their exaggerated dimensionality, the dragons had been collecting dust and dirt blown into the city from the Gobi for… well, probably since 1771. The result was a thick, dark layer of grime that topped the upper edges of the tiles. My asking to clean them off probably fell into the same category as my suggestion to repaint the doors at the Temple of Heaven. But this time it was too late for them to refuse. When the bucket of water and several rags appeared, I joined Joe and Guy who had already grabbed paper towels and were on ladders working on a couple of dragons. Meanwhile, the Chinese stood around watching in amazement.

"We can't shoot until we polish the dragons," I told them.

Within minutes, the reluctant Lao Tan and his crew had completely taken over the job from us, which made me chuckle. Years of grime had been washed away and the colorful tiles appeared brighter. The rest of us moved on to policing the grounds, picking up stray candy and ice cream wrappers left around by lazy tourists. We even swept up the ubiquitous cigarette butts dropped without thinking. The round, carved tile trash bins provided by the city were apparently thought by most citizens to be merely decorative. Even a few extras got into it and were cleaning and sweeping their areas, as if the message we'd been preaching – everything should look its best for the film – had finally sunk in.

We did two good takes and then grabbed the other eight single-camera shots. It went fairly quickly because Guy had set up the tripod on the bed of a small truck. He was able to drive me down the line, stopping long enough to film each dragon.

After lunch, we moved to our final scene of our two-month shoot: the rowboats on Qianhai Lake. Beihai Park had originally been built in about the 10th century and is also known as the Winter Palace. Signs of the Imperial Court are everywhere around the lake, such as halls, temples, and drum towers, especially on the manmade island called Jade Flower Islet. The Imperial Gardens are topped with the distinctive White Dagoba, a dome-shaped memorial *stupa* typically found in Tibet. This one, built in 1651, marks the site where Kublai Khan supposedly received Marco Polo. While I can't refute this, I came across so many places where Marco Polo was supposed to have traveled, slept, or met royalty, I suspect he must have lived three lives.

Young people in China were hard pressed to find a place where they could have a private moment away from watchful parents or grandparents. Here they could row out to the center of the lake to whisper sweet nothings to their loved one. Unfortunately, everyone else had the same idea so the lake could get crowded. I noticed that no matter the number, large or small, the boats would always be equidistant from each other. I had six pairs of extras, "young lovers" dressed in clothing as colorful as society would allow, which was still pretty muted for the rest of the world. At least no one was wearing Mao jackets. Men always rowed, women always sat in the bow, looking demure and proper, almost 19th century. All they needed were high-buttoned shoes and a parasol. We'd also rented a motorized pagoda boat and placed 18 extras on it, mixing in a variety of ages. Ding was on that boat with a walkie-talkie so I could signal them to hurry back to first positions when I wanted to do another take.

Guy decided on speed rail to box the two rowboats together like a catamaran and he set to building his one-of-a-kind rig. During this construction, he was concerned about the brackish waters of the lake. He needed reassurance we weren't being served fish from this lake at the hotel. I laughed at the comment.

"Are you kidding? This lake is so polluted nothing can live in it."

Right about then, Guy happened to drop a cable and clasp. It fell right into the water next to the public boat landing. Needing this for the rig, he took one of the oars and started fishing around for the cable. The water wasn't deep, maybe a couple of feet at the most, but so dark he could only feel the cable with the oar. He managed to snag it and carefully lift it up. What came with the cable was the foulest and slimiest black muck imaginable. The smell was awful, and I thought Guy was going to gag. Even I found it disgusting. Guy extended the oar to the Chinese crew who'd offered to get the cable washed. He gave me such a look. This was confirmation of Guy's greatest fear: we'd be floating on this manmade lake that was a cesspool of germs and bacteria.

When the whole rig was assembled, Joe, Guy, and I slowly paddled the boat out towards the middle of the lake. We were careful because the rig was a little top-heavy for the two boats. We waited for almost an hour for the sun to drop behind the tops of the trees. Any higher and the sun would have flared out the camera lenses. I was hoping to catch the shot with light rays filtering through the branches. I had both a walkie-talkie and a megaphone to cue my extras and the pagoda boat. I didn't have to worry about extraneous people on the shore who were far enough away not to matter. We managed a couple of good takes in warm, late light. Unfortunately, we missed another take in even better light because we couldn't get the pagoda boat back to its starting position fast enough. I called a wrap, thinking we had enough, and we began to paddle back to shore. I was telling myself we'd pulled this off without my own greatest concern: tipping the boats and dunking the whole camera rig in the foul water. How would I explain *that* to the studio?

Guy stood near the front of our boat and paddled with one oar slowly and carefully. I paddled sitting down from the back. As we approached the dock, we were met by our Chinese crew, always ready to lend a hand. China Joe had somehow acquired a gaffing hook from the boathouse and reached out for our boat. He snagged the edge of a rowboat and yanked us closer. It was just enough…

Guy hadn't seen any of this and tumbled off balance. Watching him go over the side was like watching a slow-motion horror film. I saw him fall in with a huge splash – he went completely under! And then he flew out of the water as if he'd been launched like a missile. He landed back up on the boat sputtering and coughing. The mortified Chinese could only stand there in shock. Guy was out of the water so quickly that he later found the inside of his wallet and the insides of his shoes were still dry! Suddenly everyone was running in different directions to find him a towel or a cloth. Lao Tan quickly offered his coat.

Onshore, Guy was shivering, not with cold but fear that he'd just been dipped into the world's largest Petrie dish. We shoved Guy, still wet, into one of the cars and had the driver whisk him right back to the hotel for the hottest shower of his life. Meanwhile, the rest of us cleaned up and stowed the equipment. I kept thinking, well, that's done it. Guy is *never* coming back to China. We'll have to get a new grip for the next shoot. There'll be lawsuits. Hospital bills. Greg's hepatitis will be *nothing* compared to this.

Because we would be having our wrap banquet right back at this same location that night, we quickly cleaned ourselves up at the hotel. I couldn't remember if this was our banquet for them or their banquet for us, but it didn't matter. I knocked on Guy's door. I could hear the shower running so I left him alone.

The rest of us returned to the 1,000-year-old Beihai Park, this time to the other side of the lake and a more opulent setting: Fangshan Restaurant. This was Beijing's oldest Imperial eating establishment and the favorite of the Empress Dowager Cixi. Waitresses dressed like Manchurian courtesans streamed out of the kitchens to serve us a multicourse meal worthy of royalty.

Late in the banquet, a surprising guest showed up: Guy Jones. In a suit, no less. He looked like he'd scrubbed off at least one layer of skin in the shower. That night he joined in the drinking (he usually abstained) perhaps hoping Maotai would kill any additional bacteria he hadn't washed off. He needed his insides scrubbed, too.

I'm not sure of the count, but we endured several rounds of toasts and shouts of *"Ganbei!"* meaning dry glass, or bottoms up. One always suspected the Chinese were just drinking water at these banquets, so I made sure my hosts were served from the same bottle of Maotai. After too many rounds, I made a decision that was diplomatically proper and otherwise foolish.

I grabbed a bottle of the local red wine and corralled Bao to follow me around and translate. Chinese wine was barely suitable for cooking but was preferable to Maotai, at least for alcohol content. I found special words to say to each member of the Chinese crew, thanking them for their outstanding contribution to our success. Then we would each take a drink. Of course, I was the one getting toasted because by the time I'd made it around the big tables I must've had a dozen shot glasses of wine. Duty calls, but oh my God.

I miraculously escaped with little hangover from this memorable banquet.

While Joe and Guy prepped our camera equipment for shipping to Japan, I was off to squeeze in one more location survey before heading home.

Leon and I caught a train with Lao Tan and Ding for Shanhaiguan on the east coast. The trip took nearly seven hours and was not unpleasant. Ding passed the time openly speaking about the Cultural Revolution in front of Lao Tan who might have objected had he understood the subject. We arrived in Qinhuangdao at nearly 8 p.m. The man who was our local contact announced that the part of the wall that reaches the ocean is considered "sensitive" and we'd be unable to photograph it at all. They couldn't have told us this before our train trip? I knew what "sensitive" meant and it wasn't their chunk of the Great Wall he was talking about. It was a PLA base tucked right up against the south side of the wall. I planned to make a direct appeal to the Army the next day, promising we'd only shoot from the north side.

On the last day of October, we drove to Shanhaiguan (literally, "Mountain Sea Gate") about 30 minutes from our hotel. While standing at the "First Pass Under Heaven," it was confirmed that I wouldn't be allowed to take pictures of the Old Dragon's Head *(Lǎolóngtóu),* the part of the wall that extends into the ocean. We argued back and forth, and they told me I might be able to see the north side as a tourist, unofficially, but I still wouldn't be able take pictures.

"What about Polaroids?" I argued. They'd at least be able to see exactly what I wanted to shoot. Ding became a bit more proactive in arguing the case and the authorities finally agreed. We were driven there via a back road, away from any military installation. Still, the air was filled with MiGs and I could hear muffled artillery explosions.

When we stood on the north side of the wall their real issue became apparent. To our left was the ocean and the last great hunk of crumbling wall and a watchtower that vaguely could be interpreted as the dragon's head supposedly drinking from the Bohai Sea. But to our right we could see one single radio mast barely rising above the wall. I doubt anyone would ever know what it was, but try convincing the PLA of that point. After all, they'd been worried I might photograph their logo on a public building in Tibet that was miles from our cameras. The final compromise, sealed with multiple sets of Polaroids to confirm, was to shoot from one very narrow spot on the beach where our cameras would not see the antenna. Literally a foot or two right or left and the deal would be off. All I could do was promise we'd return to this exact same place on the sand, even though we couldn't leave any kind of marker.

The seven-hour train ride back to Beijing was exhausting. Leon gave me some antibiotics as I felt a sore throat coming on. That's my usual response at the end of a hard shoot, my body lets down its defenses. I managed to eat some tasteless noodles at the hotel's after-hours bar before crashing.

I'd been on the road in China for three straight months, so this felt like I'd completed the marathon portion of some Chinese Ironman competition. We still had two more filming trips, one for a month in winter, then another month in spring. After all the difficulties we'd overcome so far, I wondered how hard that could be?

Three flatbed KEM editing consoles, interlocked

CHAPTER 20

Phony Receipts

After returning from China, I began arranging for the edit with the material we'd already shot. Greg had been hoping postproduction could happen down at his offices in Laguna Beach, but Bob and Randy quickly eliminated that option. Editing would take place on the studio lot which was fine with me.

I interviewed Dennis Orcutt for the position of editor. Dennis was laid back and had a quiet strength and intelligence that I appreciated. He'd been a cutter on the lot for many years, knew everyone in all departments, so he seemed like a great fit. In order to view and cut nine pictures simultaneously, we would need to bring in three KEMs. We interlocked these flatbed editing consoles into a U-shape that nearly surrounded us. This was a huge shift from how "America the Beautiful" had been edited: only footage from camera number one had been cut on an upright Moviola. When Walt gave his final signoff on the film, he had only viewed that one screen. The footage from the other eight cameras were then cut to match the first, regardless of what was happening on those other screens. Dennis and I wanted to be sure every frame of every screen was exactly what we wanted. But we endured a long wait before we could even make a single edit.

Film that was shot in China had to be developed at Technicolor, the only lab that would agree to Disney's strict specifications. Color matching is highly critical in Circle-Vision because images are projected side by side where the slightest shift in color, the merest off-tint, is readily apparent to the audience. We had strict protocols for developing and printing the films, even using the same emulsion batch for each load of raw negative, all the way through the lengthy process. Prints from our negatives had to be edge-coded, a time-consuming process. Identification was necessary so that any given foot of film could to be tracked back to which roll it came from as well as which camera. This was Disney's reliable system for maintaining synchronization of all the material and it had been developed over the years for all Circle-Vision films.

By mid-November, Leon was making it known he wanted to be considered the producer of the film. He'd already told a number of his friends and colleagues in the business that it was his title, and I had to remind him there had been no changes. Greg MacGillivray was still the producer. Leon's argument was that Greg had left early, wouldn't be returning to China, and hadn't been there every day on location like he had. It was true that Leon was handling all of the daily finances and scheduling as production manager, but Greg wasn't about to give up the credit. I had more important concerns about Leon's lack of social skills. He'd sometimes terrorized our Chinese crew with his hair-trigger temper. Yelling and screaming might have earned him points in Hollywood, but our crew had to walk on eggshells around him, hoping he wouldn't suddenly flare up and cause a diplomatic rift, maybe even jeopardizing the production. I was about to hear about a new problem with Leon, this time from Disney Studios.

I was called into a meeting with Randy and Bob. I wasn't sure whether the issue was Leon's temper or his wanting to be producer. It turned out to be his receipts.

In China, every transaction generates paperwork, usually of the flimsy variety that is stamped with multiple red seals to make it appear official-looking. The writing and printing is all in Chinese, of course, without any English identification for tracking expenses. Leon and I would usually jot a quick note in the corner of each of our receipts to identify them for totaling later. It was difficult to remember otherwise. They all looked alike – a laundry slip, a bus ticket, or a meal voucher. Leon had gathered many more than I did but where he was really getting them from was the concern of Randy and Bob. They'd heard Leon had gone to New York recently and was buying Chinese antiques and charging them to Disney. That was what had started their investigation and soon the truth came out. They believed that many of Leon's receipts, for which he'd asked personal reimbursement, were not what he said they were. I was shocked until they showed me how several of Leon's receipts were wrinkled and aged. Some had footprints on them, as if he'd picked them up off the ground or retrieved them from the trash. The studio hired a

Chinese-speaking accountant whose entire job was to verify each receipt Leon had turned in. The rumor was that he'd deliberately mislabeled several dozen.

Bob and Randy wanted to fire Leon on the spot, but I made a case to keep him at least through the coming winter shoot. It was too late to bring on someone new and hope they could get up to speed. I wasn't sure how it would look to China Co-Film, either. Later I showed Bob and Randy a rough assembly that Dennis had cut together and they both seemed very pleased with our progress.

I continued working with Dennis, pulling some temporary music from Chinese albums so we could have a screening for several of the growing team working on the China Pavilion at EPCOT. Then I got a phone call from Leon in New York. I could tell from his voice he was in wheeler-dealer mode. He was jazzed that he'd just had a meeting with the Chinese Ambassador as well as the visiting Minister of Culture! How the hell he'd arranged this I'll never know, but I'm sure he certainly didn't describe himself as the film's production manager. Shih Kuan and China Co-Film were now small potatoes to Leon, and I think he was back to imagining himself the Dino De Laurentiis of China. I wish I'd ended this sad and delusional drama earlier.

On December 3, I met with Randy and Bob again, expecting them to insist Leon be fired. Instead, they wanted to wait until they'd had a chance to talk with David Hayden. They wanted our lawyer to approach Shih Kuan first and take the temperature of how this change would affect the production going forward. I suspect they also wanted an opportunity to confront Leon with his bogus receipts and chew him out face to face. Meanwhile, Leon told me he was going to be interviewed the next day by *Newsweek!*

It got worse. Leon was preparing a personal letter to China Co-Film in which he characterized the Chinese crew as unprofessional and not up to Hollywood standards. He even sent me a copy for my records. I thought it terribly unfair and undiplomatic of him and I didn't agree at all. I shared my copy with Randy and then Bob. I got the feeling their hands were tied because we were locked into keeping Leon for the filming in China next month. I wasn't sure how I was going to face him.

In the meantime, I focused on a more refined cut of the film with Dennis, adding in more temp music that I found in a record shop in Chinatown. I'd interviewed a few possible composers, but it was early yet, and we hadn't a chance to consider any candidates in China as a possibility. I also approached the Animation Department about the opening shot, my paintings-to-real mountains in Yangshuo. They would need to rotoscope (trace) the final film images so paintings could be made to match the outlines. Randy had talked at length about the possibility of using the legendary Herb Ryman, one of the most influential artists at WED, to execute the scroll paintings. Cinching the deal was that Ryman had been trained in Chinese painting techniques. I was excited by this real coup for the production – but only because I could barely see past the next shoot in China.

I was really looking forward to filming a special performance of Peking Opera on our upcoming schedule. To record the sound, I was going to need two professional recorders and didn't want to rely on Chinese equipment, let alone the soundman supplied by China Co-Film. If need be, I had to be prepared to do it myself. I met with a pair of old-school technicians in Disney's Sound Department, Les Gear and Al Tyson. These two had seen it all and worked on countless classic shows. They grasped immediately what we wanted to do and the limited conditions in which we had to pull it off. They arranged some rugged microphones and stands, cables to connect to the theater speakers, and a pair of Nagra recorders, stacked one above the other for convenient one-man operation.

The idea would be to record a clean version of a selection from the opera on one machine, then playback through the theater's sound system for the performers to match. The other recorder would then capture sync during filming. The second recording would be noisy with cameras grinding away but that would be swapped for the original sound in postproduction. It seemed simple and foolproof to me, and these wonderful technicians wanted to make sure I was confident with the set-up before they'd let me go. They grabbed the nearest reel of tape lying around and threaded up the playback machine to give me a test demonstration. Music started coming out of the speakers and the familiar tune nearly brought me to tears. It was Cliff Edwards as Jiminy Cricket singing, "When You Wish Upon a Star."

Was there ever a better confirmation I was now a Disney filmmaker?

Actors do their own make-up

Company barber

Opera characters, scene one

Peking Opera's band

Documenting the Monkey King

The full company

The Monkey King warriors

Three of nine images from the film

CHAPTER 21

BEAR PAW AND MOOSE NOSE

Early in January 1982, just before we flew back to China for the winter shoot, I had a one-on-one meeting with Leon Chooluck to set new ground rules. They'd been worked out with Randy Bright and Bob Gibeaut and were clear and concise. Leon was *not* the producer of the film, he was not to claim to be the producer of the film, and every purchase, every receipt in his books, was going to be scrutinized by the studio's Chinese accountant. They'd already found more than $3,000 in erroneous reimbursement to him that he'd to have to pay back. Leon also casually informed me it was his intention to bring his two adult sons along this trip, but at his own expense. He wanted to give them some real on-location production experience to augment their work as assistant directors in Hollywood.

When I informed Bob and Randy, they said Leon's boys were not to be part of our crew, they could not come with us on location, and under no circumstances were they to get involved or interfere with our shoot. When I passed on this directive, Leon took it calmly and it seemed to me he was finally aware of what was expected of him. Thankfully, we'd also stopped him from sending his condemnation letter to the Chinese.

Arriving back in Beijing, Leon and I had a production meeting with Shih Kuan to review arrangements before Joe and Guy arrived with the equipment a few days later. Shih Kuan had been under the impression, perhaps because of all those friendly toasts at the last banquet, the first shoot had gone rather smoothly. I offered a few simple suggestions, just room for improvement, and came nowhere near Leon's scathing assessment of the Chinese crew.

I later discovered Leon had a private meeting with Shih Kuan, immediately following. When I questioned him, Leon offered me a lame excuse: he wanted to complain that Shih Kuan hadn't shown the "proper respect" due the film's director by coming out to meet me at the airport. *What?* That was a completely bogus notion because it never even occurred to me Shih Kuan should do that. The truth came out even later that Leon, no surprise, wanted to privately pitch ideas for films in China for which he would be producer.

We needed to get out of town, back on the road. We headed first to the ancient city of Xi'an for a survey before the start of the shoot. We'd been turned down a year earlier by local authorities when we asked permission to film the famous terra cotta soldiers. I'd remained hopeful that China Co-Film could convince them of our good intentions. We were politely shown around their amazing site, but it was not to be. One of my biggest disappointments on this film, which bothered me for years, was not getting to photograph these beautiful relics.

Back in Beijing, Leon and I were sad to learn that Ding Hai Hua, one of our most reliable and trusted translators, had left to join the Chinese Foreign Service. I'd been slowly turning Ding into a pretty good assistant director and he would be missed. Meanwhile I had errands to run. I made a quick shopping trip to art supply stores with the help of Bao who had a real passion for art. Herb Ryman had passed along a list of very specific materials he wanted us to pick up for his paintings and we shipped them back to WED.

Our American crew had been supplied with extreme cold weather gear by Disney Studios. They stored items like Arctic snowsuits and heavy thermal boots in the Wardrobe Department, where else? Leon and I, along with his two sons, were traveling up to Heilongjiang Province, near the border with the Soviet Union, where the temperatures were way below zero. Way, way below.

On our first excursion into Harbin, I wore a blue snowsuit, and a red balaclava and boots with foam liners. Despite the frigid air, the streets were full of people riding bicycles on the icy streets. Sidewalks were covered in a layer of frost. Everyone was bundled up in quilted Mao jackets or Army greatcoats and most wore surgical face masks, either to keep warm or keep out germs. Or both. We saw peasants and workers standing in orderly queues in the middle of the street waiting for one of the city's red-and-white electric trollies. Many other vehicles were still horse-drawn. A kind of leather diaper hung behind the horses to keep the streets clean and we heard manure droppings were used as fuel.

We had come to this remote, northeast corner of China to scout Harbin's famous Ice Festival. Huge blocks of ice are sliced out of the frozen Songhua River which bisects the town, then the massive cubes are hauled on horse carts to the nearby festival grounds in Stalin Park. Every manner of cutting instruments, including chainsaws, are used to shape and sculpt the ice into intricate figures, statues, castles, and other fanciful designs. Somehow they insert colorful lights into each work of art but the air is too cold for the warm bulbs to melt the ice. The impression was that of a wintry fairyland and I hoped our Circle-Vision cameras would be able to work at 30 below without snapping the film, which can turn brittle at that temperature.

The city of Harbin, like Paris and Washington, was laid out like spokes of a wheel, but with a heavy Russian influence. The area had been occupied by Soviet troops at the end of WWII. Much of the population was made up of émigrés, including nearly two million White Russians from Odessa in 1917. Remnants of this international past can be found throughout the city, such as orthodox churches with their familiar onion domes, now being used for storage or other secular functions.

My room in the Heilongjiang Provincial Guest House was very large, with a parquet floor in a zigzag pattern. The overstuffed chairs had slipcovers with the usual white doilies on the armrests and headrest. The overall flavor was rather Eastern European with a bland, uniform taupe color scheme. Like many Chinese buildings, this former railroad hotel was overheated with parched, almost desiccated, air. My second-floor room had a great view of a busy intersection and, unlike my room on Huangshan, featured a large double set of windows with full glass panes. I could open the inside windows and use the inner space to keep a few bottles of soft drinks cold.

At dinner we were served two of the local specialties which I'd read about (and dreaded). The first was Bear Paw and it was exactly as advertised, as appetizing as heavily callused animal flesh can be. The Chinese take a great deal of pride in their cuisine which has a wide definition of what constitutes "food," but sometimes you wonder if the chefs are hiding by the kitchen window to see if foreigners will actually eat what they've sent out. The second dish was Moose Nose (technically, the menu translated it as "nose of camel deer," which was equally unappetizing). The plate arrived looking for all the world like someone had sliced off the front end of a moose and it fell on a plate. There wasn't so much as a sprig of parsley to dress it up, no Chinese decorative radishes or carrots, just the nose of a moose. Mine looked like the beast had been suffering from a cold. Even Leon passed, and he had the digestive constitution of a waste disposal.

After a very quick and very frigid tour of the impressive ice festival, we took a 19-hour train ride back to Beijing, a 1,200-kilometer journey through China's northeast. We had one more location to survey before the arrival of Guy and Joe. I passed the time on the train with Bao and Lao Tan playing "Up and Up." I was either getting better at the fast-moving card game or they were letting me win.

That night in the old wing of the Peking Hotel, I saw what until now I'd thought had only been an expression: a Chinese fire drill. Alarms went off at three in the morning and I watched from a balcony as fire trucks arrived. It might have simply been a little smoke but watching disorganized firefighters running around in the snow from the fifth floor looked as funny and chaotic as the old expression implies.

We still needed to find a theater and a theater company. I went to a performance of "Havoc in Heaven" and found two scenes I thought might lend themselves to Circle-Vision filming. We saw this show in a so-called "peasant theater" where the audience was particularly rowdy, like the groundlings of Shakespeare's time. The show featured China's famous Monkey King in a very athletic role. The production is a portion of the larger "Journey to the West," one of the country's most famous Peking Operas. Beijing had eight opera companies, but only four specialized in the kind of classic "Peking Opera" I wanted to depict. When we met with the leaders of the selected company, they didn't really seem to understand what would be involved.

Our plan, suggested by China Co-Film, was to buy out an entire company for one night and they would then perform whatever scenes I wanted for the cameras instead of an audience. But where? We saw one theater that looked great but had no lights. Another one, at the Beijing Documentary Film Studios, seemed to be a perfect choice but wasn't available for a month. Why were we being dragged out to see theaters we couldn't use? We needed an empty theater already equipped with overhead stage lamps since we only traveled with a small location lighting kit. As we were to discover, those lights of ours were barely adequate for filming a makeshift insert stage in a banquet room of the Peking Hotel. We were assisted by Han, China Joe, Leo, and Lou, our Chinese grip. We had collected some great examples of calligraphy and shot most of them without difficulty using the Arriflex. Then we moved downstairs to the main dining room which had a very large scroll featuring the distinctive handwriting of Mao Zedong, considered a master of the form. We kept blowing fuses but managed to get it on film. I made a point of never identifying this particular work to anyone at the studio because I thought someone might object on political grounds. I wanted to represent Mao in the film somewhere, not for any of the horrific acts done in his name, but for his well-known artistic contribution to calligraphy. Everybody has some talent, even tyrannical dictators. Dennis and I edited Mao's famous writing into a back panel during the montage of samples, but I hoped many viewers from China would recognize his hand.

That night I took Joe Nash with me to visit an empty theater that was installing some overhead lighting. The place looked like it was going to work for us, a last-minute find, since the opera company would be joining us the next night. We would have no audience, but with the right lighting and keeping the Circle-Vision camera rig up on the stage, the film's viewers wouldn't notice. I got back to the hotel feeling like we'd solved one problem, then we ran into another, one with a nagging persistence.

Leon had secretly tried to arrange a deal with Shih Kuan to have his sons training assistants in Beijing while we were gone. When that fell through, he'd decided to bring them along on our location shoot. This resulted in a heated flare-up when I reminded Leon he was violating the ground rules he'd agreed to. I telexed Bob a detailed report and he was appropriately pissed off. He wanted me to tell Leon he couldn't do this but was quite aware we were operating a long way from the watchful eyes of the studio.

The next day we began setting up at the theater in the early afternoon. The members of the stage troupe started trickling in and, like everyone else in China, were very curious about our camera system. Some men in the company were recognizable on the street because their heads were shaved in a distinctive way that told the public they were opera stars. Hair was cut back from their foreheads in a line over the top of their scalps from ear to ear. The company had their own barber who made sure these unique shaves were maintained. The bald section facilitated the very complex make-up that was essential to each character and applied by each actor themselves. The women applied white grease paint to their faces and then blended in the colorful red cheeks that were so typical of Chinese opera. I filmed the details of this process in the theater's make-up rooms using the Arriflex. These actors went about their business as usual, preparing as they always did to put on a full show that night. Except that's not what we wanted.

When the actors learned we were only going to film snippets of two brief scenes, their preparation came to a halt. We'd run into an impasse. They felt their efforts were all going to be a waste. We'd paid for it, so why didn't we film the entire three-hour show? Obviously, the opera company administrators hadn't bothered to inform them of our intentions or our limitations. No doubt this was deliberate because it's been my experience that the Chinese will go to great lengths to avoid a direct face-to-face confrontation. I had to speak to the leader at length, to calmly explain that while we were only filming two very short segments, it was important they understand the honor we were giving them. There are many local theatrical companies, but only *their* scenes would represent Peking Opera to Western audiences for many years to come. They would be seen portraying these particular roles by tens if not hundreds of millions of viewers.

The truth seemed to do the trick and they threw themselves into staging the scenes. We had a large group of military characters onstage perform a couple of good rehearsals for us while we worked out camera movements. Peking Opera has a small traditional band play drums, gongs, and whistles from out of sight in the wings. With our cameras up on the stage, we would be able to see these musicians which I thought would add to the performance's special appeal. We recorded the music and singing for the first scene, then used our playback set-up for filming a few good takes. The dual recorders worked exactly as planned by Disney's sound department. We followed that by staging the Monkey King in a dramatic ballet fight with palace guards. We didn't wrap until 10 p.m., but we all felt we'd found a way to successfully incorporate Peking Opera into a Circle-Vision film.

The next morning, I heard that Madame Li, head of China Co-Film, had approved Leon's boys going with us on location, as if it was already a done deal. I gave up that particular fight and we packed our bags for the airport, just as we had so many times before. Whenever we had to clear security, our Chinese crew handled the details and we were never hassled over our luggage or papers – until this time.

Security wanted us to open all our bags for inspection. We weren't sure what was happening, but the special treatment we usually received was gone. Leon protested, perhaps a bit too loudly. Zhang/John, our assistant location manager, stepped in on our behalf, as if to protect us. He got into a shouting match with security, complaining that this was an insult to their American friends and so on. Not only was it one of those confrontations Chinese try their best to avoid, this one played out in public – with uniformed officers no less. Before we knew it, John was being taken away. The last we saw of him, he was being hustled through security doors and we honestly didn't know if we'd ever see him again. We looked to Bao for an explanation, but he was as spooked as we were.

On the plane, Bao told us that John would have to give a self-criticism, confessing his transgressions in a kind of public humiliation. Mao had devoted a whole chapter in his "Little Red Book" to the concept of self-criticism. But John's situation wouldn't be as onerous as the so-called "struggle sessions" of the Cultural Revolution in which members of the public would verbally and sometimes physically abuse the confessor.

But it certainly felt like we'd just witnessed an ugly vestige of that terrible time.

Songhua River, Heilongjiang Province

The Harbin Ice Festival

Leon at -20°

The river slide

A dirt street on Hainan Island

One-star hotel room

Hotel on Hainan Island

Typical fishing boats

Undeveloped beaches

CHAPTER 22

To Yi, or Not To Yi

Seeing John, one of our crew members, being led away by authorities weighed heavily on us when we arrived in Kunming, the capital of Yunnan Province. Could the incident have been prevented? Should we have tried to interfere? Or were we supposed to respond in the Chinese manner, to turn away, thankful it wasn't us?

The weather in Yunnan was colder than expected, but not like we'd seen in the far north. So much for the City of Eternal Spring. After a lousy meal at the Soviet-style Kunming Hotel, Shen took us to see a performance of ethnic dance troupes, one of which we would film in a couple of days. I selected a group of Yi people whose simple dances and gentle music seemed a good contrast with the starkness of the surrounding location where I planned to film them.

We had to leave our hotel before sunrise in order to arrive at the Shilin Stone Forest by 9:30. It took until lunchtime to verify our scouted locations and then begin to set up. The challenge was that our equipment had to be hand carried over the narrow walkways between the vertical formations. Lots of climbing, too.

The tall, ragged limestone rocks of the Shilin Stone Forest looked like a vast field of gray stalagmites. Some of the spires appeared almost like petrified trees, giving the place its name. The rocks have been eroding into these fantastic shapes since their formation 270 million years ago. Public access was along pathways with railings built over pools of water that reflected the rocks, doubling their impact. Among the towering peaks were several glyphs and carved inscriptions. The twisting pathways eventually led to a central overlook, a raised six-sided pagoda with a tiled roof modeled in the Southern Song style.

For the first planned shot at this locale, I was only given a few local National Minority women in costume. I pressed a few of my Chinese crew into service as extras to fill out the scene as "non-ethnic tourists," a common sight in this area. I positioned Shen on one of the screens and paired him with a little local girl. He shared a touching moment with her since she was not unlike his own child who'd just recovered from pneumonia. The people I did not want to see in the shot were Leon and his sons. They kept drifting into view of the cameras while we were trying to shoot, and I was happy when his boys finally got bored and wandered off.

We met that evening with the leader of the minority dance troupe to discuss how we planned to shoot the next day. It turned out the dancers had no musicians and only worked with music playing from a cassette tape and a portable boom box. More concerning, they only had the one copy, so I couldn't even borrow the tape for the film. In this remote area there was no facility for making a copy of the cassette for our use except… I hated to do it but I saw no other solution, even though it was the absolute worst way to transfer the sound. In my hotel room I played the dancer's music cassette from their boom box while recording into our Nagra with a microphone placed near the speaker. I tried it at a bunch of different sound levels in an attempt to find the one with the least amount of distortion, but I knew it was going to have lousy sound quality no matter what. Even now I cringe at the thought. I couldn't even bring myself to admit to our sound crew back at the studio that this was all they were going to have to work with.

The next morning, we began setting up in a clearing among the rock formations. There was a large open area for the dancers, and we had a decent number of extras to watch their performance. But I questioned Bao for the second time about the ethnicity of the dancers themselves. The first time was the night we auditioned them. He checked with the troupe's leaders who gave Bao assurance that everyone was a member of a National Minority. We were supposedly representing the Yi people and I wanted to be certain we were on good legal grounds without asking for identity papers. There was no mistaking the young women I used the day before as extras because, more than their clothing, they had the facial structure and high cheekbones so distinctive of the locals in Yunnan. The dance troupe, on the other hand, could have been anyone in authentic costumes. I did not want to bring an issue home to the studio if I could help it.

I decided to move the China dolly set-up much farther away from them, where we could move the cameras between some of the rock formations and "discover" the dance troupe in the distance. Another reason was the poor quality of the sound I'd recorded. From this far back, the music would be appropriately low level. But the other reason was the ethnicity question. When I asked a third time, the troupe's leader hedged his bet. Sensing my concerns that they were really Han, he guaranteed that *most* of the dancers were Yi people. This late, I had no options other than to either go ahead as planned or scrap the whole shot, so I went ahead. I've learned it's better not to edit the film before I shoot it. We can always make that cut later.

We had some trouble with the shot: getting the dolly to run smoothly over the rough terrain, a playback that didn't work all that well, and not enough control over local tourists. They seemed to come at us over and through the rocks, like water seeking its own level. One of them was an obnoxious German tourist who seemed to be drunk and refused to get out of our shot. Someone on the crew wanted to take a swing at the guy. Okay, it was me – but I didn't. We simply needed a lot more security for traffic control. I also could have used security just for Leon's boys who also kept wandering into the shot again. It took a heated discussion to convince them to stay away.

On the way back to Kunming, we stopped at a guesthouse for a late lunch. I noticed one of the young women who served us was particularly beautiful, with true movie star looks. I wondered how she'd found herself working as wait staff in this remote backwater. Then she smiled and I saw she was missing one of her front teeth. In Hollywood there would be so many people willing to help her fix her smile, perhaps making an actress out of her. But she was going to remain stuck with whatever life she could make for herself in this remote roadside restaurant. I found that rather depressing.

The incident reminded me of a time when I was discussing the phrase, "You've got to stop to smell the roses," with Bao and Ding. They in turn related a Chinese legend about a handsome soldier who was traveling through a village but stopped when he fell in love with a young woman. He was ashamed of his short stature, so he never wanted reveal this by climbing down off his horse. She felt she was so unattractive that she hid her face behind a bouquet of peonies. Unable to overcome their fears, the two of them died in love and he was never able to smell the flowers.

Their version had a kind of O. Henry quality to it that I liked.

That night in town we heard constant fireworks as Lunar New Year was approaching. It sounded at times like the noise of battle from a small war. The smell of burned gunpowder drifted everywhere. Dinner was a less-than-spectacular can of beans, followed by a can of fruit cocktail in Guy's room. I was ready to pass out by 8 p.m.

When I woke up, I found myself lying on my bed in the same clothes from the day before. I skipped breakfast and had a make-peace lunch with Leon's boys. They were okay, just a handful for Leon. And me.

We flew back to Beijing, via Chengdu, in time for Chinese New Year's Eve. I bought some champagne to share with Leon, Joe, and Guy along with a bag of tortilla chips and a jar of salsa I'd carried with me from California. City buildings were all lit up again, like on National Day, but I didn't have the energy or inclination to go out to film them. The New Year was a Dog, all right.

After performing some kind of penance for his airport outburst, Zhang/John was allowed to rejoin Shen as our assistant location manager. Together, they arranged an early flight for us to Harbin. We left our hotel at 6:30, had breakfast at the airport, and arrived in Heilongjiang Province before 10 a.m., anxious to get started. Then we discovered our hotel rooms weren't ready. All of us had to share one room until 6 p.m. Despite checking the weather reports regularly, the long-forecast snow still hadn't shown up. But it was still terrifically cold, probably 10 below zero during the day – and we were also going to shoot at night. Joe had "winterized" the Circle-Vision cameras which basically meant removing any lubricants that might freeze up.

After a production meeting to go over details, I warned our crew not to order moose nose or bear paw from the hotel kitchens unless they wished to be haunted by those images forever. We noticed tomato soup listed on the menu which sounded like a welcoming comfort food. What arrived was a bowl of lukewarm clear broth. At the bottom of the bowl was one thin slice of tomato. Minutes later we were eating canned beef stew in Leon's room. Simple fare like that worked wonders on us so far from home.

The next day we wore our cold weather gear to go out to our first shooting location, the middle of the Songhua River. We walked around stiffly, like little kids in bulky snowsuits. I just wanted to re-create what I had observed on the survey: the cutting and hauling of large blocks of ice. We waited out on the frozen river for more than an hour for the requisite horse cart, but it turned out someone had sent it to the wrong location. I had also called for a handful of extras and helpers for the cutter, but they were still in their warm apartments. We were freezing our butts off standing around waiting for them. I looked over at Leon and he was all bundled up with a scarf around his face. A cigar poked out that he claimed helped him stay warm. I noticed he'd forgotten his Disney thermal boots and was wearing leather street shoes. The chill at 20 below must have sucked the energy right out of him, so I sent him to wait onshore in the minibus.

Eventually the pieces came together and we got our shot. They sent me fewer extras than I'd asked for which looked pretty skimpy on screen. I was forced to concentrate the few that I had into limited areas of focus, making a contrast between those who were closer or farther back, letting some screens display the vastness of the area. The openness of the Songhua River location meant our crew had a very long way to go to get our boxes of equipment and vehicles out of the shot. I was also breaking in a new assistant director. Ding had been replaced as one of my translators by a very attentive and ambitious young Chinese man named Tim. The reason we always needed two was because Leon would need one when he was away from the shoot, making arrangements for the next locale.

Later I went out on the streets of Harbin to grab some atmospheric single-camera shots. I gave Joe and Guy time off to keep warm and used China Joe, Leo, and Han as assistants. As we were grabbing random street material, I could see Han had a good eye for compositions. I let him set up some of the shots himself and I think he appreciated showing what he could do. After dinner, which avoided inedible regional delicacies, the whole crew went out to the festival grounds to meet with gaffers from the local TV station. They'd been asked to help illuminate the scene and we wanted to point out where they could set up their lights without being in our shot. This was shaping up to be a brutal test of both crews in unbearably cold working conditions.

Back at our overheated hotel, we used a common feature of all hotel rooms in China: a very large colorful thermos that the staff regularly kept filled with hot water. We were never very far away from these thermoses because the Chinese wanted them available for making tea. In our rooms they were more often used for making soup mixes or hot chocolate from home.

The next day we left for the ice-festival park midafternoon and were set up on the China dolly by 4 p.m. Guy and his crew did a great job leveling out the tracks on the frozen, uneven surface. The temperature had dropped to 30 below while we were getting ready. Running cable was a real challenge for the gaffers in that frigid weather. If we'd known how inadequate their local lights were going to be, we would have brought along our Lowel light kit to at least add to the exposure. As it was, I had to shoot a couple of takes with the cameras running at half speed, down to 12 frames per second, in order to gain an extra f/stop of light. The slower speed was also helpful in keeping the brittle film from breaking, which would have been a disaster. We had not brought along any of the higher-rated Fujifilm so ended up shooting Kodak 5247, pushed one stop. By the end Joe was pretty testy, but no one could blame him. He had to constantly take off his gloves to adjust lenses or clean mirrors.

The background fireworks I'd asked for arrived just as we were packing up our equipment. A few of us later went to the river to shoot them off out over the ice. A giant slide had been set up on the shore, probably 50 feet high. We skidded down on our backsides at a pretty high speed, then spun to a stop far out onto the river ice. The crew was generally getting along well, despite the hardship of this location, and we played a big game of cards late into the night. Tim decided that a better translation of "Up and Up" should be "Escalation."

We'd always planned that after the bitter cold of Harbin we'd go south to enjoy more reasonable temperatures. Our first stop was Beijing, the hub of all travel, then we connected to subtropical Guangzhou. The city, still called Canton by some, seemed like China's mini-version of Hong Kong or even Las Vegas with lots of garish decorations and jazzy lighting, and big hotels with buffet spreads. For foreign businessmen, the city was set up to be a kind of Western fantasyland. Many of the visitors who came for industrial conventions and international markets probably thought Guangzhou was representative of the rest of China, but in those days the city was a remarkable exception, an isolated region where the central government was willing to turn a blind eye to its excesses.

Hainan Island, our real destination and the most southern point in China, was by comparison a cultural and social backwater. Many of the streets were unpaved dirt. Buildings showed the deterioration and cement streaking typical of the tropics. There wasn't a hotel anywhere on the island that measured up to minimum Western standards, despite the lure of a tropical climate with relatively pristine beaches. We ended up staying in a shabby concrete block building with mosquito nets over the beds, and the most uninspired, bland cuisine. It was a shame because the local waters provided abundant seafood, including mammoth "shrimp" that were more like small lobsters.

The trip to our remote location was hair-raising, not because of the terrible conditions of the roads or the suicidal tendencies of the driver (like the one who seemed out to kill me in Tibet). This time the problem was a vehicle with the driver on the wrong side. Our Japanese-built minibus was right-hand drive, not left-hand like all other vehicles. I usually rode shotgun because that was how I spotted the many of the elements of daily life that later made their way into our production. But on this drive, that put me on the left side of the minibus, facing oncoming traffic.

There were two basic rules of the road in China: first, pass anyone who gets in your way. Second, everyone is in your way. When our driver would attempt to go around a slow-moving truck, he'd start to pull out and I could see up the road while his view was still blocked. He was effectively blind to oncoming cars, trucks, buses. I'd frantically wave him back into our lane to avoid a collision. Then he'd slowly pull out again in order to give me a look up the road. I'd either give him a cautious go-ahead to pass or signal him to dive back to safety. This silent gamble with death continued for the better part of a couple of hours until the two of us, working in tandem, reached our location at the county seat.

We had to take a boat across a bay in order to reach the end of a peninsula, passing a naval base. I wanted to film a tropical sunset among the palm trees overlooking the sea, but we stopped filming whenever armed torpedo gunboats passed within view. We wondered how in the world was this not a "strategic" area? In those days there was an actual shooting war going on between China and her sworn enemy, Vietnam. Yet no one told us (not even Lao Tan) that we couldn't film. I stopped simply because I didn't want the military in the shot. I couldn't believe how far we'd progressed with the Chinese authorities who'd once forbidden us from even traveling to entire provinces that had a military base.

With our sunset shot wrapped, we were done filming until the spring, but first we had to get home. The after-dark drive to our one-star hotel was equally thrilling for another reason that was unique to driving in China. Besides a tendency to drift to the middle of the road to straddle the center line when traffic is clear, there was another habit of drivers that drove us crazy. At night they drove with their lights off. To see the road, we were reliant on infrequent and dim streetlights and there were none of those in the countryside. That meant we'd be driving down the middle of a two-lane road at a pretty good speed with no lights at all. This madness was topped by one other habit. When a driver saw the vague shape of a car or truck approaching in the darkness, at the last moment they'd flash their lights on while swerving to the side! As soon as they passed, they'd immediately turn off the lights again, both drivers now temporarily blinded, drifting back to the middle. As strange and dangerous as this practice seemed, being a driver was an honored and unique profession in China. These behaviors were not questioned by Chinese passengers because, as far as they knew, that's just what drivers *did*. The only explanation I ever got was that they thought they were saving the car's battery. Lao Tan and Bao found it equally hard to believe that everyone drives their own cars in America.

Soon enough we were going to be home again, driving our cars at night. With the lights on. Staying in our lanes.

Bao, Kathy, and Du Ming Xin in Burbank, CA

Han completes aerial photography

Shanhaiguan's main gate, "First Pass Under Heaven"

Remnants of the Great Wall

Shanhai Pass

Old Dragon's Head

The town of Shanhaiguan

A Forbidden City courtyard

Forbidden City details

The Hall of Supreme Harmony

CHAPTER 23

The Dragon's Head

During the months we'd had off in the winter of 1982, I'd been asked by WED to work on another Circle-Vision project: "The Eternal Sea," for the opening of Tokyo Disneyland (TDL). The completion of one film and preproduction of the other overlapped, causing occasional interferences in scheduling. It also meant I was always hearing two clocks ticking.

One of the most important elements of "Wonders of China" was going to be the film's score. By now I'd had a chance to interview a few composers in China as well as in Hollywood. I was looking for someone who could create a balance between what would appeal to Western ears and what would still feel authentically Chinese. That meant embracing the huge tonal differences in musical styles as well as very different instrumentation. I already knew the cacophony of Peking Opera's bells and gongs (let alone the screeching wails of its classical singers) could only be tolerated by Western audiences for a very short scene. I'd already experienced several operas and eventually learned to appreciate the difficult phrasing and sustained notes, but it was not going to be everyone's cup of jasmine tea. I'd collected several records of Chinese music, including examples of the different styles of the various National Minorities that would be appropriate for the film's many regions. The idea was to use the material as a reference point for discussions.

I consulted with Buddy Baker, head of Disney's Music Department, and we settled on Du Ming Xin, a composer in Beijing who'd written several scores for Chinese films. His films had the balance we were looking for and we made arrangements for him to come to the States for talks. China Co-Film arranged to send Du for a visit in March, along with Bao as his translator at my insistence. Neither of them had ever been outside of China so I flew up to meet their plane when they arrived in San Francisco. I accompanied them down to Los Angeles and they stayed in a hotel in Burbank, not far from the studio.

We quickly discovered that they'd been sent by China Co-Film with exactly $15 in their pockets to cover expenses for the better part of a week. Total. For *both* of them. That might have been an exceedingly generous amount in China, but it wasn't going to last through their first meal. I informed Bob Gibeaut and he subsequently reimbursed Kathy and I after we'd covered all their expenses. For the record, none of our receipts had footprints on them.

Kathy was their personal driver, shuttling Du and Bao around to famous sights like the LA Zoo and even Forest Lawn Mortuary. I joined them on a trip to Disneyland to get their first sense of what a theme park experience is like. Of course, we viewed "America the Beautiful." I watched Bao's face as he reacted to the 360 film. Suddenly what we'd been doing on location with the big cameras made sense to him. From this moment on he became a great spokesperson for our project and I only wish we could have shared what we were doing earlier. We capped off a great day with a meal, arranged by the studio, at Club 33. No doubt this very exclusive and private club was not appreciated by our Chinese friends nearly as much as by Kathy and me.

Another day, I took Du and Bao over to WED where we could show off scale models of EPCOT. They were particularly impressed with the miniature of the China Pavilion and its theater entrance fashioned after Beijing's Hall of Prayer for Good Harvests. We also toured Disney Studios where they met Dennis Orcutt. My editor showed them what we had assembled so far of the film on the interlocked KEMs and Du wanted to see it several times, scribbling notes. I could tell he was already motivated, as if he were already hearing imaginary music in his head.

Then we gave him a chance to hear real music. I walked them across the lot to the scoring stage where they were welcomed by the ever-gracious Buddy Baker. A true Disney legend, Buddy invited them in to witness a music recording session that I think was the highlight of the trip for Du Ming Xin.

We sat around for a half-hour on the recording stage, empty music stands and chairs filling the area. Du grew worried that the musicians were not going to be on time. About ten minutes before we were scheduled to begin, studio musicians began to trickle in one by one and take their seats. They opened their cases, took out their instruments, and then chatted quietly, some read newspapers, some ate donuts. They could not have been more casual or blasé. When Buddy took to the podium at the top of the hour, everyone suddenly became alert. The musicians picked up their instruments and the concertmaster led them in tuning. Right at the appointed hour, Buddy gave the downbeat and they began playing. Du couldn't believe how thoroughly professional they were. After the first tracks were laid down, he wanted to know how much rehearsal time they'd been given. When Buddy said this was the first time they'd even seen the sheet music, Du couldn't believe it. No one gets to play in a studio session without being an excellent sight-reader. Du said Chinese orchestras have to rehearse for many weeks to be this proficient and he didn't know any who could sight-read this well. The experience was as amazing to him as all the wondrous dreams of EPCOT.

I'd just come from touring the TDL construction site when Kathy and I met up with Joe and Guy on the flight from Narita to Beijing. It was the first of April and our spring shoot was about to begin. China Co-Film had extended invitations to the American crew's wives so that they could accompany us on this last leg. Gloria Nash, Ginny Jones, and Edna Chooluck were finally going to see the China they'd heard so much about.

One of my first stops was at a music conservatory where Du Ming Xin was already working on the score. He played some lovely themes for me on a piano and I could tell he had been inspired. Whatever that trip to America had cost had been worth it because he was going to reach for new heights in his composing.

When I rejoined my crew, one of our first tasks was to check out the helicopter landing sites near the Great Wall. We had to make sure there'd been no further snags with cooperation and the location. The new site was now only fifty yards from the PLA's previous selection. Spring weather turned out better than the last time we thought we were ready to shoot. I met with the CAAC crew and learned further restrictions had been placed on which parts of the wall they could overfly. Han, our aerial cameraman, remained confident, but I'm not sure why.

I also rechecked our proposed filming locations inside the Forbidden City with Shen. Unfortunately, one spot would have to be changed because of yet another restoration project in the vicinity. More bamboo scaffolding. But the Forbidden City offers so many angles and opportunities within its various halls and palaces that a substitute was easily found.

The next day was the start of aerial photography. We caravanned out to the wall and by 9:30 we were beginning to set up. Joe needed a clear area for prepping the cameras relatively close to the landing platforms. That meant the helicopter couldn't just fly in and land. The rig has to be secured, mirrors covered, all the open boxes shut because of the whirlwind of dust and debris. One problem we discovered was the video camera, which worked so well in the garage that morning, just died. We couldn't get it working again and this was my lifeline, the only record to tell me what Han and the pilot were shooting. Guy, who always finds ways to solve problems, stepped up and offered us his own personal video camera. This was a VHS recorder, the size of a large briefcase, with a thick umbilical cord to the clunky video camera. Guy grabbed some gaffer tape and somehow wedged all this equipment into the helicopter mount so at least I had some kind of eye for the shooting. I told him his personal home movies flying over the Great Wall might be valuable someday.

I sent the helicopter up a number of times and at least we didn't suffer the same bug problems as we had down in subtropical Guilin. After a reload and a lunch on location, I sent the crew back up again. They were strictly following the limits that had been imposed by the military. We eventually got what I thought looked like a couple of good passes towards the end of the day. That night I reviewed the video footage in Guy's room. It seemed to me this was as good as it was going to get.

We traveled by train the next day to the far eastern end of the Great Wall at Shanhaiguan. I wondered if we'd be able to find the precise spot on the sandy beach that had been preauthorized by the military. Our crew and their wives were in good spirits, but I think that was mainly because I'd asked Leon and Edna to remain back in Beijing and not make the trip. Leon jumped at my "suggestion" and planned to show Edna the town.

During the seven-hour ride, our train passed the town of Tangshan. All we could see were a few smokestacks that poked above a high brick wall that blocked views of the town. Tangshan had been devastated by a massive 7.8 earthquake in 1976 that killed over 240,000 people. The industrial city of one million had been mainly made of unreinforced brick buildings because no one knew it was sitting on top of a major fault. The city was literally and figuratively sleeping when the quake hit. The reports of the toll and the devastation, not to mention any plans for rebuilding, were kept as state secrets but rumors were rampant. I think if the government hadn't hastily erected that cosmetic brick wall along the railroad tracks, there would have been more of a public outcry. News photos I've seen of the leveled city reminded me of the devastation of Hiroshima.

Our hotel in the nearby town of Beidaihe was quite a decent resort. This area was famous as a vacation spa for dignitaries and high-ranking politicians in government. Not far away was Qingdao, the city made famous by its German brewery.

After a western-style breakfast, we were off to the end of the wall where it juts into the Bohai Sea. Some on the crew were a little disappointed that the view wasn't more impressive. I thought it was going to work well within the planned montage: three screens each of the dragon's head at the sea, the middle at Badaling, and the dragon's tail lying far away in the desert. In order to make the image of the head fit in with the other two, I planned to later flip the screen direction, as if we had filmed from the southern side of the wall.

Considering we only needed a three-camera shot at this end of the Great Wall, the locale had been problematic from the start. While setting up the cameras for the shot, I told the crew what we'd gone through to get this approved. Lao Tan said he'd had to make eight subsequent trips here to secure final permissions from the military. I recall the look on Guy's face that said he wouldn't trade jobs with me for all the tea in…

Lao Tan was very involved, as expected, in our precise camera placement. He was under the watchful eyes of uniformed PLA soldiers who hovered nearby, checking the checker. The military were quite curious about our camera system, much more than the typical man on the street. They stayed close until we had to hustle them out of the shot. I wasn't sorry to finally wrap at that location.

After the train trip back to Beijing, we found that the city was in the midst of a dust storm that had blown up out of the desert. We were told the dust could be expected every afternoon and I wondered how it would affect our shooting.

The next morning, we loaded our truck which was too large to enter the Forbidden City directly through the Gate of Heavenly Peace. The vehicle had to come in the back way and then negotiate many turns and alleyways to come out near our first location, the Hall of Supreme Harmony. A vast courtyard surrounds the palace with a layout of rigid symmetry, but I'd chosen a camera position away from the central axis on the eastern side. I wanted to use some close foreground elements, but I also needed to block the low morning sun with a wall that would be at our backs. We only had a handful of extras, but I used them fairly close to camera. I wasn't worried about tourists off in the distance or groups of very young school kids strung together with rope. One of our extras was a "visitor to the set" from China Co-Film. Mister Li was their company accountant, an uptight character whose personal style was as rigid as any in a Dickens novel. I placed him in the mid-ground, far enough away from the cameras that he wouldn't get into trouble but close enough that the Chinese crew thought the sight of Mister Li walking alone through the courtyard hilarious for some reason. We set up efficiently on the China dolly and finished the first shot by 9:30 a.m., a record for us. I felt we were once again clicking as a team.

During our filming in the Forbidden City I heard the odd sounds of a strange whistle. The haunting notes seemed far away, yet they moved about on the wind, coming from different directions but I couldn't pin it down. Some on the crew could hear the high-pitched sounds, others thought we were crazy.

We found out later they were pigeon whistles, small devices made of bamboo that dated back to at least the Qing dynasty. Bird owners attached them to tail feathers to ward off predators. I thought they added another layer to the unique atmosphere of these majestic grounds.

Our second location wasn't going to be available to us until after lunch, but by then the dust storms had started drifting in, depositing a very fine grit over the city. I tried shooting with the single-camera Arriflex to capture some of the intricate architectural details of the palaces and halls, but even that became problematic when dust affected the light. We'd have to try again the next day.

I was able to shoot more architectural details in the Forbidden City in the early morning while Guy and Joe set up the full rig on the China dolly at the Hall of Central Harmony. We filmed that shot before the dust moved in. The extras were manageable, the lighting was pretty good, and Leon only ruined one take by walking into the shot. I think we had more Circle-Vision footage of Leon than we did of Li Po.

My problems with him going rogue as "producer" flared again. Leon arranged another private meeting, this time with Madame Li of China Co-Film, and he hadn't bothered to inform me. I contacted Sally, David Hayden's assistant in Beijing, and she said she understood this had been planned for some time. I suspected Leon set this meeting up during our last banquet with Madame Li, again to promote the idea of films that Leon would produce using his impressive Hollywood Rolodex. He liked to throw around big names and he'd even promised me a meeting with Frank Capra Jr. when we got back.

I telexed Bob to keep the studio in the loop. We agreed that, for better or worse, we were stuck with Leon for the duration.

The Great Wall, western terminus

Kathy at the wall's end

Jiayuguan, "The First and Greatest Pass Under Heaven"

Weathered pillars

A roof detail

Brick repair

Fort entrance

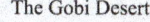
Leon's ride

The Gobi Desert

Caravan, take two

Caravan, take one

Lunch in the desert

Circle-Vision set-up on China dolly

Jade leftovers

Breaking jade on the factory grounds

A wooden threshold

The Ming Tombs entrance

Ancient trees

The "Avenue of the Animals"

Filming single-camera with Shen

Chapter 24

The Dragon's Tail

After a confrontation with Leon about his no-longer secret meeting, the crew and their wives flew on a charter flight from Beijing to Xi'an and then, after refueling, on to Lanzhou, the capital of Gansu Province. Lanzhou was supposedly another fabled hub on the Silk Road but, in reality, it was just an undistinguished industrial town on the shores of the Yellow River surrounded by desert. The city had been fought over for centuries by various dynasties, but the reasons why it was so important were not apparent to the casual visitor. Lanzhou was subject to fierce seasonal flooding and some of the worst pollution in China. The air from factories and Gobi dust storms was thick enough to blank out the mountain just south of town. This spot certainly wasn't the kind of place to show off to our wives.

Leon was in a foul mood, for various reasons including the fact that I'd pointed out he'd forgotten his little stove on which we'd grown so dependent. We were also concerned that our charter flight was stuck in Lanzhou, no doubt because of more damned dust storms. Lao Tan told us we'd have to stay over one night, and I already knew from the survey that the food was terrible.

Our hotel room was really awful, like an Albanian dorm room, but with ubiquitous white doilies on the stuffed furniture. The overhead light worked with a dangling pull cord, we had a wash basin on a stand behind the door, thin towels draped over a wooden rod. I found a cheesy bathrobe, the kind unlikely to be stolen as a souvenir. The room was so cold that Kathy and I slept in our clothes under two comforters.

Leon's bad mood continued the next morning, which was uncharacteristic for him. He usually had the ability to start each day fresh, as if he'd mentally wiped the slate clean during the night. At breakfast, we had some decent news for a change: our charter flight was allowed to proceed to Jiayuguan.

We landed in the desert outpost and were taken by minibus to our hotel. It turned out to be the same spartan accommodations we'd had on the survey with memorable communal toilets. Lao Tan announced that our permissions had come through for filming at the fort, but there were still doubts about going to the Gobi Desert locale. He claimed he was still working on the problem which seemed like he was cutting it close.

Jiayuguan is known as the "First and Greatest Pass Under Heaven," which is not to be confused with the "First Pass Under Heaven," used to describe Shanhaiguan at the other end. The supposed dragon's tail tumbles down out of the surrounding hills in broken sections of heavily compacted earth and mud brick. Crumbling edges had flaked off the wall, while chunks were completely missing in other areas. What's left of the Great Wall out in this province seems a mere echo of the finer structures around Beijing. It gives the impression it could wash away in a good flood.

The nearby frontier fortress was decorated with Chinese embellishments, but the colors had been abraded by the constant winds and harsh sun. Pillars look unfinished, as if made of untreated wood, like telephone poles but with faded murals. A wonderful legend says that when the structure was designed during the Ming dynasty, the architect was told he had to specify the exact number of bricks he needed. He said 99,999. When questioned if he was sure that was enough, he added one more brick to the total. When the fort was completed, according to the legend, there was one brick left over. Allegedly, it can still be found on top one of the two gates, but I never saw it.

We filmed a dolly shot up on the parapet of the fortress, using some of my crew as extras, including my translator Tim. That went smoothly and we got three good takes. We then hurried down to try to set up near the foot of the dirt wall for the final three-camera shot that would complete the wall montage, but the light had faded by that time. The wives, and Leon, killed time riding on rental camels that were available for the few tourists who came out this far.

That night Lao Tan gave me some bad news: the Public Security Bureau had said we couldn't go on to our next location, the sand dunes of the Gobi. The PSB is in some ways more powerful than the People's Liberation Army. Our production already had an all-clear authorization from the highest levels in Beijing as well as from our local officials in Jiayuguan. Apparently, we lacked the necessary paperwork from the provincial authorities back in Lanzhou. In effect, we were being hung up by the middlemen. Lao Tan confided that the central issue was that to get to the Gobi Desert locale we would have to drive past a super-secret military base. There was no other route, so we had to wait for the papers to come through.

Our group visited a factory where they made wineglasses out of the local jade. The stemware was ground so thin they became translucent. Kathy and I bought a set. We found the manufacturing process fascinating: machines very slowly core through a chunk of jade which looks unremarkable until it's highly polished. A rock the size of a basketball might make a half-dozen cores, but when they were done with it the workers tossed the remainder away. Outside the factory building we saw an enormous pile of these cored and discarded rocks. Perhaps they were useless to a factory that only made stemware, but these leftovers with their distinctive two-inch holes were still *jade*, weren't they? Each rock weighed about 30 or 40 pounds and we all came to a conclusion about the same time: that's a lot of jade just lying around on the trash heap.

What a sight we Westerners must have been as we picked up these heavy chunks and crashed them onto the pile in hopes they'd break up into smaller pieces we could take back to the States. The Chinese just laughed at us – until they got in on the act. Everyone was trying to smash off a fragment. In the end, the only jade that made it home was the set of wineglasses we'd bought.

That afternoon the crew returned to the foot of the earthen wall to reshoot the last segment of the Great Wall montage. We had to wait a few hours for better light on the dragon's tail, but it was worth the wait. We received official word that evening that our papers had come through, meaning we were good to proceed the next day. No one was more relieved than Lao Tan because he'd supposedly arranged these details long ago. He was laying down railroad tracks just ahead of the onrushing train.

We were going to have at least two more nights in our local hotel and were slowly being driven mad by the PA system outside. It broadcast the "The Internationale" over speakers starting at 6:30 in the morning, followed by ninety minutes of a high-strung, nasal-voiced woman reading the news. Then they played Peking Opera selections and local music. In the evening, it started all over again. Even our Chinese crew wanted to move on as soon as possible.

By 7:30 the next morning, I was in a Beijing Jeep-o with Lao Tan, Tim, and a local man headed towards the Gobi Desert. As we approached the supposedly secret base, a couple of Chinese MiGs flew very low right over us following the road. By this time I felt I could joke freely with Lao Tan. I told him, through Tim's translation, "Wait, I have to go back. I forgot my CIA notebook."

Lao Tan got a big laugh out of that, but the local man didn't.

It took a couple of hours to reach the end of the road. Then we four-wheeled the last 20 kilometers over rolling hills which had less and less scrub and more and more sand. When we could go no farther in the vehicle, we hiked about

200 yards to the top of a massive dune. From there the vista of undulating sand dunes reached like ocean waves towards the snow-capped Taishan Mountains in the distance.

Our equipment truck drove as close as it could, then we transferred our many boxes onto the camels we'd hired to be in the shot. They lumbered their way up to the top of the dune where I wanted to set up the Circle-Vision rig on the China dolly. Guy used stacks of split bamboo to make a bed for the dolly which distributed its weight out over the sand. By the time we were ready to shoot and had removed our cases out of sight down the dune, the area around us was a mess of footprints. I'd brought along a broom from the hotel and whisked away most of the markings, painting myself into a corner with Joe and Guy at camera. We did a take with the camel caravan slowly passing by us right to left and then disappearing over the edge of a dune. Among the camels was a baby that tagged along after its mother, a real Disney touch that I can't take credit for. The young camel came along as a package deal. After I called cut, I radioed to Tim that I needed the camels to return to their first positions. As they were coming back, I decided to film the string of camels going left to right as an alternate take.

After we'd returned the cameras to their cases, we had a box lunch sitting at the base of the dune in the shadow of our truck. It wasn't a very satisfying meal, as usual, but we were in no hurry to rush back to our crappy hotel just to hear the evening news on loudspeakers.

Our charter flight was scheduled to rescue us the next morning, but we found out it was delayed leaving Lanzhou by mechanical problems. As anxious as we all were to leave, my attitude about a delay like that is, "Please – take your time. Get it right." When that aircraft did arrive to get us out, it only meant we were going to spend another freezing night in the crummy airport hotel in Lanzhou.

Our flight was delayed the next morning due to even more engine problems. We finally made it as far as Xi'an before we had to stop for fuel. We were growing desperate to get back to Beijing as we hung out at the small local airport. This was a casually run airfield with no security, people just wandering in and out like it was a train station or bus terminal. After an hour the call came that our flight was finally ready, and we quickly boarded the plane. Then we just sat there. Several minutes went by and I thought it strange. Another engine problem? I looked out the window and saw our two Chinese camera assistants, China Joe and Leo, had wandered into a big field of wildflowers next to the runway. China Joe was snapping photos with his twin-lens reflex like he'd lost track of time. Lao Tan stood at the top of our plane's loading ramp and yelled at them. I think he used his Little Miss Pu voice. The young men came running through the flowers and up the steps. The rest of the Chinese crew ribbed them all the way back to Beijing.

We got back to the capital in time to find out the Temple of Heaven was now undergoing renovations that would delay our shoot. More damned bamboo. Shanghai couldn't be advanced on our schedule either, so what was left? We couldn't even shoot the travel shot at the Ming Tombs because the limousine wasn't available. I spent a couple of hours with Shih Kuan sorting out the mess and coming up with some possible alternatives. During the meeting I received a message from Bob Gibeaut to call the studio right away. Communication by phone was very expensive compared to telex, so I knew it must be really important. Leon had already given me a report from the studio that the helicopter footage from the Great Wall aerials had been processed and looked "excellent," in his words. When I had Bob on the line, he said he was worried we'd changed our arrangements with the customs broker. He saw red and green flashes on the edges of some of our dailies which might indicate the film had been X-rayed by mistake. Well, which was it, Leon's excellent footage or Bob's ruined footage?

Despite the somber mood, I passed out gifts to the crew: red-white-and-blue baseball-style caps that I'd had made with a cartoon image of Li Po. The slogan surrounding the logo was *"Mei Guan Xi,"* the most common expression we heard during the shoot. It meant "Don't worry about it" or "It's not important," or perhaps the Australian "No worries!" Even Joe and Guy, who claimed not to speak a word of Chinese, found it handy. When I left MacGillivray-Freeman as an independent filmmaker, that's what I named my corporation. My business cards for Mei Guan Xi Inc. never fail to get a smile or a laugh out of Chinese clients.

I was still trying to find options for filming the Ming Tombs, but it was proving difficult. The necropolis of several Ming Emperors is found at the end of a seven-kilometer road called the "Sacred Way" because legend says it leads to Heaven. The road was forbidden to all except the Emperor's funeral cortege. It is lined with 36 large stone statues, 24 of which were animals such as lions, camels, elephants, unicorns, and horses. Some standing, some kneeling, all have symbolic significance. The other 12 statues were of noted people, such as a famous general, civil officials, and others of merit. This long double row of carved stone statues was often called the "Avenue of the Animals." Unfortunately, whatever its name, it didn't fit into a good Circle-Vision shot because the statues were too far apart. The road at that time was in bad shape so we couldn't do a driving shot, even if we'd had the limo convertible. I had no option left except to film the statues individually using the Arriflex. I planned to assemble them into some kind of nine-screen montage later. At least each of them got the big close-ups they deserved.

When we'd returned to the hotel, I called the studio to learn they were now backtracking from their earlier concerns about X-ray fogging. There may have been some light leaks when loading the magazines, but not into the picture area of the negatives. *Mei guan xi!* However, Dennis informed me that much of the calligraphy needed to be reshot with better lighting. I was thinking it'd be a pain to do again and how was I going to find time to fit the reshoot into our schedule.

We were fast running out of shooting days.

CHAPTER 25

BEYOND THE BUND

On Saturday, April 17, I left my crew behind and traveled First Class on a CAAC jumbo jet to Shanghai. China might have only just acquired their first 747 to enter the modern era, but I noticed they were still reliant on serving champagne with a Russian label.

The city was a sprawling mess. Even the Shanghainese would admit that. Historically this metropolis was ground zero for invasions, civil unrest, and foreign influence. The biggest scar left by the interference of other nations was also the city's great pride: the Bund. This waterfront along the Huangpu River was dominated by stolid, neoclassical buildings that housed banks, trade associations, and mercantile exchanges, built by Westerners. Just a block or two beyond the Bund, the city's chaotic streets and crowded back alleys were a different world, but one that I found vibrant with daily life. The waterfront seemed more stodgy museum while the rest of the city had the heartbeat.

The British East India Company had been in Shanghai for over 100 years, dating back to the Opium Wars. White Russians fleeing the 1917 revolution found their way here, taking jobs other Europeans would not. The Treaty of Nanjing opened the floodgates to exploitation by French, German, and eventually American interests. They formed their own "concessions" where they weren't subject to local Chinese laws. The Japanese would leave their own indelible wounds on Shanghai and its people during WWII. The International Settlement put up buildings and parks reserved exclusively for foreigners where the myth began about signs supposedly reading: "No Dogs or Chinamen." Of the ten park regulations that were actually posted, #1 read: "The Gardens are reserved for the Foreign Community." Then #4 stated: "Dogs and bicycles are not admitted." The settlements ended with the Japanese invasion right after Pearl Harbor.

The city continued to have a split personality. Shanghai was a major trade port, making it stronger economically than Beijing, but the city had to remain subservient to the capital because it was directly administered by the central government. The local accent was strong and not always looked on kindly by Beijing's leaders who insisted their Mandarin was the only acceptable way to speak in government. The Shanghainese liked to think of themselves as more forward-thinking in fashion and culture. "Shanghai girls" was perhaps a pejorative in Beijing but it meant cool, stylish, and hipster and was embraced by local teens, even in the time of common Mao jackets.

The weather was overcast and drizzly as Shen and I walked the Bund looking for a new location along the waterfront. Our local contacts had rejected my first choice without ever saying why, reminding me of that distant PLA logo in Lhasa that had to be hidden. Checking a map of the city I noticed a prominent pier that belonged to the Chinese Navy. Well, if that isn't "strategic," I don't know what is. The information at least gave me the coordinates of the area I'd need to keep from being photographed.

At one time we'd considered filming a shot from a junk in the middle of the Huangpu River. You could throw a rock into the Huangpu and would likely hit a passing junk, but Lao Tan could only come up with a 70-meter cruiser. Yikes! Our last remaining option to film the classic old European-style buildings was going to be a travel shot down the main thoroughfare. Shen set to work getting permissions.

I called Leon in Beijing to check in. He reported that the Forbidden City footage looked good, according to Bob. I had to inform him I wasn't making much progress with the local Shanghai authorities who seem inclined to argue about everything. They'd probably prefer we just go away and didn't represent their city in the film. I wondered if this was part of the general Beijing-Shanghai rift.

I continued walking along the Bund with the local police to designate which areas would be seen in a travel shot. I thought it was pretty clear the cameras could see 360 degrees, but they wanted it spelled out for them specifically, as if they couldn't quite imagine what I was proposing. Then I threw them and Lao Tan a curve.

Back at the Peace Hotel I'd seen a rooftop terrace that wasn't being used. The view from up there showed much of the waterfront and skyline of Shanghai to the west and conveniently faced away from the naval dock. The off-limits pier would be blocked from view by the hotel itself. What if we shoot from the ninth floor of the Peace Hotel? My idea was to turn the open terrace into a fancy restaurant for one night. Lao Tan seemed willing to exchange the rooftop for the more troublesome Huangpu boat shot and set about convincing the locals.

Meanwhile I toured the backstreets of Shanghai through various old quarters with our hosts to pin down areas where I could shoot single-camera details. Again, the authorities resisted most of my suggestions, trying to limit my options. Everywhere I looked were wonderful scenes of life: young boys marching in file wearing the red scarves of Young Pioneers; laundry hanging to dry on shafts of bamboo in the cramped, narrow streets; rooftops cluttered with potted plants and herb gardens; and old gray-haired men kibitzing or slapping down Mahjong tiles on a board resting on their knees. On nearby streets I saw a 16-story building that was completely covered in bamboo scaffolding, top to bottom. Police manned elevated yellow stations in the middle of intersections to direct traffic with hand signals. Along the city's tributaries of the Huangpu, barges were tied up sometimes four abreast. In a public square, a hundred citizens performed tai chi exercises in hypnotic synchronization. I found these details fascinating but had to convince authorities that we wanted to embrace them in the film.

That evening the rest of the crew and their wives flew in. I treated myself to a T-bone steak in the hotel dining room which I felt I'd earned.

The next morning before breakfast, we tried filming the travel shot along the Bund's historic riverfront. We had access to another Red Flag limousine. The hefty vehicle gave us confidence that its boat-like ride would smooth out the bumpy old pavement. As we were rolling cameras during the shot, our driver suddenly accelerated, and we found ourselves zooming along the busy street dodging pedestrians and bicycles. I was ineffectively shouting *"Màn man de!"* (slowly), but maybe this time it was my Mandarin accent he reacted to. In any case, Tim straightened him out for takes two and three. These took place in overcast light, but I thought this acceptable under the circumstances. I was more concerned about our driver breaking traffic laws.

One more area of concern came up when the police tried to stop us from using our walkie-talkies. We'd not had a hassle anywhere else in China because we had proper permissions *from Beijing*. But that was the problem: we were now in Shanghai where they had very different rules and attitudes. We left it to Shen and Lao Tan to put out the fires of political rivalry.

There were so many single-camera shots I wanted to include that we split up into two crews, each with an Arriflex. Joe operated one with Guy acting as director (while shooting behind the scenes with his video rig). Joe's biggest problem was when he tried to film a panda at the local zoo. The deep black and brilliant white animal gave him such wildly different light meter readings that he nearly freaked out. Meanwhile, Han and I filmed a pipa player in a park, and then two kids in a ping-pong match. I set it up as two opposing shots so that I could edit the ball bouncing across more than one screen. We also filmed old men playing Army Chess, a very popular strategy game. Despite the restrictions placed on me by my local minders, I was able to shoot in the old part of town until I ran out of light at sunset.

Rain poured all the next day. I checked on the preparations at the hotel for our rooftop terrace shot. I wasn't surprised to learn the area had actually been a restaurant at one time, many years ago. That night Leon tried to arrange a small dinner party for the American crew and their wives, but his plans grew into a full-on banquet. Guy just wasn't interested, especially if his presence wasn't required for diplomatic reasons, and he bailed out which left Leon upset. I later found Guy in the hotel's nightclub listening to the old musicians playing 1940s American standards.

The split crews shot more Arriflex footage the next day even though it was overcast and cold enough to see our breath. I shot subjects such as four old men playing checkers on the side of the road and some stylish "Shanghai girls" going shopping on Nanjing Road. As the sky started improving in the afternoon, I decided we should give the restaurant scene a try at sunset.

The hotel staff efficiently set up several tables with linen cloths. I'd also asked them for a number of large potted plants which we could use to hide roof air conditioning ducts. Our crew replaced the dim lights in the table lamps with brighter bulbs so we would be able to better see the faces of our diners. Twenty extras had been brought in, male and female, young and old, and they'd been told to dress for an elegant dinner. Not one Mao jacket in sight. I kept an eye to the west as the sun was dropping while Joe and Guy prepped the cameras with the help of China Joe and Leo. The idea of the shot was to slowly dolly among the diners towards the edge of the terrace where we'd be able to see down the length of the Bund.

I called for a quick rehearsal, which went well, and then I noticed the extras were not faking. They were wolfing down the hotel's best dishes and didn't stop when I called cut! I guess I'd forgotten what kind of limited diet these people were used to at home. We had to bring in a lot more food from the kitchen for actual takes. Through my translators, I told them to pace themselves until the finish, then they could take home any leftovers.

I thought we filmed two acceptable takes where the lights of the city matched the sunset as well as the table lamps. These kinds of shots require a tricky balance as the sky fades. We were also fighting exposure because opening up the lenses to let in more light shortened the depth of field needed to keep all the tables in focus.

The city was lit up, but not directly across from the Bund where there was only a dark muddy field. It was absolutely black on the other side of the Huangpu, except for the dim lights on a couple of billboards. I wanted to believe those signs were advertising the promise of the futuristic new world that was coming in less than 20 years… Ah, who am I kidding? Those old billboards were probably just reminders of the "One Child" policy or some faded political slogans.

Our own dinner that night came very late, was served cold, and mine had a long black hair in it, so the restaurant extras made out better than I did.

That night we packed up to leave for Suzhou and I wasn't sorry to leave the difficulties and problems of Shanghai behind.

Chapter 26

Suzhou Unrefined

We left in the early morning with Guy in a bad mood. Leon was still giving him a hard time about not joining us for his "banquet," the one no one else wanted.

We had pretty good weather on the one-hour ride to Suzhou. As we passed through farmland, areas of the roadway appeared to be covered with straw or hay. Right after we drove over the grain, the farmers would sweep or shovel the material back into the road. Then they'd wait for the next vehicle to do the same thing. We were told this was part of rice harvesting. The farmers were using the heavy cars and trucks to "thresh" the husks from the straw. After hearing that, Guy refused to eat any rice if he found the tiniest speck of black in his bowl, convinced it was tire tread.

Our hotel in Suzhou was rather civilized compared to so many we'd endured. We revisited the Fisherman's Garden in order to make sure nobody had just started construction, renovation, or some other bamboo-related disaster. I also wanted to check out the canal boat the locals had arranged. They proudly showed us a barge, probably one of the biggest on the canals. *Bu hao.* No good. As a result, we got the usual runaround from our local fixers when we tried to replace it. I had to repeat for the umpteenth time, through my translators, what we were looking for. Just walking along the canals, I spotted one the right size. A quick financial deal was made on the spot in *renminbi*. The owner was happy and I was happy.

We mounted the cameras in the front of the barge so we could cruise along the narrow canals and the boat would not be visible. However, in the back screens we'd see the small cabin and our driver. I asked for some fake cargo so that it looked like our barge was hauling a load. All we needed were a handful of empty cardboard boxes or some lumber in order to fill in the space near the cabin, not an entire boatload. The cameras didn't see but a foot or two below the cabin windows. My request set off a search throughout the city for cargo and it took quite a bit of wrangling by my crew to pull the locals back. We finally settled for a pile of bricks that was just sitting there beside the canal. We briefly "rented" them from a man repairing his wall.

Personal homes along the canal were a uniformly dirty white stucco with black tile roofs, typically only single story. The buildings backed up against the channel with stone steps leading down to a level where sometimes kids played, launching paper boats into the polluted waters. The walls of the canals were made of crude brick and concrete which was contrasted by the city's distinctive and rather elegant half-circle bridges and walkways. Traffic on the larger canals included "trains" in which a string of barges was towed by one boat with a motor. Other vessels looked similar to those we'd seen on the Li River. They were little more than rafts with a half-round woven rattan shell that served as living quarters, with cooking implements stacked on the foredeck.

Once we were set up, we did a few lengthy takes navigating through the canals, but then I decided to wait for more interesting light later in the day. After reloading the cameras, we were able to shoot a lovely sunset shot with the warm sky reflecting off the water. The darkness of the deep shadows helped hide some of the canal's unsavory details. Not a bad start, but there was one traumatic incident that would probably linger in the crew's memory for years.

During our canal travels we would occasionally pass long shallow barges coming the other way. Some of these wide, open boats carried a liquid the same color as the muddy river but with a horrific, pungent smell. Suzhou had no septic tanks or sewer systems, so these particular barges passed with regularity, loaded to the brim. The polite Chinese term for this cargo was "night soil" but essentially this was liquid human waste, effluent destined for sewage treatment. In the narrow confines of the smaller canals, with one boat giving way for another, the "cargo" would slosh up and over the gunwales and mix with canal water. Guy's video camera captured the horrific sight of this type of spillage – right next to the stairs of a cramped house where a little old lady was squatting down on the last stone step. She was preparing a meal, scrubbing and "cleaning" some raw pork in the river water, just as a ripple of sewage washed out of the barge. My stomach turned watching this so I can't imagine how Guy reacted. He had already been referring to this particular canal as "shit alley," but Joe, who was in many ways just as squeamish, wasn't bothered. Maybe it was because this kind of sight was already baked into Joe's views of China. Besides, he'd been dining pretty much exclusively on canned tuna over rice, so what did it matter to him? That night Guy and I didn't eat anything that hadn't been prepackaged in the States.

Far, far removed from the sights and smells of the canals was the peaceful world of Suzhou's Classical Gardens. Some of these have been around for a nearly a thousand years while others date to the Ming and Qing. They were mainly built by scholars looking for a personal retreat from their busy Suzhou court life in a beautiful setting that delicately simulated rocks, mountains, trees, and rivers. They wanted a metaphysical atmosphere of isolation from the rest of the world. The high white walls enclosed courtyards, corridors, foot bridges, pools, stone rockeries, carved brick gates, intricate carved wooden furniture, and stone tablets. Garden designers used techniques and craft to blend art, nature, and architecture into serene and aesthetic masterpieces. Windows and archways were used as framing devices for the bushes and plants that lay beyond. The same plants could be seen and framed from different angles, resulting in vastly different impressions. Roof lines of the walls and pagodas flowed like a carefully controlled composition while the reflecting ponds magnified the limited space. Every element had its symbolic value as well as contributing to a harmonious whole.

On the survey I'd selected the Master of the Nets Garden for a scene in which Li Po addresses the cameras. Shih Kuan, in full costume and make-up, looked very much like he belonged in this setting. I'd chosen a place for him in a six-sided pavilion called The Moon Comes with the Breeze. Other colorful names in this garden are the Beauty Within Reach Tower, Rosy Clouds Pool, Washing My Tassels in Water Pavilion, and the Hall of Ten Thousand Volumes library.

Master of the Nets, usually just called the Fisherman's Garden, was first constructed in 1140 during the Southern Song dynasty, but it had been destroyed and rebuilt through the years. It was restored with that time period's distinctive and exaggerated curving roof lines.

The gardens might have been designed as an escape, but we couldn't get away from our problems with local authorities. The park people decided, despite our protests, to let paying tourists in while we were shooting. As expected, they swarmed all over us. When Lao Tan tried to restore order and get them out again, the local police and the Public Security Bureau got into some sort of jurisdictional dispute, which didn't help the situation. I let the Chinese crew sort out the issues while we tried to focus on a more immediate problem.

When I'd scouted the location a year earlier, I'd used a tape measure to check doorway access for our hefty Circle-Vision cameras. I wanted very much to be able to dolly out from one of the halls to find Li Po in the pavilion. The problem was the ancient doorway (measured a dozen times) was exactly the same size as the camera rig's minimum width. I'd warned Guy about this in advance and he said he'd see what he could do on the day. I think he measured the opening as many times as I did. He laid out the China dolly to run through the doorway while we assembled the cameras inside. Then Guy slowly inched the rig forward to see if it could safely pass through. He realized that even a quarter of an inch more room might make the difference. There was no way to make the cameras any smaller, so Guy tried leaning on the carved wood of the doorway, as if he were doing an isometric exercise. He used his big size to see if he could stretch out the remaining fraction we needed. After a couple of attempts, our cameras were able to magically slide through the opening. *Just.* The effect of the final shot was wonderful as we glided effortlessly from inside to outside.

Filming Li Po with his dialogue required a soundman and the latest addition to the crew from Beijing proved professional enough. Li Po's words on camera would have to be replaced in postproduction because of camera noise, so I was only concerned we could hear his words well enough to record a sync guide track. The soundman lay hidden on the ground at Shih Kuan's feet which did the trick. The scene worked very well and created one of the warmest moments for his character in the film.

However, we didn't escape the gardens without an official reprimand about how we had "altered" the carved wooden doorway. The production was fined 200 yuan (about $25) which Leon paid on the spot. For all the times this garden had been destroyed and rebuilt through centuries of war and repression, I thought our quarter of an inch alteration was worth it.

Back in Shanghai, I went out with the Arriflex and grabbed a few more shots of European-style buildings, scenes of crowds, a circular police booth elevated above the traffic, and an old church that looked forlorn and forgotten. Meanwhile, our soundman recorded some very useful effects along the Bund. I wish we'd had him from the beginning.

For a change of pace, we took our Chinese crew to one of only two restaurants in Shanghai that served Western food. Hong Fang Zi Restaurant (literally "Red Party House") was established in 1935 when Louis Revere, a Jewish Italian with a French wife, first opened the doors of the red brick building. Revere had been imprisoned in a concentration camp during the war. When he got out, he sold the restaurant to a local Shanghainese man for less than $350. Lao Tan and Shen had never had Western food, unlike Bao who'd had his chance in Los Angeles, so there was great anticipation for them. I ordered the dishes, simple but hearty fare: pork chops and mashed potatoes with string beans. Unfortunately, all the food was served Chinese style. First came several plates of string beans. Later came a second course consisting of bowls of mashed potatoes. Naturally, we finished our meal with platters of pork chops. As much as we tried to explain this was *not* how to eat Western food, there were no complaints from the Chinese. They didn't want to embarrass us, I think.

The crew moved on with an hour's train ride to nearby Hangzhou. I'd planned to shoot an early morning scene along the beautiful West Lake with 120 tai chi exercisers. I'd been influenced by witnessing morning exercise in Shanghai, but this seemed like a better locale. As soon as we arrived, I learned my location had to change for a variety of reasons. That meant another quick survey along the lakefront for an alternative. The lake is divided by the narrow Su Dongpo causeway with six curved bridges for boat access to both sides. In this area I found a spot we could use near some willow trees. The local man who took me around seemed to be trying very hard to cooperate, unlike the resistance we faced in Shanghai.

We set up the Circle-Vision cameras on the China dolly in the late part of the day while there was still enough light for me to line up the shot. I needed to look through the viewfinder to be certain of the framing because when we came back predawn, it would initially be too dark to see. Joe and Guy covered the cameras in a weather-proof tarp, and we posted a couple of Chinese guards to stand watch overnight.

Needless to say, we had a *very* early call in order to be ready to film by sunrise. The crew hiked from the Hangzhou Hotel along the narrow strip of land and down a few hundred yards to our position. We were met by many of the tai chi extras who were already there and warming up. I gave them their final positions after watching their routines by flashlight. I picked a couple of likely "stars" and made sure they were closer to the cameras. By first light it was obvious the weather was not going to be great but at least there'd be no rain. By the time I had three good takes, there was about a two-stop difference in lighting from the brightening sky in the front screens to the shadowed background. We put the scene in the hands of Eastman Kodak and hoped we could balance the exposure in the final print.

After we returned to our hotel for a well-earned breakfast, we went out to do a travel shot along the West Lake. Guy had rigged the cameras on a local Beijing Jeep-o and did a little trick I hadn't seen before. He let quite a bit of air out of the tires so they were rather saggy. This balloon-like quality absorbed the bumps and made for a much smoother ride on the uneven pavement. Having raced in the harsh conditions of Baja, he knew what to do.

By the time we'd packed up and returned to Beijing, we thought we were on the home stretch. Unfortunately, Lao Tan and Shen informed us there was still bamboo scaffolding up at the Temple of Heaven. Completing the last scheduled Circle-Vision shot of the film would have to wait.

CHAPTER 27

A Great Poet Rewritten

While beginning to write the narration for the film, I altered and paraphrased several quotations from Li Po's poems to flesh out the script. I had been seeking particular word choices of his that might be appropriate even if taken out of context, such as describing the jagged landscape of Guilin as "scattered dragon's teeth." I didn't think of this as stealing from the great poet as much as asking him for his advice on how he'd describe modern China. I considered him my collaborator.

I thought it appropriate for Shih Kuan to read one final Li Po poem on camera to conclude the film. The only one that seemed worthy of the special moment was called "Taking Leave of a Friend." I found it in the book "The Works of Li Po, The Chinese Poet" translated by Shigeyoshi Obata.

Here's Obata's original translation of the entire poem:

> *Blue mountains lie beyond the north wall;*
> *Round the city's eastern side flows the white water.*
> *Here we part, friend, once forever.*
> *You go ten thousand miles, drifting away*
> *Like an unrooted water-grass.*
> *Oh, the floating clouds and the thoughts of a wanderer!*
> *Oh, the sunset and the longing of an old friend*
> *We ride away from each other, waving our hands,*
> *While our horses neigh softly, softly…*

When Shih Kuan and I met to go over the last scene, he brought along his collection of Li Po's poems written out in Chinese. He proudly showed me his own translation into English which wasn't bad at all. It would form the basis of our joint effort. But I'm a visual learner so what I needed was to be able to see the original Chinese, to go back to the real source. Chinese is not exclusively, as some think, pictograms, or even ideograms. Technically almost 95 percent of Chinese characters are "logical aggregates" or, more often, "phonetic complexes." On my travels I'd only learned to recognize a few of the more simplified characters, but as Shih Kuan broke the "words" down for me into their component parts, the process opened up a whole world.

Li Po's poems were written in a very formalized way, almost as rigid as a haiku. Understanding the true meaning required stringing the individual characters together in the mind, then doing a lot of interpreting. For example, one line of the poem contained five items: the sun, the direction for down, the character for departing or leaving, another representing emotion or feeling, and finally the symbol for friend. That's it! But an experienced reader of Chinese poetry might come away with: "The sunset lingers like the parting of a friend." This enormous leap in meaning and context from such simple characters was an inspiration to me as Shih Kuan and I did our own translation of the film's final poem. We agreed right away that, for Western audiences, it just wasn't going to be perceived as "poetry" if it didn't rhyme.

The script called for Li Po to say: "We are now at the Temple of Heaven, where we have come full circle. I wrote a poem many years ago; it's like this:

> *This is the place where we must sever.*
> *You go thousands of miles, my friend, once forever.*
> *Like the floating clouds, we drift apart,*
> *The sunset lingers like the feelings of my heart."*

At that point, the plan was to have the huge red doors behind him swing open. Li Po would magically fade away, returning to history as we revealed the real Hall of Prayer for Good Harvests beyond. The back panels would sequentially fade out until we're left with just this one final image of the hall directly over the theater's exits. I'd hoped the audience would immediately recognize that this was the same building Disney craftsmen lovingly re-created as the entrance to the theater, the "full circle" Li Po referred to.

But getting this final scene on film was one of the bigger struggles of the shoot. When I went out to the Temple of Heaven site to check on preparations, the local park manager, a petty bureaucrat at heart, figured we could do our crowd control with just park people. But the area we planned to shoot had several public access points. Experience told me that we'd need a dozen policemen. The manager's idea of a compromise was to suggest adding only two policemen. At that moment I realized he didn't have a clue. Despite our planning this shot for a year, the local man in charge still didn't understand the complexities of what we were shooting. A meeting with Lao Tan reminded him of our expectations from the Chinese side.

On April 29, we had our chance to film. The weather was a dreadful fog at first light, but I knew it would eventually lift. After we'd set the cameras for the final composition, we closed the big doors and did a few rehearsals. The "magic" would really just be two of our Chinese crew pulling the doors open with ropes when I cued them. Their speeds were different, and the action hardly looked majestic, so I put them to practicing under the supervision of one of my translator/assistant directors.

Meanwhile Shih Kuan was decked out in full make-up and costume, ready with our revised poem. The immediate problem was where he needed to stand: under a huge roof that left the actor in deep shadows. We could either film with an exposure for Li Po in low light, or for the temple in full sunlight when the doors opened. We couldn't do both in one shot. We'd have to balance the light on Shih Kuan and that meant we needed lights. Heavy-duty lights balanced for sunlight temperature. We'd anticipated this as far back as the survey, but the equipment brought from the Beijing Film Studios by China Co-Film was inadequate. By the time their lamps were filtered to match the daylight, there wasn't enough light to increase the exposure. We sent for our Lowel light kit which was simple, crude, but effective.

But even that wasn't enough to balance the light on the actor. Our only solution was to move the lights much closer, so close that the lighting units and stands were going to be right in the shot. I had originally planned the scene as a dolly shot, but I could see I needed to compromise. I changed the set-up to a lock-off, meaning the cameras wouldn't move at all. This one change would allow me to shoot the first part of the scene with Li Po, properly lit, and let him do as many takes as it took for him to say his lines right. We would film with all nine cameras, knowing eight of them would be no good because of the light stands. Once I was satisfied with his performance, we would then continue with the second part. This time we would remove all the lights and stands from the shot. Because the cameras weren't going to move, the footage would be combined back at the studio to make it appear to be all one take, the same way we did with the Potala zoom shot. This technique would also allow the soundman to get much closer to the actor, as long as his microphone stayed out of camera number one.

I filmed four or five takes of Shih Kuan. The timing with the doors opening was looking pretty good, but by then we were close to 5 p.m. I went ahead and shot again to create the matching background on the other eight cameras, which simply required clearing the frames of extraneous people and equipment. But this shot was the film's last key emotional moment, so I wanted a back-up.

Unfortunately, we were told we couldn't shoot the next day. With the May Day holiday coming up (again!), we wouldn't be able to return to this same location until May 3.

I'd been on my feet all day and wanted to go back to the hotel to collapse, but then I was told I needed to deliver a speech at an upcoming press conference. Did I have an advance copy of my remarks? What a laugh. Why don't you let me *write* it first?

The following day I filled in a lot of single-camera shots that had been on my list: close-ups of workers in an ivory-carving factory, a female construction worker building the Great Wall Hotel, a doctor examining X-rays in a hospital, close-ups of an acupuncture procedure, a traffic cop directing bicycles on the streets of Beijing. I had to skip dinner to get cleaned up for a lengthy evening at the Great Hall of the People featuring songs, ballet, and National Minority music. I was exhausted which didn't put me in the best mood to write an uplifting speech about filming in China.

The next day brought good news – for Joe and Guy. A new place had just opened up down Chang'an called the Jianguo Hotel. Compared to the old Peking Hotel, this was modern and had classy Hong Kong-trained service people who were responsive and reliable. Best of all, they featured an actual honest-to-God hamburger on the menu. Guy and Joe, who up until then had been reliant on our Chinese crew to get around the city, proved to be very enterprising. They had someone at the hotel desk write "take us to the Jianguo Hotel" on a card, then they showed it to a taxi driver out front. The other side of the card had the address of the Peking Hotel for their return. They ended up talking about the joys of that burger for days.

The formal announcement of our project to the press had to be coordinated by telex with Bob Gibeaut back in Burbank. He was adamant that I avoid getting too much into who did what on the film. It's been a longstanding tradition with Disney theme parks that their films never have credits on them, but this press conference might force the issue out into the open. What was I to do if a reporter specifically asked? I couldn't very well claim the information was secret or privileged or say I didn't know who wrote and directed.

The announcement at the Ministry of Culture went very well, certainly as far as I was concerned. Representatives for the Associated Press, UPI, and the *Los Angeles Times* attended, along with some foreign and local press. Michael Parks of the *Times* gave us a very detailed and accurate write-up as our hometown newspaper. Leon visibly choked when I introduced him as our American production manager. He'd been hoping, unreasonably perhaps, for more. One of the more interesting quotes in Parks' article must have occurred when I wasn't around:

"You can't stand behind the camera," said Leon Chooluck, *the veteran production*

manager Disney hired for this film. "Often you are squatting underneath and praying as you try once again on the eighth or ninth take that another peasant does not wander into frame."

The cameras didn't hold enough film to ever go anywhere near that many takes, of course. And Leon never squatted under the cameras. Plus, he was the one who occasionally wandered into frame, not some random peasant. Other than that, good quote.

High winds over the next couple of days threatened our second attempt at filming the Temple of Heaven. When we got the chance with good weather, we were well-practiced enough that the set-up went smoothly. It didn't take us long to get a few more good takes of Shih Kuan. We then spent the rest of the morning shooting the remaining background panels, but we had to film between heavy gusts of wind. We took a break and made a mad dash to the Jiaguo Hotel for burgers. After lunch the winds picked up again, but we squeezed out a few more good takes.

To top off a pretty good day, we received permission to film an elusive subject that had been off limits for our entire stay in China: the Empress Dowager's clocks.

Stored in an anteroom in the Forbidden City is a collection of elaborate and intricate timepieces that had been gifts to Empress Cixi from foreign dignitaries and kings and queens. They remained locked up and were not part of the regular public tour. When President Nixon made his famous trip, he'd specifically asked if he could see her clocks, so they showed him. But when he asked if he could see the fanciful creations *working*, he was turned down cold. We were going to do much better than Nixon as the museum officials were going to let me film them in their full animated glory.

During a historic time when women had little to no power, Cixi was the woman behind the throne, the Empress who rose from the low ranks of Imperial Consort to become a strong-willed 19th-century ruler of China as the Empress Dowager. Her skill set included political maneuvering, incarceration, and even assassination, but she was also a cultured artist as well as patron of the arts. Her tastes influenced the style of traditional Asian art for a century. The bejeweled clocks in her collection were larger and more elaborate than Fabergé eggs. Each was precision animated with moving, spinning, and twirling mechanisms. Playful, beautiful, and mesmerizing, they were as well-crafted as any timepiece made in Switzerland or Germany.

I set up the Arriflex on a tripod and used just a few lights to create a backdrop within the museum as a display. Curators of the collection brought out each piece and set them up one at a time, then wound them up and set them in motion. I shot a dozen clocks with the plan to choose the best nine.

Besides making the elements of a wondrous montage, it was a rare privilege just to be in the same room with these one-of-a-kind devices.

By comparison, filming an acrobat show the next night was pretty ho-hum. This kind of entertainment is found all over China, even in smaller towns, so by this time we must have seen a half-dozen such shows. The thrills had lost their thrill. China Co-Film arranged permission for me to put the Arriflex in the middle of a working theater and shoot during a real performance. It felt a little weird because there were lots of paying guests, some even seated directly behind me. I apologized by telling them I was sorry in Chinese and they responded with *"Mei guan xi, tóngzhì."*

That same evening, Madame Li hosted our final banquet. It was a pretty emotional moment for both American and Chinese sides. I remember Shih Kuan feeling rather sentimental about the project coming to an end. He said to me privately, "You have experienced so much of China, been everywhere, seen each province." Then, like a well-timed joke, he added, "Oh, we forgot to film in Taiwan!" Funny stuff, Shih Kuan.

I got pitifully drunk that night, going around the room toasting everyone again and have no recollection of how I got back to the hotel.

Unlike the last time this happened, the next day I had a massive hangover. I was sorry I didn't get to see off Guy and Ginny at the airport. When I was feeling human again, I met with Du Ming Xin and listened to his entire score for the film on piano. I made a simple recording in order to see how his music would work against the edited pictures. Even though we were the ones indebted to him, Du offered Kathy and me going-away gifts.

On May 7, the filming portion of "Wonders of China" was over. Joe and Gloria, Leon and Edna, and Kathy and I traveled out to the airport. The Chinese crew came along for goodbyes. Joe was in a terrific mood now that his work was finished. He didn't even seem to mind when customs wanted to go through everyone's bags. We parted ways in Japan. Joe and Gloria were headed home while I was just beginning a new survey for "The Eternal Sea" that would take us across the Pacific and more Circle-Vision adventures.

It would be weeks before I could get back to the studio to see just what kind of film we'd made.

Classical Chinese landscape paintings

Keye Luke, 1976

Keye Luke as "Number One Son" in "Charlie Chan on Broadway" with Warner Oland (1937)

1930s publicity photo

A publicity poster for the 1984 Disneyland premiere

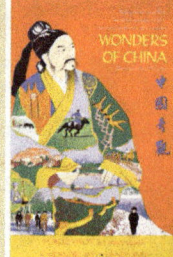

Wonders of China
中國奇觀

The main title artwork

CHAPTER 28

NUMBER ONE SON

Postproduction began in earnest once I returned to Burbank. Dennis Orcutt had completed an assembly of all our scenes in the general order of the script. Editing would be a continuing process of finessing every take, every cut, until the picture was locked and no further changes could be made. I continued to work on my drafts of the narration script which I was now seeing as a cultural and political minefield.

The regions of Xinjiang and Tibet, even then in the early 1980s, were still in dispute. The People's Republic of China listed them both as "Autonomous Regions," rather than outright declaring them provinces. They further isolated these people by referring to them as National Minorities. Words of description applied to the land and the people were critically important to avoid political conflicts, so I felt great pressure to select mine carefully. My only cover was that these words and phrases would be spoken by a poet who'd been dead for 1,200 years, so that would give me a little distancing. But the Chinese knew they originated with me and there was no hiding that fact. Put another way, the apparatus of the Chinese Communist Party would be reading and approving my narration script, word by word. I asked myself again how I was supposed to be qualified to speak for both East and West. What hope did I have to satisfy both?

There were two concepts I used to fudge what the narration was *really* saying. Li Po states: "Even within her borders, there are distant lands." This was a kind of chapter heading, my way of acknowledging that Xinjiang and

Tibet may be technically *within* the borders but that they remained distinct lands, not quite an integral or historic part of greater China. It was a dodge which I hoped wouldn't cause controversy among the audience or the Chinese government. Either side could point to that line and read it as they liked. There was no question China controlled their frontiers with an iron hand but there was a certain amount of deference paid to local customs, traditions, language, and history. History knows the People's Liberation Army went into Tibet with force and, as a result, the Dalai Lama went into exile. In Xinjiang, there were already rumors that many ethnic Han Chinese were being relocated into the region in order to shift the balance of minorities. Today's policies – including subjugation of the Uyghur people by the use of widespread monitoring through facial recognition as well as relocation and re-education camps – are direct descendants of what we witnessed in its earliest stages. That's what I was trying to dodge and fudge.

The second concept I used was another chapter heading or narrative category I called "Legacies of the Past." I saw this as a way to navigate around lingering bitter feelings in the aftermath of the Cultural Revolution. Mao had unleashed his Red Guards on wild forays to destroy certain elements of Chinese culture that pre-dated Communism called the Four Olds: Old Customs, Old Ideas, Old Culture, and Old Habits. The term first dates to a June 1966 newspaper editorial entitled: "Sweep Away All Monsters and Demons." These fundamental components of life and society were called out in the newspaper as anti-proletarian, that they were "fostered by the exploiting classes," and they supposedly "poisoned the minds of the people for thousands of years." Exactly *which* customs, ideas, cultures, and habits were left to mobs of local cadres to define, but the recent destruction of China's past stems from this one horribly misguided policy. The Four Olds also happened to encompass a great deal of what I was trying to include in "Wonders of China." I was going to need to thread a political needle with the narrative words chosen for Li Po.

In 1989, after the so-called Tiananmen Square riots, I got a rather frantic phone call from Michael Eisner, head of Disney Studios. He said he was thinking about removing all the scenes I'd filmed in the square because of the recent deaths and repressive crackdown which was worldwide front-page news. His suggestion would have required an extensive re-edit and leave quite a hole in the film. I was also concerned the studio would be perceived as having a knee-jerk reaction, which this was. I told Michael I didn't think there was a problem with what was depicted. Visually we only showed people gathering in the square to celebrate a holiday, no marches, no political or military parades. Li Po's narration, which I quoted to him from memory, said: "Gone are the warlords, landlords, and Emperors. This is now a place for all Chinese."

Michael's reaction was, "Oh?" After a moment he said, "Okay. Never mind." The sequence remained in the film for many more years.

⁂

I still had very practical concerns about completing the film, such as the opening shot with the paintings-to-mountains transition. Herb still hadn't begun work on our project. I cornered Randy Bright to talk about it one day in a hallway at WED. At the time Randy was supervising so many projects that if you had a question for him, you first had to give enough preamble for him to mentally shift gears. If I'd just walked up to say I had a problem with Herb Ryman, it would take him a moment to know what I was talking about. Instead, I'd say, "Randy. Question for you about EPCOT. 'Wonders of China.' The opening shot. The one where the scroll paintings turn into real mountains…?"

"Oh, yeah. Right, right…" he'd say. From that point we could have a meaningful conversation.

I knew Herb was extremely busy, creating EPCOT concept art for The American Adventure in addition to the China Pavilion. But those commitments, and the same deadline, meant he had little time for the paintings I needed for the film. Herb Ryman was already considered a living legend, having worked on "Fantasia" and "Dumbo." Walt Disney even had Herb do the sketches that secured financing for Disneyland. He went on to design conceptual art for Main Street and many attractions like Sleeping Beauty Castle and the Jungle Cruise. Herb had come from a film background, having been an art director at 20th Fox as well as MGM on "The Wizard of Oz" and "The Good Earth." This last film sparked his lifelong passion for China where he'd traveled after the war and made many sketches. And therein lay my problem.

I'd have meetings with the very personable Herb in his studio, which was cluttered with memorabilia and paintings from various parks. But he'd just want to swap stories with me about places he remembered in China. What was it like there now? Or he'd tell me that he'd just purchased a set of the finest camel-hair brushes, or how he'd acquired some 300-year-old rice paper that would be *perfect* for this project. None of which really moved us any closer to what the film actually needed. I continued to meet with him only because Randy and his boss Marty Sklar felt Herb was the right man for the job. He certainly was, according to his history and experience, but I could hear Empress Cixi's clocks ticking the countdown to the film's hard opening date.

In that hallway, I told Randy that Herb seemed to be delaying or dragging his feet for some reason and hadn't made any useful sketches in the months since I'd approached him. I feared Herb would miss the film's deadline. Randy, who prided himself on being able to make quick, decisive decisions, said, "Then just cut the scene!"

No. I wasn't about to throw out any babies or bathwater just yet.

I said, "I have one last idea I want to try first."

I approached Jack Boyd, another longtime animator at the studio, to tell him my situation. I knew that background artists on every Disney animated film had to adapt their own individual and personal styles to that of the overall production design. Imitating other artists was part of their job description. If I presented them with samples of Chinese art (from several art books I'd collected), couldn't they copy the various dynastic styles and apply them to the mountains of Yangshuo? Jack was willing to try. Within a week his artists had executed wonderful watercolor and ink paintings that looked like they dated to the Tang and Ming Dynasties. They'd even duplicated the look of authentic red chops that stamp an artist's signature in the corner. I couldn't have been more pleased with their efforts and the fact that they'd literally saved the opening scene of the film. Randy thought the paintings looked great and we never spoke of Herb Ryman again.

Meanwhile, I needed main title artwork for "Wonders of China," but I wanted it to represent a number of China's languages, including the beautiful Mongolian, Uyghur, and Tibetan scripts. I had asked for these authentic samples while I was still in-country, but it was taking a long time for China Co-Film to track down and assemble the scripts.

The musical score was also still in the works and it was decided that Du Ming Xin would record the ethnic parts in China with his musicians, then studio musicians on the Disney lot would record his more "Western" cues as orchestrated by Buddy Baker. It was going to be an interesting mix to get Chinese instruments to overlay against the lush backgrounds recorded afterwards in the States. I began making plans to travel to Beijing to supervise the recording sessions there. But first I had to keep updating Du on the film's timings. Every time we made the slightest editing adjustment, the time codes changed and I'd have to send him a long telex with new numbers.

Meanwhile Dennis and I had finished editing all of Li Po's scenes so that we could begin looking for an actor to replace his dialogue. That same actor would also record all of Li Po's voice-over narration. The studio casting department came to me with the suggestion of Keye Luke, a wonderful character actor who'd been around Hollywood for a long time. Younger people knew him from the "Kung Fu" TV series while older audiences might remember him from the Charlie Chan movies where he played the detective's "Number One Son." I had a meeting with him, and he couldn't have been easier to work with. He observed Shih Kuan's unique way of speaking English and recognized right away that there would be some issues matching his unusual cadence and rhythm. He wanted to know when we'd record the narration and I had to tell him I honestly didn't know. Disney had a contractual obligation to have the Chinese government sign off on the narration script.

This had been a huge sticking point in the negotiations so there'd been a lot of pressure on me to finish a draft early enough to submit via China Co-Film. But after I sent it to them, all we got in return was silence. China's enormous and intricate bureaucracy has a lot of moving parts. I imagined my script slowly working its way through the gears of government machinery, wondering if I'd recognize my own words in the end. While I understood the delay, I couldn't help but think that the long silence meant the worst.

With a temporary mix in place by mid-June, we planned to show the latest cut of the film to Randy and Marty Sklar down at Disneyland. This was the only Circle-Vision theater where we could watch a show with all nine screens at once. But we had to get in and get out before the park was open to the public. That meant getting up at 4:15 a.m. to get to the studio by 5 where their drivers would take us down to the park and in the back gate. A Circle-Vision film is typically projected with the film threaded through nine large loop cabinets. For a screening like this, a projectionist has to thread up and synchronize all nine film reels. What many park visitors don't appreciate is that the physical film may be in the theater, but the soundtrack is playing back in a basement building across the park. A separate reel of sound required someone to thread it up on a playback machine and then synchronize and interlock it with the theater. Normally this isn't too much of a hassle. However, on this very important morning, the soundtrack was loaded on the reels facing the wrong way. The resulting sound was muddled and dull because the track was playing through the base side of the magnetic material. Despite the muffled sound, Randy and Marty really liked the film. We screened the front screens of the film later that day on Stage 2 at the studio, using five projectors and it went even better. I invited Greg MacGillivray to this screening, the very first time he'd seen any footage, and I expected copious notes. But Greg had no negative comments, which I took to be a very good sign.

We set up a test screening with an invited audience of about 80 people. They ranked their opinions of the overall film as well as their personal feelings about Li Po. Nearly 70 percent said they'd see the film again, a high mark indicating they liked our Tang dynasty poet. The gamble of including a "storyteller," as Randy liked to call him, had paid off. No one jumped up to label him a Communist, at any rate.

Dennis and I could then lock the picture, which kicked postproduction into a higher gear. I sent the final telex to Du Ming Xin with his score timings. Meanwhile I got called into Bob Gibeaut's office to put out a recent fire about the film's narration.

We'd still heard no reaction to my script. I wanted to go ahead and record with Keye Luke, cut in his voice tracks, and then mix the final film, a process that would take a full six weeks. My argument was that we had to move forward, even if we hadn't received a signoff from the Chinese. I convinced Bob that in a worst-case scenario, we might have changes to make down the road, but at least we would have the film in the theater for the park's opening. That was the ultimate argument – make the deadline – so he agreed.

More screenings helped us feel we'd pass the test. "Wonders of China" was shown to Ron Miller and other Disney higher-ups: Donn Tatum, Card Walker, Gil Grosvenor, and Caroline Ahmanson who had been a steady and influential supporter of the project for the past year and a half. Unfortunately, the soundtrack again didn't play properly and so I had to narrate live, filling in for Li Po's missing voice from memory.

In early July I left for China, this time with a sound engineer named Clark who had never been out of the country before. Our flight was met in Beijing by Bao and Shen. Tim was away at the Foreign Language Institute while Lao Tan was "doing his own rubbish," according to Bao. We checked into the old wing of the Peking Hotel. I could only hope that the jury-rigged process we'd proposed for recording the film's music on two continents was going to work.

Why wouldn't it? For starters, this had never been done before.

CHAPTER 29

Patchwork

I took Clark, our audio engineer, for a quick tour of the Forbidden City and Tiananmen Square on the 4th of July. I'd brought my own video recorder, a model just like the one Guy Jones used. We were caught in a bad rainstorm but were surprisingly rescued by my camera assistant, Leo, who happened to have access to a government car that day.

I then had a meeting with Madame Li to discuss China's plans for the premiere of our film at EPCOT. She was expecting the Chinese Ambassador and other dignitaries to fly from Washington to Florida for the occasion, especially since the festivities fell around the time of National Day on October 1, which was considered auspicious.

We visited Du Ming Xin's music conservatory where his best students had been rehearsing his film music for weeks. They were certainly skillful and enthusiastic players, but they were young college kids. I was suddenly struck with concern that perhaps we should have searched for more professional ethnic Chinese players in the Los Angeles area. I was also worried about the timings they were using. Had he received my telex with the latest changes?

Clark and I visited the recording facilities at the Beijing Film Studios, and Shih Kuan dropped by to say hello. I think he also wanted to make sure there were no screw-ups that would reflect badly on China's abilities to achieve high technological standards. Clark gave their equipment a very thorough inspection and ran a few audio tests. He gave me a thumbs-up: we were good to go. The plan was to start the next day, but the time would depend on Du's students completing some of their final exams in the morning!

That night I took solace in a burger and a Coke down the street at the Jianguo Hotel. Clark couldn't understand what the big deal was about such a simple meal.

The next morning, we had the expected: Du's students arrived late, and the unexpected: technical issues to overcome. I'd brought my own small video monitor which we mounted on the podium. It allowed the conductor, a friend of Du Ming Xin from the conservatory, to match tempo and timings to screen one of the film. Clark and the local engineers, working without translators, had to fiddle with settings and cables to sync up with the two-inch AMPEX tape we were using to record.

When the musicians were in place and ready to go, Du looked a nervous wreck. He was probably that way for every one of his film scores and I could relate. On the downbeat, Du's music had a very authentic and naturalistic feel. I particularly loved the emotional sound of the Chinese violin called an *erhu* (literally "two string"). It was late morning before we had the first cue laid down to everyone's satisfaction. The piece was for the Xinjiang sequence, one of the most complex for the musicians, so there was relief on everyone's part when we broke for lunch. I thought it sounded pretty good and we got another thumbs-up from Clark. I couldn't help but notice Du's conductor bore more than a passing resemblance to a Chinese Buddy Baker.

Later we recorded the cues for Suzhou, Hangzhou, Huangshan, and the Great Wall. Using the video track for reference, it seemed to me the timing was lining up really well. Du's melodies were quite beautiful and I admired the varying rhythms and colors he'd worked into the score. Like me, he'd had to encompass all of China in 20 minutes! Clark and I celebrated the first day's success with one more burger feast at the Jianguo that cost 98 yuan (about $12).

Another full day in the recording studio resulted in seven more cues, despite another late start due to student exams. The most complex part was still to come, the combining and overdubbing of separate Western and Chinese elements, especially for the Guilin sequence. After his students left, Du laid down separate piano guide tracks for Buddy Baker. The opening of the film also called for the same kind of overlap of styles, but it looked to me like there might be a timing issue that didn't get resolved. Buddy would probably have to make a slight adjustment on his end.

We came across a handful of kids from Inner Mongolia who happened to be on the studio lot, so I brought them in to record some authentic ethnic "walla." I gave them specific directions to fill in the audio for certain scenes. There'd definitely be no source for this kind of sound back in the States, so this felt like a very lucky find. It reminded me of the local Chinese film we saw that used English-speaking extras and I hoped we could avoid that kind of mistake.

The next day we scrambled to find last-minute items before our flight home. I picked up some silk for scrolls and three printed titles from the National Minorities Institute that read "Wonders of China" in Tibetan, Mongolian, and Uyghur.

When I got back to the studio, Dennis and I began to cut the music cues into place for Buddy Baker. Du had sent along his sheet music for these Western cues but Buddy and his music department needed time to map out orchestrations and instrumentation. Meanwhile, I handed over the ethnic artwork to the studio art department. They combined the scripts into a very striking main title layout. Pieces were finally falling into place.

As we drew closer to our deadlines, I was asked at the studio to speak to employees about the difficulties of making films in China. Sheesh, where to begin? How about the days of difficulties I was experiencing at that moment getting Bao and Du their visas to come for the music recording? I thought of the invitation to do the studio talk and presentation as a bit of an honor, until I found Leon Chooluck had also been invited. He was remarkably low-key, considering his dreams of a $15-million deal to become a producer in China had recently fallen through. Disney had also hit him up for even more expense reimbursements that he needed to pay off.

Without any official word yet from China, I recorded the narration with Keye Luke in mid-July at Goldwyn Studios. He imparted a warmth and sympathy to Li Po's readings that would go a long way to humanizing him for audiences. There was still the fear some might think his words were propaganda coming directly from the Chinese government. And maybe they would be right. Until I saw how extensive the CCP's changes were, there was no way to deny those kinds of charges with any certainty.

I took Keye Luke to lunch across from Goldwyn at the Formosa Cafe, one of his old Hollywood haunts where the staff recognized him. We recorded dialogue replacement (ADR) in the afternoon and, as he'd pointed out, it was a challenge to match Shih Kuan's unusual rhythms and cadence in English, but the old master showed his experience. When we left the stage, I was very happy with the sync. But I wouldn't feel that way after the tapes had been transferred to Disney's Sound Department.

Once Dennis and I had cut together all the narration and dialogue tracks, we got a signoff from Marty and Randy with three very minor changes. At least no one was talking about redoing the narration should we hear from the Chinese government before the film's opening. Marty mentioned that Card Walker was thinking of running "Wonders of China" at Disneyland in Anaheim over the Christmas holidays, which was another vote of confidence in the project.

At the same time, I finally heard from our own government: the visas had come through. On July 23, I picked up Du and Bao at LAX. After I'd set the two of them up in a local hotel, I left them in Buddy Baker's capable hands. I was leaving for the first brief shooting trip on "The Eternal Sea" so I'd be out of the country for the final music recording sessions.

There was one small error in timing right at the start of the film. The first ethnic cue turned out to be a few seconds short. Buddy and Du fixed it with a clever repetition of the first few bars. This fit so well musically that I think they were the only two people who would ever notice.

I returned from Japan in time for the mixdown of the Western tracks. I found a slight problem with the Yangtze River cue. This time it was Buddy's music editor that came up with a fix.

Since Du and Bao were still in town, I took them to see "E.T." in Hollywood, followed by a dinner at the Hamburger Hamlet on Sunset Boulevard. Du kept trying to use a knife and fork because he had a hard time with the concept of food being eaten with the hands.

During our music mixdowns, Ron Miller and Bob Gibeaut stopped by the stage to give a listen. It was all sounding great and the blend of East and West was working.

I couldn't say the same for Li Po's on-camera words. We had one of the studio's longtime dialogue editors working on it and frankly, I hadn't seen that the sync needed any adjustments. It had been fine on the stage at Goldwyn, but this editor kept trying to "finesse" the ADR tracks and was only making them worse. I eventually had to tell him in no uncertain words that he needed to stop and put it back the way it was.

The start of a marathon dubbing session was yet to come.

At the time of "America the Beautiful," the studio only produced a single monaural soundtrack which was pumped out of all nine screens. The philosophy for this, reflected in Walt's approach to many elements of the park, was that everyone should get the same experience. Every time. No matter where one stood in the theater. But times and technology, not to mention the expectations of park-goers, had changed dramatically.

The mixing facility set up on Disney's Stage 1 consisted of a standard audio console on a platform surrounded by a circle of nine video screens. Each screen had its own individual speaker, one through nine, with an array of overhead speakers assigned to channel ten for narration only. The eleventh was reserved for a mighty subwoofer. The stage also had dozens of 35 mm audio playback machines where reels of edited sound effects, foley footsteps, and backgrounds could be fed into the system.

Every sound for the film, including the music, had to be assigned to an individual channels as appropriate. That meant that when Li appears in the fields of Inner Mongolia on screen one, his voice needs to sound like it's only coming out of screen one. Except – Li Po walks as he talks, into screen nine, then eight, seven, and he finally lands for the last of his dialogue on screen six. The monaural track of Keye Luke's replacement dialogue had to be panned from screen to screen to screen to match the images. But so did the sound of his pony's footsteps, the jingling bell on the horse's collar, the horse's whinny, the rustle of Li Po's robes.

These many elements for one small moment had to be accounted for within the volume of the 360-degree space of the film. Each sound had to be amplified, digitized, equalized, and modulated to fit the picture. And there were hundreds and hundreds of such elements in what was really a rather straightforward soundtrack for "Wonders of China." A small team of sound technicians and audio engineers worked for several weeks on the tracks that had been edited by dozens of other technicians and editors. The paper cue sheets were like a roadmap several feet wide. Every individual element had to be accounted for, checked off, and assembled into pre-dubs.

Over the weeks of mixing, all the atmospheric backgrounds were assembled into one pre-dub, a kind of complete collection of just those sounds. Foley footsteps went in another. Hard effects into still another. These each became what's called a stem. In the end there'd be four or five stems that had been premixed and balanced and that simplified the last step of blending them together into the final soundtrack. By that stage, another console would be added with controllers, faders, and EQ for a total of 120 tracks.

Some days were like watching paint dry as it seemed to take hours to lay down just three or four effects. Other days went quicker, but it was still going to take the better part of six weeks. I tried to be on the stage as much as I could because creative questions came up frequently, especially if the editors had given us options or alternates for certain effects. When we premixed the music, there were a couple of places we decided to slip the sync a half second or so, in order to make a better impact with the visuals. The film had been arbitrarily divided into reels one and two for our convenience. The last days on the stage, August 26 and 27, each reel took a full day to finalize. The exhausted sound crew broke out the champagne, but it turned out that was a little premature.

Randy and Bob came by the dubbing stage to see the final mix. The images, which had been transferred to video for interlocking with the sound machines, recorders, and consoles were blurry and indistinct. Definitely not the way the film was meant to be seen, but we'd been living with these degraded visuals for so long it didn't bother us. However, this was the best the film would ever sound. Randy really liked it and was very complimentary. Bob had one comment and it bothered me all day. Maybe even longer than that. He said he thought there was too much of Shih Kuan in the film. After I got over my shock (there wasn't any more of Li Po's character than had been scripted), I realized the possibility that Bob saw him as his old rival, the man who'd faced him during negotiations and won a few rounds while *speaking English*. Perhaps that hurt a bit.

The next night Randy showed his gratitude and class by throwing a huge party at his house in Yorba Linda, featuring catering and a live band. He'd said he wanted to honor nearly 100 guests who had worked so hard on EPCOT.

For the next few weeks, as further production shoots drew near for "The Eternal Sea," my focus was on getting the best print of the China film for the opening. We had a few opticals that needed to be redone and a couple of scenes that needed better color-correction (like that Fujifilm at Tiananmen Square), but this was standard film finishing.

I went down to Florida in mid-September to meet up with Glenn Barker, the head of sound at WED. Buddy Baker joined us to screen the film a few times in the new installation. I'd rank the sound about a B+ compared to how the film played on Stage 1, but theater acoustics are an art, not a science. Betsy Richmond, who had her hands full with publicity and promotion, gave a group of us a complete tour of EPCOT's World Showcase in its unfinished glory. We met with Dumonts Grant, the architect for the China Pavilion, who said they would be ready in two weeks. Looking over a site filled with bulldozers and construction people in hard hats, I didn't see how. As it turned out, that last-minute rush was normal for every theme park opening, as was confirmed for me at TDL and Disneyland Paris.

After quick trips at the end of September to London, Venice, and Mykonos for the other Circle-Vision project, I met up with Kathy in Orlando for the grand opening of EPCOT. I'm so glad my wife was there because, with all the press events and worldwide publicity surrounding the opening of a major Disney theme park, I was a nervous wreck. "Wonders of China" was a high-profile entertainment that was about to be carefully scrutinized and critiqued by a number of important people, each with their own agenda. There were sure to be cultural and political ramifications layered on top of the simple question of whether I'd made a worthy film. Would it actually *please* anyone?

No pressure.

CHAPTER 30

ONE THING WRONG

No one can gear up to generate publicity and promotion quite like Disney. They can spew out press material like those machines that gush clouds of colored confetti at football bowl games. Roving bands of reporters from all over the world were kept fed by hourly press releases and handouts, a regular media maelstrom. I was asked to do my share of interviews with print, TV, and radio. You tell the same story enough, it gets highly polished and easier to repeat, but after two days of the whirlwind I was starting to feel I was on autopilot. The questioners also seemed to be going through the motions, barely getting to the surface, let alone under it. So many interviewers seemed content with a quick recap, a few clichés, and on to the next.

I thought I was in safe hands when I was accosted by a reporter from an LA TV station who wanted to ask me a few questions on camera. They were from my hometown, so why not? By now I'd summarized my production tales so often it was like ordering from a menu. I figured I could start her off with a little of this incident, followed by that funny story, then a wrap-up with a known winner that always elicited smiles. Plus, there was always our fallback: "The spirit of cooperation between our two countries."

An assistant gave me a touch of make-up even though I'd been powdered and primped all day. The cameraman arranged his tripod and adjusted his lights while the reporter told me she was going to ask about any production problems I might have faced. Sure. That's number three off the menu.

A moment later we were rolling, and she stuck a microphone in my face.

"Mister Blyth, you represented an American studio while you were in China making a film. What problems did you see that were of a political nature?"

All I could do was smile and try to steer the answer back to safer subjects. I said, "We had a few problems in terms of permissions, especially authorization for helicopter work, but I wouldn't characterize them as political. More logistical. For example, when our crew was off in –"

"– Did the Chinese Communist Party dictate what you could and could not shoot?" she interrupted. "What kinds of areas were they keeping off limits?"

"Well, we had negotiations early on with China Film Co-Production Corporation, that's a unit of their government, to come up with a list of acceptable locales…"

"Acceptable? So you admit they censored the film?"

I gave her a halfhearted smile and said, "You know what? I think we're done. This isn't the interview I agreed to." I walked away without looking back.

In my mind this had been some kind of "gotcha" interview which was out of place on Disney property in the middle of a massive celebration for a new theme park. But what bugged me for the rest of the day was whether the Chinese government *was* going to have the final say about the film. They still had the option to edit the wording of the narration. The very next day the film would be seen by His Excellency, Chai Zemin, Ambassador of the PRC. A press conference was planned for the moment he came out of the theater. Who knew what he might say, inadvertently or otherwise, that might doom the film? I started wondering where the ambassador was from. Had I represented his province in the film? If so, would he be happy with how I'd shown it? Or upset I'd left it out? What was clear was that if there were questions about the film's narrative content, there was no one to share the blame with me.

October 3 was Dedication Day for the China Pavilion. My own day didn't start that well when I came across a full-color Disney brochure. It promoted the film but featured a shot of Greg MacGillivray in Tiananmen Square beside the Circle-Vision camera rig. I had to wonder, was my exclusion deliberate or inadvertent?

During the opening ceremonies of the China Pavilion, several people got up to speak at a podium, including former Chairman of the Board, Donn Tatum and Dick Nunis, President of Disney's Outdoor Recreation Division. Dancing lions and Chinese acrobats entertained the crowd of press and the public. I was immune to their charms, so the spectacle didn't lighten my mood. I couldn't help but notice the somewhat unfinished nature of the area and the rather barren gift shop.

Finally, after two full years, it was time for the film. Someone encouraged me to accompany the entourage into the theater for the ambassador's official screening. Already uncomfortable in a suit and tie in the Florida heat, I tried to blend in. If none of the Disney executives who live for such moments wanted to single me out, that was just fine. The film was the film. Too late for changes. If someone didn't like it, well I saw no point stepping into the line of fire. Maybe, as Bob Gibeaut had wanted, we could claim the film made itself…?

The presentation actually played very well, the final print looked quite good, Du Ming Xin's music was wonderfully appropriate, and I could see the ambassador looking around, trying to absorb the many scenics and vistas from his country. I was surprised when Li Po's little joke in the Fisherman's Garden went over so well: "I suppose if I had traveled to Europe, they would now call Venice, the Suzhou of the West." Even the ambassador chuckled, which was more than I could have hoped for. Maybe he really liked the film and would say so when he faced the reporters outside. I repeated that to myself like a mantra.

The theater doors opened at the end and we streamed outside, walking out under the image of the Hall of Prayer for Good Harvests. I listened for comments, but the Chinese delegation was silent, probably one of those "don't say a word until the big boss speaks" moments.

A large gaggle of press had been assembled out front with a podium of microphones. The ambassador went straight for them as I felt hands pushing me, urging me forward, even though that was not where I wanted to go.

Ambassador Chai Zemin was introduced by Dick Nunis. Someone in the press simply called out, "Mister Ambassador, what did you think of the film?"

He looked down for a moment, as if gathering his thoughts. Then he said in clear English, "There is one thing wrong with this film."

My heart sank in the silence that followed. What had I left out? Worse, what had I left in? Was Bob right that there was too much of Li Po?

The ambassador smiled and said, "It's not long enough! There is so much more of China to see!"

My relief was palpable. That particular "mistake" I could live with. The *China Daily* reporter who'd said I was trying to cram all of China into 20 minutes was right. The following moments took place in a haze as the ambassador shook my hand and we exchanged a few words about what parts of the film he really enjoyed. I never got to ask which province he was from, but suddenly it was *"mei guan xi,"* it didn't matter. Two years of build up for one minute in the spotlight and I'd escaped.

I later stood outside the theater's exit doors for a number of screenings. I wanted to hear the immediate comments of Guests coming out of the film. As they streamed by, their opinions and reactions fell into two distinct camps. They either said, "That's it – now we *have* to go to China!" or they said, "Well, that's it – now we don't have to go to China!"

There were other pavilions and other shows that premiered that day and had their own dedication ceremonies. Kathy and I toured World Showcase until we could walk no more. The evening's big event was a grand banquet on the Empress Lilly steamboat, about as anachronistic a setting as possible. Dick Nunis and Donn Tatum hosted China's delegation, including Ambassador Chai Zemin, and Cao Guisheng, Consul-General of the PRC. Maotai flowed but I didn't need feel a need to prove myself to anyone and abstained. The gala affair quickly became a blur anyway. I don't remember the food or the speeches or the personal comments they delivered to me that night. Nothing.

It was over. Time to move on to my next project.

In 1990, everyone at Walt Disney Imagineering was saddened by the tragic death of Randy Bright in a traffic accident at the age of 51. He was a great friend and a creative powerhouse who left an indelible mark on the film and everyone with whom he worked.

I was also sorry to hear of the passing of Joe Nash. For all his faults (and mine), we successfully worked together on a number of films after "Wonders of China."

I will also miss my China travel companion and would-be producer who tried to start every day with a clean slate: Leon Chooluck, who died in 2002.

Shih Kuan at EPCOT

Reception for Disney team members at SARFT

The new Li Po at Jinshanling

The Shanghai travel shot

A camera set-up on Nanjing Road

The skyline of Pudong

CHAPTER 31

Reflections

A couple of years after "Wonders of China" began playing in Florida and Disneyland, I received a call from the studio about a Chinese VIP arriving in the U.S. They offered to pay my expenses if I would escort him to EPCOT. Was I interested?

Talk about coming full circle. If there was one person who deserved to see this film as it was meant to be seen, it was Shih Kuan. I accompanied him from San Francisco to Orlando. He looked much older and had certainly lost a step. Most strange was seeing Shih Kuan in a suit and tie. I suspected he had more than $15 in his tailored pockets.

The two of us strolled around World Showcase, sharing stories, taking our time to savor our approach to the China Pavilion. As we entered, he admired the Imagineering craftsmanship that created the half-scale Hall of Prayer for Good Harvests.

No surprise, Shih Kuan loved "Wonders of China" and his part in it. He was especially pleased we'd selected a famous actor to re-voice him. Waiting for a second viewing, I introduced him to a young Chinese hostess. She brought him up to the preshow podium as "the man who portrays Li Po." Guests applauded him, before and after the show. This direct acclaim must have made the lengthy trip worthwhile to Shih Kuan. The many production problems we'd endured together had vanished, a legacy of the past.

We stepped outside to take pictures. He wanted his backdrop to be the large China gate that had been modeled on a similar one at the Summer Palace.

I got up the nerve to ask the question that had nagged at me for so many years.

"The Chinese government reviewed my narration script. They could object to anything I wrote, but we never received a response. What happened? Why didn't you get back to us?"

Shih Kuan chuckled. The former bureaucrat (and former actor) was also my *tóngzhì*, a comrade. He smiled knowingly as he said, "Oh, if we'd wanted to change a single word of your script, we would have told you."

❧

None of us who experienced that earlier time could have foreseen the architectural wonders of Pudong, the worldwide influence of a Chinese stock market, or the jaw-dropping sight of millions of bicycles replaced by millions of privately owned automobiles. Instead of standing or running, perhaps now it's more appropriate to say: "The Chinese people have learned to drive – really fast."

During the making of "Wonders of China," our crew had frequently traveled on the surface streets that encircled Beijing. The city has grown like a tree, resulting in five concentric traffic ring roads. These highways are now choked with private cars, but at least no drivers are straddling the center line. The desert dust storms and smoke from charcoal fires we'd experienced seem like minor inconveniences compared to the blanketing smog of a post-industrial China. Hainan Island, that once southern backwater, is nearly overdeveloped with spectacular beachfront hotels rivaling the best of Hawaii. Visitors to Huangshan have the option of a cable car that whisks them to the summit, bypassing those many stone steps. What they gain in speed, they lose in a sense of physical accomplishment and the thrill of discovering unfolding vistas at every turn. My old place, now called the Huangshan Beihai Hotel, had been remodeled many times, with glass in every window. Anyone looking for the battered fortress across from the Potala Palace would discover that the ruins of broken stone that signified Tibet's military takeover have been scrubbed from history, replaced by a mundane TV tower. When so inclined, the Chinese can literally move mountains. Or dam up the Three Gorges of the Yangtze. Steam engines have become gleaming bullet trains. Even far-off Lhasa and Inner Mongolia have four-star hotels. The dual currency that effectively kept villagers rooted in their communes is long gone, but so is the fundamental security of the Iron Rice Bowl. I'm sure none of China's millionaire and billionaire class have inclinations to return to that simpler time. There was no stopping the Chinese once they rose to their feet. There was no going back.

But then that's exactly what I did.

❧

I'd been approached many times by visiting Chinese delegations who never failed to ask, "When will you update 'Wonders of China'?" They'd always say, "We love it, but China's not like that anymore!" Their requests got more strident and I dutifully passed them along, right up to Michael Eisner. What I got were nods of understanding, followed by shrugs. Disney had been willing to foot the bill to get a Chinese Circle-Vision film ready for EPCOT's opening but had no intention of self-funding more filming without corporate sponsorship.

That changed on June 20, 2001. I got a call that day asking if I would be interested in filming an update, limited solely to Shanghai, Tiananmen Square, and Hong Kong. I never say "No" to any film offer. Three weeks later, Walt Disney Imagineering (WDI, formerly WED) had changed the scope to only helicopter aerials of Shanghai, Hong Kong, and Macau.

This didn't make a lot of sense because what bothered the Chinese government the most were shots of Shanghai's backstreets. These lifestyle images upset them even more than seeing Mao jackets and bicycles. The Chinese government wanted to showcase Pudong and its futuristic architecture and turned down Disney's offer of an aerial update. Once more they were saying "No" to helicopters.

I was told by an influential insider that one of the sticking points was the man hired by Disney as corporate liaison for negotiations. He was Chinese-American, a slick corporate type who some government hardliners privately called "a running dog." This was a Mao-era epithet of the worst sort. More than a mere lackey, it meant an "ally of counterrevolutionary imperial forces." I watched the proposed shooting date slip nearly a year, then had a private meeting at Theme Park Productions (TPP) to express my concerns about this roadblock. I was told my information (not mentioning the man's name) would have to be passed up the ladder.

At the top was Tom Fitzgerald, creative executive at TPP, a 1988 offshoot of WDI. Tom had no interest in tilting at political windmills, but he did write a conciliatory letter to the Chinese. Two months later, with the project finally gaining some momentum, I was invited out to Disney's Tujunga facility. Using their projectors, we watched the front five screens of "Wonders of China" followed by the back four. We had to decide exactly what needed to be reshot. This was WDI's initial plan, to reshoot problematic scenes, not to add new material. But a few days later, I got a call from a Vice President for Creative Development at TPP. He threw cold water on the whole project, saying it might not happen. Besides, he added, there were internal discussions about replacing Li Po in the film with Mulan!

I was so shocked that I couldn't even bring myself to discuss the call with anyone. I was numb, but I'd endured lots of other crazy "suggestions" along the way. After the shattering events of 9/11, a return to China was the furthest thought from my mind. But it turned out the project was still alive.

I went to China in January 2002, with David Katzman, a TPP creative executive, and Jim Bice who oversaw WDI's film quality and distribution. Beijing was such a marvel: four-star hotels, first-class restaurants, tens of thousands of commuters in their own cars, and familiar landmarks swept away by progress. Hotel staff, who'd adopted western names like Gloria and Charlie, were courteous, bilingual, and efficient. David and Jim merely expected that level of service, but I was very impressed.

We met with Li Shuping, Senior Engineer of China Research Institute of Film Science and Technology. I found Li to be sharp and enthusiastic, with a can-do spirit. He showed off the institute's pride: their own 360 camera – the direct result of Leo and China Joe's clandestine measurements and photos. It was a complete duplicate of Disney's rig, down to the smallest detail. They'd even included the label that identified the system by its earliest name, "Circarama."

Li was also proud of their own 360 theater at Badaling, in the shadow of where we'd filmed the Great Wall. When we screened "Wonders of China" there, some institute guests broke into laughter at odd moments. But not at the film. It turns out Leo had made a number of 360 films for the institute and had stolen some of my creative ideas. When Leo's associates finally saw the original, they realized his source. Maybe that's why he didn't attend the screening. I told Li that I considered Leo's efforts more of a "tribute" than a theft.

While we were in Beijing, the Harbin Ice Festival was again in progress. David and I were invited to survey some new single-camera shots. I used my video camera to create a storyboard of images in Stalin Park and at the Harbin Snow and Ice World, a kind of frozen fantasyland. One of the institute's cameramen, Wang Yuan Chao, would return later to film in 35 mm. I didn't mind missing out on the frigid night shoots. Wang did such a good job matching my visuals that later I hired him for another project.

In May and June 2002, I was joined by David Katzman, Linda Folsom, (a production coordinator at TPP), and Steve Spiegel, (the film's writer), on a wide-ranging location scout. We had many of the same logistic challenges as 20 years earlier, but we at least had more comforts, including much better food. The Chinese wanted us to incorporate so many elements that the film had to rely on more single-camera images. Montages like these require a tremendous amount of effort to acquire each image: finding a location, managing crowd control, bringing in extras, and waiting for the right light. Each montage needed nine such images, plus alternates. But the biggest problem of the survey was the discovery we'd been operating under a wrong assumption.

By July we were back at TTP, preparing a presentation for Tom Fitzgerald. Our updated 360 images were mixed into the existing imagery of "Wonders of China" and mounted on large boards. We had simply followed the original continuity, replacing old shots with modern. Tom really liked what we'd come up with, but then dropped the bomb: he wanted to promote this as *a new film*.

I just wished we'd known earlier. The first new scene was going to fall about four or five minutes into the old continuity. How would an audience feel this was an updated version if they had to wait that long? Tom announced his intention on a Friday, and I spent the weekend deconstructing the old film, putting individual shots on 3x5 cards, then made another set for the new scenes. I changed the sequence order to move many modern shots up front. I quickly realized this proposed continuity needed an unplanned addition: an opening scene of Li Po on the Great Wall. Shih Kuan was 20 years older and getting pretty frail so that would also mean recasting. Oh joy.

The following Monday, I presented my case to David, Linda, and Steve, using my taped-together 3x5 cards. There was a lengthy silence. No one wanted to be the first to comment. I also felt in that moment I might have crossed a line, short-circuiting TPP's internal creative processes. No one ever accused me, but I felt echoes of that breach as a lingering tension during production. On the first film, I'd performed all three of their duties by myself. This time, I was an outsider, hired solely as the film's director. But when Tom was presented with my reconfigured outline, he bought into it right away. Feeling vindicated, I suggested that while we were at it, why not do a "goodbye" scene with Li Po as well?

In August 2002, we did a full dog and pony show for Michael Eisner, hoping for a signoff. The room was full of WDI and TPP people, along with his usual studio entourage. Michael, always no-nonsense, cut the presentation short. He said, "I just want it to be as artistic as the first one." I let out a huge sigh of relief. Thank you, Michael.

For the production, we were using the latest version of the Circle-Vision rig: new lenses that could focus remotely and independently, four small video taps that I could monitor and record on tape, and a motorized panhead. Mounted on a Panther dolly, the enhanced rig had the ability to boom up and down during a shot.

But before we could start, we had to endure a formal meeting at the State Administration of Radio, Film, and Television (SARFT). The meet and greet was covered by the news. The Vice Minister was anxious to hear my opinions on changes since "Wonders of China." Easy, that was number five off my diplomatic speech menu…

Casting for a Li Po replacement started out so much better than the first time. We had four candidates – a choice! But on the day of the casting session, only one actor showed up. And Mister Liu spoke not a word of English. I was assured by Li that they would use a technique that had proven workable before. English dialogue would be broken down phonetically and the actor would be speaking Chinese words that were similar in mouth shape and tone. That meant he would actually be reciting a long list of gibberish: "shoe, laundry, sky, airplane, rabbit, blanket, yellow, thirteen." How was I supposed to direct random words into a performance?

For Li Po's hello and goodbye scenes, we chose a recently restored section of the Great Wall at Jinshaling. But the dramatic locale was so far from Beijing that the crew had to stay in a local hotel as bad as any we'd suffered on the first show. My bathroom, with no stall or tub, had a shower that sprayed brown water all over the room. Radical changes transforming China had yet to reach this shabby guesthouse.

Filming at Jinshaling took a long time because, no surprise, Mister Liu had trouble remembering his nonsense words. There was little I could do to help, other than directing him to turn away from camera earlier than planned, delivering his "lines" to the open vista. We could fill in his dialogue while looking at his back. His second set-up took even longer, requiring cue cards under the camera, which forced us to shoot late into the afternoon. China could usually be counted on for a thick layer of haze in the distance, but not today. The sun remained bright all the way down to the horizon, throwing a sharp shadow of our camera onto the wall behind us. We would have to erase it later with CGI.

Xinjiang Province had gone through many changes in 20 years, but not always for the better. When our crew arrived in Ürümqi, we didn't sample the local *shashlik* or *Hami* melons, but instead had authentic tacos. Two touring Mexican chefs happened to be staying at our Holiday Inn. They whipped up flavors never tasted before in that part of the world. Our filming of an open-air market had as many problems as before, but with the added complications of night shooting. We'd arranged nearly 100 Uyghur extras, paid many more vendors to appear in the film, and used a lighting crew from a local TV station. But it still took until 2 a.m. to get a barely useable shot. The issue was with random shoppers who kept wandering past our cordon of plain-clothes police. They seemed to be drawn to the bright lights of our filming like moths.

We executed many single-camera set-ups of street scenes in Shanghai and also planned four major Circle-Vision shots. The vibrant city boasted freeways and interchanges that gave spectacular views of Pudong, the modern metropolis that has replaced the previously empty field across the Huangpu River. We used a camera car to capture a travel shot on the highway that swept along the Bund. Just like with our Beijing bicycles, we hired several cars to surround our vehicle to keep back the civilian onlookers. Aggressive drivers still tried to pass our little flotilla. One got through on our best take, showing up in the front cameras. We also filmed along the Bund at night, catching a lucky break with a well-lit yacht that added some free production value. Our crew constructed a 30-foot-high camera scaffolding on the incredibly busy Nanjing Road, the famous shopping district. During both day and night shots, I slowly panned the cameras so the two parts could be blended together with a seamless transition.

The last Shanghai scene took place on the top of a wealthy bank building which had an unobstructed view of the futuristic TV tower and skyscrapers of Pudong. Similar to my staging at the Peace Hotel, we turned the rooftop into a catered office party, complete with extras in business attire. The view towards the front was so compelling that I often wondered if anyone ever saw our efforts in the back panels.

In Hong Kong and Macau, we filmed dozens of single-panel images to create a montage of horseracing, bird and jade markets, temples, shrines, hydrofoils, and neon. What held the sequence together was a 360 shot on the open water between Victoria Harbor and Kowloon. We filmed from the front of a large yacht while passing a classic red-sailed Chinese junk that had been rented for an hour. All the while, we had to avoid constant boat traffic from the Star Ferry. I resisted the suggestion of a Disney executive who asked for sunbathers on the deck of our yacht.

One of the more difficult Hong Kong shots made for the longest survey. To capture a 360 view of the famous architecture, we had to find access to a clear rooftop at the proper height. After many failed searches, we eventually found a 44-story high-rise in what the locals call the mid-levels. We were surrounded by modern buildings that rose above us, but we could see down to the streets as well. A special crew was needed to hoist our heavy equipment to the roof using only a block and tackle. As usual, I worried they couldn't pull it off, but they were as successful as their counterparts on Huangshan. We filmed a lock-off scene in time-lapse, an added feature for the cameras, but the iris controls failed right in the middle of a lengthy take. I elected to shoot short pieces at intervals through the day and night. For the last scenes, we captured the brilliant lights of Hong Kong by filming at a very slow three frames per second. In postproduction, the short snippets were blended together to create an effect similar to what we'd originally planned. Then we added a soft-edged wipe that transformed the scene from day to night.

I once again found the entrance to the Forbidden City wreathed in scaffolding, but this time it wasn't bamboo. When they'd finished repainting, we filmed a driving shot emerging from the Meridian Gate. The only challenge was a limit of one hour to film while the water fountains were operating out front.

One other Beijing Circle-Vision set-up proved much more problematic and kept getting postponed. A tremendous amount of effort was expended arranging what was, for us, a fairly straightforward dolly shot.

The location was the upper levels of the Monument to the People's Heroes in the middle of Tiananmen Square. Li had to arrange the approval and coordination of 32 separate government units, each with some measure of control over the sensitive area. We'd even had to arrange special dispensation just to take survey photos after the memorial's military patrols warned me of snipers.

For the scene itself, I asked to have large red flags flying from every pole, not just in the massive square, but on the tops of the surrounding Great Hall of the People and the National Museum of China. It was a thrill to watch all those flags rising and unfurling exactly on time. Li Shuping's plan was working, and I was getting the shot I wanted – until it suddenly fell apart. Just as our limited window for filming was about to expire, nearly 20 large sweeper trucks showed up around the square – and into our shot. My local assistant directors flew into action and somehow managed to get the trucks to regroup behind the monument and out of camera view. The drivers were angry but waited until we finished our take. Li humbly apologized afterwards. Apparently, there was one more government committee – number 33 – that had been overlooked. No one had thought to consult the monthly cleaning schedule for Tiananmen Square.

During postproduction, we reprinted a few outtakes from "Wonders of China," using Joe Nash's detailed logbooks. There were only a few locales that hadn't been used, but we found a dolly shot on the fort at Jiayuguan. The Mao jackets weren't too prominent. There were also outtakes of Guilin helicopter aerials that felt fresh. We also found an alternate of the Gobi camel caravan. Using the left-to-right version, instead of the original right-to-left, wasn't exactly Tom Fitzgerald's idea of "new," but it hadn't been seen by audiences before.

WDI cast locally for an Asian voice to replace the gibberish of the new Li Po and to add rewritten narration. What was strange for me was directing the ADR of the continuing scenes featuring Shih Kuan. We were giving voice to him for the second time in Li Po's study, the Suzhou garden scene, and inside the cave.

In December 2002, Li Shuping led a small technical group from China to see the first edited assembly. As a filmmaker himself, Li asked to watch "Reflections of China" three times, front and back. He gave us an enthusiastic thumbs-up.

I dug out my copy of Du Ming Xin's original score and handed it over to a composer who would incorporate many of Du's themes into the updated soundtrack. The recording, at 20th Fox, turned out to be a synthesis of styles that Du would have enjoyed.

※

The following March, after many editing adjustments, tweaks, and general tightening, "Reflections of China" was screened at the Tujunga facility for the Chinese government. Bob Iger, Disney's President and COO, hosted the official delegation. At the conclusion, everyone's relief was palpable, even Bob's. He quietly thanked me for my work on a difficult update. The Chinese felt we'd managed to capture the spirit of their modern country which had evolved so dramatically since the first film. How great was their relief? They said they didn't even need to screen the back panels.

Bob Iger officially rededicated the China Pavilion at EPCOT on October 9, 2003. "Reflections of China" played continually for nearly 17 years. Hopefully, it was as artistic as the first one.

About the Author

Jeff Blyth has made films all over the world in a number of unusual and technically challenging film and digital formats.

The Blyth family moved from Canada to the west side of Detroit in 1956 where Jeff celebrated his tenth birthday. His father, Kenneth, a sales executive with the Chesapeake and Ohio Railroad, made train trips a regular vacation tradition. One of Jeff's most prized Christmas gifts was a basic 8 mm camera that had no options at all, not even a lens that focused. After years of struggling to overcome its limitations, he saved his money for a more advanced camera. Jeff shot dozens of short films with it and was encouraged with an Honorable Mention in Kodak's nationwide teenage movie contest. As the first to go to college in his family, Jeff was faced with a dilemma. He wanted to make films, but his parents insisted on a more secure and "reasonable" career. The compromise was to study Television, Radio, and Film at Michigan State University. He continued to make his own independent short films in addition to his class requirements and found a paid position as an editor at the university's film unit while also hosting his own campus radio show for four years.

After graduation, during the height of the Vietnam War, Jeff spent two years as a teacher in the Peace Corps in Liberia, West Africa, but felt he could justify the time if he came home with footage for a documentary film. He had to coordinate a shipment of 16 mm film into and out of the country during his two-month school vacation period. He received help from his supervisor, Tommy Kelly, the former child star of "The Adventures of Tom Sawyer" and a man who became his friend of many years. While working on his own film in Liberia, Jeff was asked by the Peace Corps to make a training film called "One Day – Two Volunteers."

Returning to the States, he completed his documentary, "Birth-Rite," which won a Ten Best of Festival and Best Editing in Toronto. Jeff began work at a TV station in Cadillac, Michigan, shooting and editing dozens of commercials and documentaries, but he never stopped making his own short films. At Omnicom Productions in Lansing, Jeff broadened his experiences as a writer, producer, director, cameraman, and editor making a wide range of industrial films for clients.

After he and his wife Kathy moved to California, Jeff worked on the IMAX production of "To Fly" and became an integral part of MacGillivray-Freeman Films where he worked on several productions, including "Wonders of China" for Disney. That show led to more independent work for Disney, including "The Eternal Sea" (a premiere attraction at TDL), "American Journeys" (played at Disneyland, the Magic Kingdom, and TDL), and "Portraits of Canada" for

EXPO 86 (also played at EPCOT). Jeff directed the feature film "Cheetah," a G-rated family adventure filmed on location in Kenya for Disney Studios, executive produced by Roy E. Disney. Jeff then wrote and directed an IMAX film for a Dutch sponsor, "Light and Life," which was photographed on locales around the world. Jeff also directed the most ambitious Circle-Vision production ever made, "From Time to Time" (a premiere attraction at Disneyland Paris). This film, with a few revisions, also played as "The Timekeeper" at TDL and the Magic Kingdom.

Jeff has been back to China many times, documenting remote World Heritage sites, slowly checking off his list of places China Co-Film wouldn't let him photograph. Each trip he learns the exact same lesson: the more you know about China, the more you realize how little you know.

Jeff moved into television as a director for Nickelodeon, including several episodes of "The Secret World of Alex Mack" and the Montreal-based sci-fi kids' show, "Space Cases." Jeff is a proud member of the Writers Guild of America, the Directors Guild of America, and the Documentary Branch of the Academy of Motion Picture Arts and Sciences.

Lately Jeff has focused on his work as a writer with three of his scripts produced as TV Movies of the Week. He has a feature film script in preproduction in New Zealand and two novel manuscripts lying in wait for just the right publisher.

"Polishing the Dragons" is Jeff's first book.

www.ingramcontent.com/pod-product-compliance
Lightning Source LLC
Chambersburg PA
CBHW061603110426
42742CB00039B/2701